MICHEL SAINT-DENIS AND THE SHAPING OF THE MODERN ACTOR

MICHEL SAINT-DENIS

and the Shaping of the Modern Actor

◆ ◆ ◆ ◆ ◆

Jane Baldwin

Contributions in Drama and Theatre Studies, Number 104

LIVES OF THE THEATRE

D. G. BEER, SIMON WILLIAMS, and CHRISTOPHER INNES, *Series Advisers*

Westport, Connecticut
London

Library of Congress Cataloging-in-Publication Data

Baldwin, Jane.
    Michel Saint-Denis and the shaping of the modern actor / Jane Baldwin.
        p. cm. — (Contributions in drama and theatre studies, ISSN 0163-3821 ; no. 104. Lives
    of the theatre)
    Includes bibliographical references and index.
    ISBN 0-313-30566-8 (alk. paper)
    1. Saint-Denis, Michel, 1897—Criticism and interpretation. I. Title. II. Contributions in
drama and theatre studies ; no. 104. III. Contributions in drama and theatre studies. Lives
of the theatre.
    PN2638.S27B35 2003
    792′.092—dc21   2003053565

British Library Cataloguing in Publication Data is available.

Library of Congress Catalog Card Number: 2003053565
ISBN: 1-313-30566-8
ISSN: 0163-3821

First published in 2003

Praeger Publishers, 88 Post Road West, Westport, CT 06881
An imprint of Greenwood Publishing Group, Inc.
www.praeger.com

Printed in the United States of America

The paper used in this book complies with the
Permanent Paper Standard issued by the National
Information Standards Organization (Z39.48-1984).

10 9 8 7 6 5 4 3 2 1

CONTENTS

COPYRIGHT ACKNOWLEDGMENTS

For material reproduced in this book, the following publishers, institutions, and individuals are gratefully acknowledged:

Text

The Shakespeare Institute, publisher of *Theatre Notebook*, for material from "Chekhov, The Rediscovery of Realism: Michel Saint-Denis' Productions of *Three Sisters* and *The Cherry Orchard*" by Jane Baldwin (*Theatre Notebook*, vol. 53, no. 2 [1999]), copyright © 1999 by Jane Baldwin.

Theatre History Studies, Theatre Department, Central College, for permission to include material from "The Compagnie des Quinze and the Emergence of Michel Saint-Denis" by Jane Baldwin (*Theatre History Studies*, vol. 14 [1994], pp. 49–72), copyright © 1994 by *Theatre History Studies*.

Pierre Lefèvre, for permission to include excerpts from the author's personal interviews with him on January 13, 1989 and August 11, 1990.

Georganne Mennin, for permission to quote from Peter Mennin's letter dated 14 February 1963 to Michel Saint-Denis.

Catherine Dasté, for permission to include the following material: documents concerning the life and career of Michel Saint-Denis archived at the Copeau home; excerpts from the author's personal interviews with Catherine Dasté; and information concerning C. Dasté's career sent to the author by her.

Christine de la Potterie, for permission to include the following material: documents concerning the life and career of Michel Saint-Denis; excerpts from M. Saint-Denis's *Theatre: The Rediscovery of Style* and *Training for the Theatre*; and extracts from the correspondence between Michel and Suria Magito Saint-Denis.

Bibliothèque nationale de France, Département des Arts et Spectacle, for permission to include material concerning the life and career of Michel Saint-Denis in the library's archives.

Illustrations

Bibliothèque nationale de France, for permission to reprint figure 4.1, *Le Viol de Lucrèce*, which appears in chapter 4, page 47.

The Harvard Theatre Collection, The Houghton Library, for permission to reprint figure 5.1 in chapter 5, page 70: Edith Evans in *The Witch of Edmonton* (1936), The Old Vic, Angus McBean Photograph, Copyright © The Harvard Theatre Collection, The Houghton Library.

The Harvard Theatre Collection, The Houghton Library, for permission to reprint figure 5.2 in chapter 5, page 72: Laurence Olivier and Judith Anderson in *Macbeth* (1937), The Old Vic, Angus McBean Photograph, Copyright © The Harvard Theatre Collection, The Houghton Library.

ILLUSTRATIONS

SERIES FOREWORD

Lives of the Theatre is designed to provide scholarly introductions to important periods and movements in the history of world theatre from the earliest instances of recorded performance through to the twentieth century, viewing the theatre consistently through the lives of representative theatrical practitioners. Although many of the volumes will be centred upon playwrights, other important theatre people, such as actors and directors, will also be prominent in the series. The subjects have been chosen not simply for their individual importance, but because their lives in the theatre can well serve to provide a major perspective on the theatrical trends of their eras. They are therefore either representative of their time, figures whom their contemporaries recognised as vital presences in the theatre, or they are people whose work was to have a fundamental influence on the development of the theatre, not only in their lifetimes but after their deaths as well. While the discussion of verbal and written scripts will inevitably be a central concern in any volume that is about an artist who wrote for the theatre, these scripts will always be considered in their function as a basis for performance.

The rubric "Lives of the Theatre" is therefore intended to suggest both biographies of people who created theatre as an institution and as a medium of performance and of the life of the theatre itself. This dual focus will be illustrated through the titles of the individual volumes, such as *Christopher Marlowe and the Renaissance of Tragedy*, *George Bernard Shaw and the Socialist Theatre*, and *Richard Wagner and Festival Theatre*, to name just a few. At the same time, although the focus of each volume will be different, depending on the particular subject, appropriate emphasis will be given to the cultural and political context within which the theatre of any given time is set. Theatre itself can be seen to have a palpable effect upon the social world around it, as it both reflects the life of its time and helps to form that life by feeding it images, epitomes, and alternative versions of itself. Hence, we hope that this series will also contribute to an understanding of the broader social life of the period of which the theatre that is the subject of each volume was a part.

Lives of the Theatre grew out of an idea that Josh Beer put to Christopher Innes and Peter Arnott. Sadly, Peter Arnott did not live to see the inauguration of the series. Simon Williams kindly agreed to replace him as one of the series editors and has played a full part in its preparation. In commemoration, the editors wish to acknowledge Peter's own rich contribution to the life of the theatre.

D. G. BEER
SIMON WILLIAMS
CHRISTOPHER INNES

ACKNOWLEDGMENTS

I am indebted to many people in the United States, France, England, and Canada, without whose help this book would not have come into being. Particular thanks go to Christine de la Potterie, Marie-Hélène Dasté, Catherine Dasté, Suzanne Maistre Saint-Denis, Marius and Prudence Goring for their generosity in allowing me access to their private records, letters, photographs and other archival materials, as well as sharing their memories with me. Many thanks to Pierre Lefèvre and Jeremy Geidt for giving of their time, reminiscences, advice, and knowledge of Saint-Denis's teaching methods. I am grateful to Fritz Weaver for sharing his correspondence and documents with me.

Appreciative thanks are due to those I interviewed, who provided invaluable information. In alphabetical order: Stephen Aaron, Peggy Ashcroft, Norman Ayrton, John Barton, John Blatchley, Victoria Boothby, André Brassard, Robert Chapman, Judi Dench, Abd'el Kader Farrah. James Forsyth, René Fugler, Blaise Gautier, Hubert Gignoux, Edward Gilbert, Gerald Gutierrez, George Hall, Dylis Hamlett, Margot Harley, Margaret Harris, Jocelyn Herbert, Nick Hutchinson, Clare Jeffery, Michael Kahn, Alain Knapp, Michael Langham, Jeanne Laurent, Dominique Lecoyer, Eliza Hutchinson, Loiseau, Pauline McGibbon, Janet McLaren, Paul-Louis Mignon, Norman Paul, Claude Petitpierre, Marc Proulx, Tod Randolph, Raymond Ravar, Lesley and Peter Retey, Jean-Louis Roux, Chattie Salaman, Perry Schneiderman, Claude Schumacher, Sylvia Short, Fernand Simon, John Stix, Harold Stone, Peter Streuli, Henry Tarvainen, Irving Wardle, Edgar Wreford.

I would also like to express my appreciation to the helpful personnel at the Juilliard Archives, the library of the National Theatre School of Canada, the Shakespeare Centre Library, the library of the École Supérieure d'art dramatique de Strasbourg, and the Bibliothèque nationale de France (Département des Arts du spectacle).

I wish to express my gratitude to my editors, Christopher Innes, Josh Beer, and Simon Williams, for their careful reading and invaluable suggestions.

Finally, my thanks go to my husband Lawrence Baldwin for his patience, support, insights, and editorial comments. And to my daughter Kathryn Syssoyeva for her encouragement and useful discussions of this work.

Previously unpublished and/or untranslated French documents have been translated by Jane Baldwin.

CHRONOLOGY

Year	Events in Saint-Denis's life	Saint-Denis's productions	Relevant theatrical events	Selected political events
1895			Adolphe Appia, *The The Staging of Wagner's Musical Dramas*	
1896			Alfred Jarry's *Ubu roi*	
1897	Born in Beauvais, France			
1898			Moscow Art Theatre founded. Lilian Bayliss becomes manager of the Old Vic	Dreyfus Affair in France
1899			Appia, *Music and Stage Setting*	
1905	Moved to Versailles		Gordon Craig, *The Art of the Theatre*. Georg Fuchs, *The Theatre of the Future*	Abortive Russian Revolution
1911			Copeau's début, *The Brothers Karamazov*. Stravinsky, *Petrushka*, dir. Fokine, Paris	
1913			Vieux-Colombier founded	
1914	Writes a play and fails baccalaureate exams		Vieux-Colombier closed	World War I begins
1916	Passes exams and is drafted			
1917	Sees combat		Vieux-Colombier company in New York	Russian Revolution
1918	His division sent to fight Red Army			World War I ends

Year	Events in Saint-Denis's life	Saint-Denis's productions	Relevant theatrical events	Selected political events
1919	Released from military			League of Nations established
1920	Begins work with Copeau		Vieux-Colombier reopens in Paris	Women's suffrage in the United States
1921			Vieux-Colombier School founded	
1922	Acting début, *Twelfth Night*		Charles Dullin founds the Atelier. Moscow Art Theatre tours to Paris	Fascists seize power in Italy
1923	Marries Marie Mroczkowski-Ostroga	Directing début, *Amahl ou la lettre du roi*, Vieux-Colombier School	Moscow Art Theatre tours the United States	
1924	Father dies. In Burgundy, Saint-Denis becomes leading figure in the Copiaus. Son Jérome born		Copeau closes Vieux-Colombier; Moves to Burgundy. Louis Jouvet founds his own troupe. Stanislavsky, *My Life in Art*	
1925	Creates first masked character, Jean Bourguignon. Daughter Christine born	Collaborates with Copeau and Jean Villard on *La Célébration du vin et de la vigne*	André Breton publishes his first surrealist manifesto	
1927			Copeau directs *The Brothers Karamazov* for Theatre Guild in New York. Cartel des Quatre formed	
1928	Creates masked character Oscar Knie	Writes and directs *La Danse de la Ville et des Champs* in collaboration with J. Villard		
1929		Creates *Les Jeunes Gens et l'Araignée ou La Tragédie Imaginaire* collaboration with J. Villard	Copeau dissolves the Copiaus	New York stock market collapses
1930	Founds la Compagnie des Quinze. Son Blaise Gautier born			
1931		*Noé. Le Viol de Lucrèce. La Mauvaise conduite. La Bataille de la Marne. La Vie en rose*	Quinze first London tour. American Group Theatre founded. Rupert Doone founds Group Theatre in London	

Year	Events in Saint-Denis's life	Saint-Denis's productions	Relevant theatrical events	Selected political events
1932		Les Lanceurs de graines. Vénus et Adonis	Motley/J. Gielgud collaboration begins	Height of the Depression
1933		Violante. Loire	Tyrone Guthrie directs 1933–34 season at Old Vic	Hitler takes power. New Deal in the United States
1934		Don Juan	Socialist realism declared proper style in Soviet Union	
1935	Disbands the Quinze. Moves to London; establishes collaboration with Motley	Noah (J. Gielgud). Sowers of the Grain	Romeo and Juliet with Laurence Olivier, John Gielgud, and Peggy Ashcroft. Federal Theatre Project inaugurated in the United States	Purges in the Soviet Union
1936	Establishes London Theatre Studio (LTS)	The Witch of Edmonton		Germany reoccupies the Rhineland. Spanish Civil War breaks out
1937	Adjudicates Dominion Drama Festival (DDF) in Canada	Macbeth. L'Occasion, LTS. A Woman Killed with Kindness, LTS. Judith, LTS. Hay Fever, LTS		Italy leaves League of Nations
1938		Three Sisters. The White Guard. Twelfth Night. Electra, LTS. La Première famille, LTS. Ariadne, LTS	Antonin Artaud, The Theatre and Its Double	Anschluss unites Germany and Austria. Munich agreement dismembers Czechoslovakia. Kristallnacht
1939	Production of The Cherry Orchard interrupted by the war. LTS dissolved. Returns to France to serve in the military	The Marriage of Blood. Weep for the Spring. The Confederacy, LTS. Alcestis, LTS		Germany invades Poland. France and Great Britain declare war on Germany
1940	Begins BBC wartime broadcasts		Meyerhold executed. Old Vic wartime tours initiated	Dunkirk retreat. France conquered by Germany and divided into two zones
1945	Son Jérome dies	Oedipus		United States drops atom bomb on Japan. World War II ends. United Nations founded. Nuremberg trials. Fourth Republic, France. Women's suffrage, France

Year	Events in Saint-Denis's life	Saint-Denis's productions	Relevant theatrical events	Selected political events
1946	Suffers first stroke		J.-L. Barrault and Madeleine Renaud establish troupe	
1947	Old Vic School opens	*Noah*, Young Vic	Centre de l'Est founded. Jean Dasté named director of 2nd drama center. Avignon Festival created. Actors Studio founded in New York	Marshall Plan instituted. India and Pakistan gain independence
1948		*The Snow Queen*, Young Vic (S. Magito was co-director). *Our Town*, Old Vic School	International Theatre Institute (ITI) founded	Communists seize power in Czecho-slovakia. State of Israel established
1949		*A Month in the Country*	Copeau dies. Berliner Ensemble formed	People's Republic of China founded
1950	Adjudicates Canadian DDF	*The Black Arrow*, Young Vic	Ionesco, *The Bald Soprano*	Korean war erupts
1951		*Electra. The House of Bernarda Alba*, Old Vic School	Jean Vilar appointed director of the Théâtre National Populaire. Jean Gascon founds Théâtre du Nouveau Monde (Montréal)	
1952	Adjudicates Canadian DDF. Old Vic School closes	*King John*, Old Vic School	Stratford Festival (Ontario) founded, Tyrone Guthrie, director	
1953	Assumes directorship of the Centre de l'Est (CDE). Acting division, Ecole supérieure d'art dramatique opens in Colmar	*A Midsummer Night's Dream. On ne badine pas avec l'amour*	Beckett, *Waiting for Godot*	Stalin dies
1954	School expands and moves to Strasbourg	*Tessa. Une femme qui a le coeur trop petit. Romeo and Juliet. La sauvage*		Algerian revolt against French rule
1955	Second severe stroke	*Voleur d'enfants*		
1956	Les Cadets (student touring company) created		George Devine founds English Stage Com-pany. Brecht dies	Russia crushes Hungarian revolt
1957	Resigns and turns CDE over to Hubert Gignoux		Roger Planchon founds Théâtre de la Cité	Sputnik I and II
1958	Marries Suria Magito. Begins Juilliard consul-tancy. Lecture tour in the United States			Fifth Republic, France; de Gaulle elected president

Year	Events in Saint-Denis's life	Saint-Denis's productions	Relevant theatrical events	Selected political events
1959	Adjudicates Canadian DDF. Appointed Inspecteur Genéral des Spectacles (France). Second U.S. tour		Grotowski founds Polish Laboratory Theatre. Ford Foundation gives grants to regional theatre companies (U.S.)	André Malraux appointed French Minister of Culture
1960	*Theatre: The Rediscovery of Style* published. National Theatre School of Canada inaugurated	Stravinsky's *Oedipus Rex*		
1961	Adjudicates Canadian DDF	*The Cherry Orchard*	Royal Shakespeare Company (RSC) established	Berlin Wall
1962	Designs theatre program for the Institut national supérieur des arts du spectacle (Brussels). Director with Peter Hall and Peter Brook of the Royal Shakespeare Company (RSC). Runs RSC training program		"Maisons de la culture" inaugurated	Algeria gains independence. Cuban missile crisis
1963	Conducts training symposium at ITI		British National Theatre opens. Tyrone Guthrie Theatre (Minneapolis) created. Peter Brook's Season of Cruelty	John Kennedy assassinated
1964	Conducts training symposium at ITI		Ariane Mnouchkine forms Théâtre du Soleil	United States sends troops to Vietnam
1965	Conducts training symposium at ITI	*Squire Puntilla and His Servant Matti*		
1966	Conducts training symposium at ITI. Third severe stroke		George Devine dies	Chinese Cultural Revolution instituted
1967	Conducted training symposium at ITI. Has mild stroke			Israel defeats Egypt in "Six-Day War"
1968	Juilliard Drama Division opens. Suffers two strokes		Richard Schechner founds the Performance Group (New York). Theatrical censorship abolished in England	French students, workers, artists revolt. Soviet troops crush "Prague Spring"
1971	Dies in London			
1982	*Training for the Theatre* published			

chapter one

(Re)claiming Michel Saint-Denis's Place in the Theatre

A T THE HEIGHT OF HIS CAREER, the director, teacher, and theatrical reformer Michel Saint-Denis was a leader in the field whose work was respected, admired, and closely followed. Several of his productions—*Oedipus, Three Sisters, Le Viol de Lucrèce*, Stravinsky's oratorio *Oedipus Rex*—set a standard that has seldom been equaled. The five major theatre schools he founded profoundly affected and improved theatre practice, particularly acting. He remains a pervasive influence, but an unrecognized one, his achievements scarcely remembered except by his few remaining colleagues, former students, and scholars of twentieth-century British theatre. No extended investigation of his practice has been published (although he has been the subject of several dissertations). More often than not, he appears only as a passing reference in a theatrical biography or study of modern British theatre.

One of the many paradoxes surrounding Saint-Denis is that while he was well known, little was known about him. This is due in part to a reserve that seems old-fashioned to our obsessively confessional age. What emerges from descriptions of those who knew him well is an intellectual who was highly intuitive, a person of great dignity with a ribald sense of humor, a fighter who, in moments of stress, sometimes deserted the arena, an autocrat capable of genuine kindness and warmth, an astute planner who frequently bogged down in detail, a pragmatic idealist, a man determined yet vacillating. While loved and revered by many of his students and co-workers, he was feared by others. He was rigorous, often authoritarian, but always in the service of an ideal of theatre. He never demanded more from others than he demanded of himself. Those with whom he worked more peripherally in offering advice or helping to set up a theatre program enthuse about his generosity. Those who knew him best testify to his lack of interest in personal glory.

Saint-Denis's tangible legacy lies in the extant schools he founded, but his productions may have been an equal force for propagating his vision of theatre. Like the early reformers who were his guides, Saint-Denis saw the theatre in a state of transition. Unlike them, he was not a utopist; he was aware that the transition is on-going, that the theatre at each phase of its being must respond to a constantly changing culture. It is this conviction that informs his conception of style, the ruling principle of his teaching and directing. So many of his ideas on style have been incorporated into the contemporary theatre that it is difficult to appreciate the striking, almost revolutionary effect they had on those who first heard them in England in the 1930s, in Canada in the 1930s and later in the '50s, and in the United States in the late 1950s.

Yet, Saint-Denis is not always clear what he means by "style," possibly because of its broad implications. In some of his writings it is discussed in practical terms, in others, almost philosophically. He often conflates style with reality and/or realism, sometimes linking the concepts; at other times he uses the words interchangeably. To approach his point of view, it is useful to take a glimpse at the world of art that Saint-Denis found when he entered the theatre. It was in the midst of a paradigm shift: The advent of anti-naturalist movements in the late nineteenth and early twentieth centuries had altered the function of art from an attempt to reflect the world around it to creating its own reality. It was also a period in which the leading experimentalist directors were struggling to raise the standards of theatre, to reclaim it as an art, unique in itself, which had an indispensable role in society.

The inherent contradiction is that a theatrical production may integrate a host of art forms: acting, poetry or literature, visual arts, music, and dance, among others. How then can it be an autonomous art form? For Saint-Denis, a production's integrity derived from the director's understanding, vision, and unified interpretation of the play's text. His respect for the text precluded the development of a characteristic production style. He rejected the addition of any element that could be considered extraneous to the play's organic wholeness. The following account illustrates Saint-Denis's understanding of style. In 1946, Peter Brook directed *Love's Labour's Lost*, which was well received by the critics but not by Saint-Denis. The reason: Brook had chosen to use Watteau's paintings as a visual motif. As Saint-Denis explained to the young director, this choice was an imposition because "the theatre is theatre in its own right and should not refer to anything outside itself."[1] What Brook had presented was an accretion, a gimmick that was essentially untrue to the play.

For Saint-Denis, finding and presenting the style of a play was akin to creating an encounter between two worlds—that of the author's original world and that of the audience. He frequently said that each period has its own style. Style is both internal and external: it is composed of language, behavior, fashion, prevailing aesthetic(s), social structure, and belief system(s). All these elements are filtered through the play's text. Style is not static; the playwright's world is fixed in time but not the audience's perception of it. Although Saint-Denis believed that universality was the test of a play's greatness, he realized that a given style's contemporaneity is related to the anxieties, fears, desires, and values of the audience. If a director were to attempt to reconstruct the culture (of even a modern work) into which the play was born, the production would be both artificial and dead: artificial, since it is impossible to free oneself completely of one's own time and/or place; and dead, since the audience would not identify. Conversely, to ignore the playwright's world is to do irreparable damage to the work's meaning. The director's inventiveness lies in the way he or she connects and/or blends the two worlds.

Style informs every aspect of theatrical presentation—architecture, design, performance—and Saint-Denis, the complete man of the theatre, was involved in each one. His long theatrical apprenticeship gave him a thorough training and expertise in all areas. He became engaged in the twentieth-century experiments in theatre architecture beginning in 1931, when he rebuilt the stage of the Vieux-Colombier (with André Barsacq) for his first troupe, the Compagnie des Quinze. By then, Saint-Denis had assimilated how the shape of the stage and auditorium not only affects the staging and style of a play, but influences the actor–audience relationship and the way the public receives the production. His earliest directing experiences (1920s to early 1930s) took place on untraditional stages: the trestle stage of the Copiaus and the presentational stage of the Vieux-Colombier. It was not until he arrived in England in the mid-1930s that he directed specifically for a proscenium theatre. Despite his previous rejection of fourth-wall illusionism, he came to appreciate the proscenium's inherent appropriateness for realistic dramas, such as Chekhov's. On the other hand, he found it unsuitable for more presentational theatre. Ideally, Saint-Denis would have liked to create a specific audience–actor configuration for each production. But being practical he did not try for the impossible, given his continually limited financial resources. He developed multipurpose stages for the Old Vic Theatre, the Centre de l'Est in Strasbourg, and the Juilliard Drama Division in New York.

It follows that as Saint-Denis modified his ideas on stage architecture and broadened his repertory, his views on design would also change. The kind of permanent and abstract set he developed for the Compagnie des Quinze seldom reappeared after his move to England. Different conditions, different perceptions, different collaborators also demanded other approaches. In England, he experimented with realism and surrealism, among other styles. He worked closely with his designers, always in a supervisory role. Indeed, he preferred long-term partnerships such as he had with André Barsacq, Motley, and Abd' Elkader Farrah, if possible with designers he had trained himself. Saint-Denis's model of unified production presupposed a director in charge of every element.

His influence on English stage design through Motley, Farrah, and his former pupil Jocelyn Herbert was considerable.

Saint-Denis saw himself as part of an experimental European community of theatre artists that had begun in the early twentieth century and was still evolving. In his youth, the leaders of this community he so admired were Jacques Copeau, Charles Dullin, Louis Jouvet, and George Pitoëff in France and Stanislavsky, Meyerhold, Tairov, and Vakhtangov in Russia. They shared a similar attitude toward the theatre as an art, especially the French practitioners. Saint-Denis's artistic principles were also based on "the search for beauty and style as taught by Gordon Craig and Adolphe Appia."[2] He felt immeasurably enriched by having had the experience at the beginning of his career of being "in contact with men of the theatre and writers who were beginning new theatre movements," namely, modernism, even if he was sometimes at odds with their opinions.[3] (Among them were the surrealists including Antonin Artaud who, following his attendance at Compagnie des Quinze performances, explicated at length to Saint-Denis his formulations on the theatre of cruelty.)[4] In his maturity, this community grew wider because the artists within it had been nourished on similar theories and practice. The movement had become more internationalized, partly due to Saint-Denis's work.

An internationalist, he nonetheless recognized that he was a man of his era and particular cultural experiences, acknowledging that his most immediate influences were the French and the English. For him, to deny one's culture was to deny experience and identity, which leads to anomie. In his own words, "It is only our traditions which tend to create any sort of unity."[5] Ever paradoxical, Saint-Denis's career was far more involved with the modern than the classical theatre despite his passion for classical and ancient texts, such as Shakespeare and the Noh, and his emphasis on the classics as a tool for training actors. Of the approximately forty productions he directed, twelve were original scripts and seven were classics. The rest came from the modern repertory—a repertory he endeavored to increase. Throughout his career he encouraged new dramatists, but to little apparent effect. The exception was André Obey, Saint-Denis's collaborator-playwright, with the Compagnie des Quinze.

The drama he was drawn to was "poetic"; that is, it sought and/or exposed a deeper reality than that of the day-to-day. His aesthetic derived largely from the symbolist ideas prevalent at the time of Saint-Denis's initial exposure to the theatre in the first decades of the twentieth century. For Saint-Denis, a play's poetry was not necessarily dependent on words, although he deeply appreciated heightened, metaphorical, and lyrical language. A poetic theatre can be a theatre of images, one that uses the language of the body in space. He looked for plays that present vast or universal themes, as opposed to heavily plotted dramas that emphasize the detailed psychology of individual characters. He held that a true artist "can create worlds that have an existence of their own and are not directly governed by the laws of living nature."[6] For much of his professional life he bemoaned its paucity in modern theatre. For a period in the 1940s he believed that T. S. Eliot and Christopher Fry would usher in a new era of poetic drama. In the 1950s he found many of the qualities he admired in the work of Eugène Ionesco and Samuel Beckett, in contemporary form.

Counterbalancing Saint-Denis's call for a poetic theatre was his desire to revivify popular theatre. Other twentieth-century theatre reformers looked to old and new popular forms—circus, commedia dell'arte, street performers, puppetry—as a means of revitalizing contemporary theatre practice and expanding its audience base. The difference was Saint-Denis's extensive experience in that realm. With the Copiaus he wrote, directed, and acted material that was created for and enjoyed by Burgundian peasants. His close connection with his audiences and familiarity with their lives were reflected in the productions. His success with this untutored public stayed with him and he continued to explore and delight in popular forms, both their roots and their modern expression, mostly through his teaching but also in his work for the BBC.

If one were forced to reduce Saint-Denis's directorial, pedagogical, and political ideas to a precept, it would be *balance*. He believed that the theatre should be practiced with passion, but also detachment.[7] Without passion it is emotionally meaningless, without detachment it is intellectually void. Saint-Denis tried under all circumstances to keep his critical detachment, although his students and actors frequently found his assessments more cutting than detached. At the same time, even those who were hurt by what they experienced as excessive harshness were impressed by his ability to penetrate to the heart of a problem—a quality dependent on detachment. Admittedly, some found his approach off-putting, but most of those who worked with and under him thought him inspiring. "Genius" and "great man of the theatre" are words used repeatedly to describe him, not only by his students, but by artists of the caliber of Laurence Olivier, Peggy Ashcroft, and Peter Hall. His intellectual acuity in combination with his fervor to search out and develop what he termed "theatrical truth" drew followers to him.

Throughout his professional life Saint-Denis remained convinced that the renewal of the theatre could be brought about by the establishment of theatrical research organizations composed of drama schools teaching the complete range of the theatrical arts working in close coordination with experimental theatres, staffed by teams of dedicated professionals. His professional life was committed to the implementation of this ideal and, despite repeated setbacks, he tenaciously continued the struggle while instilling his students with the same values. As a teacher, he knew that the aspirations of one generation may be fulfilled by the next.

NOTES

1. Peter Brook, *Threads of Time: Recollections* (Washington DC: Counterpoint, 1998), 34.

2. Michel Saint-Denis, "Naturalism in the Theatre," *The Listener* (4 December 1952), 928.

3. ———, *Training for the Theatre*, ed. Suria Saint-Denis (London: Heinemann, 1982), 38.

4. ———, "Artaud for Artaud's Sake," *Encore 11*, no. 3 (May–June 1964), 21.

5. ———, *Theatre: The Rediscovery of Style* (New York: Theatre Arts Books, 1960), 28.

6. ———, *Training for the Theatre*, 37.

7. ———, *Theatre: The Rediscovery of Style*, 48.

◆ chapter two ◆

A Call to the Theatre

I just received your letter. . . . To say how unhappy it made me is useless. . . . You know that you are everything for me; you are my ideal, you are my future, you are the only person in whom I can totally confide. You alone know me, to you alone I have unveiled my plans which now have become very firm decisions. What joy your letter brought me when full of enthusiasm you wrote me about everything that we would build together. . . . Yesterday I was happy when I found I had a letter from you. I opened it expecting to find the usual comforting words and instead, I read a page of reproaches and threats about the future. I cried and I couldn't work all day.[1]

CONTRARY TO APPEARANCES, the object of these passionate words, written by an eighteen-year-old Michel Saint-Denis, was not a rejecting sweetheart but Saint-Denis's uncle Jacques Copeau. Today this letter strikes us as puerile, hysterical, and sentimental, but in the France of 1914 Copeau, as the family patriarch, was owed obedience and respect. Saint-Denis, a stage-struck schoolboy, was impatiently waiting to begin working alongside Copeau, the brilliant director.

It is difficult to assess Saint-Denis without reference to Copeau, his strongest influence. Theirs was a complex and enduring relationship. For Copeau, the younger Michel was a devoted acolyte, the older an occasional apostate. For Saint-Denis, Copeau was an idol, mentor, and sometimes oppressive authority figure. In his youth Saint-Denis internalized the ideas espoused by his uncle. In adulthood he brought his personalized adaptation of Copeau's theories to England and then to North America. His ambivalence about the relationship is reflected in an anecdote Saint-Denis often recounted. He and Louis Jouvet, another Copeau follower, were traveling by train one day when Jouvet suddenly said: "You know Michel, we're screwed, wherever we go in the future, anything we do will be attributed to Copeau."[2] To the child Saint-Denis pleasing his uncle was crucial. Copeau offered a future that contrasted sharply with the shabby life Michel felt he led with his parents. In order to appreciate the intensity of the boy's emotions, hopes, dreams, it is important to understand how Copeau came to assume such a position vis-à-vis his nephew.

Michel Saint-Denis was born on September 13, 1897 in Beauvais, a city about fifty miles north of Paris.[3] His birthplace was a comfortable home that had been in his father's family for several generations. He was the first child of Charles Saint-Denis and his wife Marguerite, Jacques Copeau's elder sister. A sister Suzanne was born four years later. Affable and easy-going, his father was also feckless and irresponsible. Educated at a Jesuit academy Charles planned a career in government, but failed the civil-service examinations. He entered the family business for which he had neither taste nor aptitude. By the time Michel was seven, the business had collapsed and the house was sold to pay off debts.

Saint-Denis's maternal grandmother offered assistance, prompting the family to move to Paris to live with her. After several months, Charles secured a job and they found an affordable apartment. Charles turned to selling, at one time representing a company that made grindstones, and, at another, peddling hernial trusses. At first, Michel remained in Beauvais; a bright boy, he won a scholarship to a local Catholic boarding school. But after six months, loneliness caused him to fall ill and he was withdrawn from school to rejoin his family. Nonetheless, Michel found living at home taxing. His father unsuccessfully attempted to augment their meager income through gambling, while his mother struggled to put food on the table and dress her children adequately. She also had difficulty coping. Her daughter Suzanne remembers her as "a good woman, but weak."[4] From his earliest years Michel despised his father for his frailties. In 1910, Charles found steady employment at a lumberyard in Versailles, fifteen miles outside of Paris, but continued gambling. Overcoming her misgivings, Marguerite joined her husband, bringing the children with her. Despite family conflicts, Michel continued to do well scholastically, winning scholarships to the lycées he attended. The classroom provided a positive atmosphere in which he could excel.

School was not Michel's only refuge. The Saint-Denis family's arrival in Paris coincided with Jacques Copeau's return to the capital in 1905, after a sojourn in Denmark. In Copeau, Michel found his spiritual father. This relationship served to weaken further the role Charles played in his son's life.

It is significant that in Saint-Denis's writings, his memories begin with the advent of Copeau into his life. Charles is mentioned only in relation to Saint-Denis's esteem for Copeau. "I was proud that he was my uncle—my mother's brother. It was he who, after my father's early death, began to take care of our family."[5] Contrary to Saint-Denis's assertion, Copeau, concerned for his sister, intervened in their lives well before Charles's death in 1924. When Michel was fourteen, household tensions reached a crisis. His mother could no longer tolerate the economic hardships, her husband's uncontrollable gambling, and the constant fighting. Copeau tried to persuade her to leave her husband, further

FIGURE 2.1   *Michel Saint-Denis (top row), Marie-Hélène (left), Jacques Copeau (center), and Suzanne Saint-Denis (right).*

inflaming the situation. In spite of the desire to be free of domestic strife, passivity and a sense of propriety restrained her.

Importantly for the theatre's future, Copeau took a strong interest in his nephew. With the Copeaus Michel spent school vacations either in Paris, the country, or at the seaside, playing with his cousins and listening to the adults' conversation (see figure 2.1). He particularly enjoyed the company of Copeau's daughter Marie-Hélène, called Maïène. Although she was five years his junior, their mutual adoration of Copeau and passion for the theatre brought them closer. While not wealthy, the Copeaus lived on the fashionable avenue Montaigne, not far from the Champs-Elysées; to Michel the book-lined apartment seemed luxurious, their life glamorous. At his uncle's residence, Michel mingled with France's intellectual elite. As one of the founders of the prestigious *Nouvelle Revue Française* (1908) and director of the experimental Theatre of the Vieux-Colombier, Copeau was at the center of Paris' literary and theatrical world. Among his colleagues were the leading twentieth-century writers: André Gide, Roger Martin du Gard, Jules Romains, Charles Péguy, and Paul Claudel. These men were a formative influence on the young Saint-Denis, who absorbed their cultural values and dreamed of becoming a writer. But more than anyone else, Copeau was the teacher to whom Michel listened, devouring the books he recommended. An apt pupil, he assimilated what he saw and heard.

At the time when Michel grew close to his uncle, Copeau was moving towards establishing the Vieux-Colombier, an endeavor that would permanently change the French theatre. Other than a love of the theatre, little in Copeau's early background had prepared him to be one of its preeminent reformers. Just eighteen years older than Michel, Jacques Copeau was born in Paris in 1879 into a bourgeois family of no intellectual pretensions. By contrast, Copeau was attracted to literature and the arts, eventually becoming a drama critic. In this capacity from 1905 to 1914, Copeau attended nearly every Paris production— no easy task given the approximately fifty playhouses in the capital. As Michel matured, he accompanied his uncle and gained an invaluable theatrical education, developing his critical skills, learning what to accept, to discard, and on occasion preserving images.

The Paris theatre Saint-Denis encountered was in decline, whereas in other parts of Europe the avant-garde was in its ascendancy. In less than a decade Paris had ceded its position as Europe's leader of theatrical innovation and was living complacently off its reputation. The work of the first wave of French experimentalists had been watered down and integrated into the mainstream. As directors, those early reformers had emphasized theatre practice, while literary movements provided their inspiration. Driving the demand for change was the perception of the theatre as a second-rate art—if indeed an art at all—that lagged behind music, painting, and literature, which were not only more responsive to social transformations but at times heralded them.

In founding the Théâtre Libre in 1887, André Antoine, the first of the reformers, set the theatre on a path, which had repercussions for generations. Influenced by Émile Zola's writings, Antoine made his playhouse a venue for realism and naturalism, introducing the works of foreign playwrights including Tolstoy, Ibsen, Hauptmann, and Strindberg to frequently unappreciative French audiences and critics. Audiences accustomed to the world of make-believe that the era's theatre offered often found realism and naturalism, with their emphasis on social problems and fidelity to everyday life, raw, poorly constructed, and tendentious. For many, Antoine's productions struck too close to home to be considered art. Conversely, with a potential outlet for their work, numerous French playwrights turned to naturalism.[6] Because Antoine's theatre operated on a subscription basis, in effect transforming it into a private club, productions were able to escape censorship.

Arguably, Antoine's most important contribution was in finding a production style for his repertory. To create the illusion of everyday life, he particularized sets, costumes, acting, giving the characters' social milieu an authenticity heretofore unknown. Props assumed new importance, set pieces were three-dimensional, and lighting effects became more natural. The accepted romantic and/or melodramatic presentational acting style was incompatible with lifelike behavior, necessitating the development of an alternative approach. This, in turn, altered time-honored blocking patterns. In Antoine's theatre actors no longer played to the audience, but retreated behind the invisible fourth wall of the box set. Relationships to other characters and the environment motivated their movement.

The Théâtre Libre became a model for other theatres throughout Europe and in the United States in terms of philosophy, repertory, directing, and acting style. The Freie Buhne in Germany, the Independent Theatre in England, the Moscow Art Theatre in Russia, and the Provincetown Playhouse in the United States were only a few of its offshoots.

But almost simultaneously an anti-illusionist theatre challenged the realists and naturalists' claim to reveal the truths of human life. Its proponents argued that naturalism and realism tended toward the simplistic by focusing on the externals of human experience. Symbolist theatre, the first of these movements, emerged in Paris at the Théâtre d'Art in 1890 under the direction of Paul Fort. Ambitious but inexperienced, Fort allied himself with literary figures who convinced him to produce the works of symbolist poets and dramatists. He also forged a relationship with a group of symbolist painters—the Nabis—who became designers for the Théâtre d'Art.

Their settings reinforced the symbolist concepts of synthesis and synaesthesia, originally put forth by the composer Richard Wagner and the poet Charles Baudelaire, respectively. Various ideas of Wagner's were advocated by the symbolists, but none more than his view of theatrical performance as a *Gesamtkunstwerk* or total art work that would combine and give equal value to music, poetry, movement, and set design. Implicit in this idea is one overriding vision whose effect was to buttress the power of the director. In his proto-symbolist poem, "Correspondences," Baudelaire evokes the links between the material and the mystical, the visible and the invisible worlds, guiding the reader through mysterious "forest of symbols." For Baudelaire, our senses are not only connected but interchangeable: "perfumes, colors, sounds correspond."

Obviously, the stage has always made use of symbols, as even the realists and naturalists were aware. Despite their concern with the accurate representation of contemporary life, dramatists such as Ibsen, Strindberg, and Chekhov, even in their most realistic/naturalistic phase, utilized realistic objects, situations, and language to evoke ideas and emotions in their audiences. The symbolists differed in that their use of symbols was a conscious aesthetic, at once more veiled and more direct. Although the symbolist movement encompassed a variety of subtly divergent concepts, it had certain basic characteristics. The artist's task was to celebrate the mystery of life, a mystery fundamentally unknowable. Truth existed for the symbolists but differed from the naturalists' objective reality, being intangible and unprovable. Symbolist drama generally minimized plot, stripped away detail, employed evocative and/or poetic language, idealized and/or universalized relationships, metaphorized characters, and rendered time and space ambiguous. It also drew on Nietzsche's *Birth of Tragedy*, which posited a ritual origin for theatre. Although Freud's insights were not a motivating factor, the symbolists were fascinated by the unconscious.

As had Antoine, Fort created a production style specifically for the type of works he presented. His was the world of a dimly lit dreamscape with stylized and minimal scenery featuring gauze scrims and draperies. Often costumed in robes, which contributed to a mystical or mythic aura, actors chanted and moved with measured pace, using stylized gestures. Interestingly, despite the Théâtre d'Art's dictum that "the word creates the décor," the actors were directed to privilege the musical and tonal aspects of the text over the meaning. Most likely, this acting style resulted from the symbolists' distrust of the rational. Likewise, the greater attention paid to movement on the symbolist stage was an antidote to realism and naturalism. Unfortunately, Fort's results were sometimes laughable, partly because of bad amateur acting. Yet these early productions, with their emphasis on movement, may have informed the work of later theorists and practitioners who came to believe that the theatre's salvation lay largely in the actor's body, rather than the playwright's words.

While Fort's production ideas were revolutionary, his theatre suffered from mismanagement and dilettantism, leading him to abandon theatrical practice for poetry in 1893. The symbolist banner was picked up and carried further by the professional Aurélien Lugné-Poe who in 1893 opened the Théâtre de l'Oeuvre. In spite of their opposing views, Lugné-Poe borrowed more than a page from Antoine, under whom he had acted. He established his theatre on a subscription basis. And he too welcomed a new generation of Francophone dramatists—in this case symbolists—and dedicated himself to introducing significant contemporary foreign plays. But since Lugné-Poe accentuated a play's symbolist potential regardless of its style—even in as naturalistic a drama as *The Lower Depths*—his productions could prove particularly detrimental to the meaning of foreign works. Four years later, Lugné-Poe renounced symbolism for what he believed was its failure to produce any important dramatists (with the exception of Maurice Maeterlinck) and closed the Théâtre de l'Oeuvre.[7]

It was thought that the closure of Lugné-Poe's theatre sounded the death knell for the symbolist movement, but it continued to reinvent itself; its permutations were many and its influence far-flung. Following World War I (and beyond), France's primary dramatists would continue to reject Cartesian rationalism and the scientific model. As Eric Bentley writes, "The French highbrow theatre became a theatre of dreams."[8]

Artists in other countries, most notably Russia and Germany, began developing their own variations on the French theme. After Chekhov persuaded Stanislavsky to put on an evening of Maeterlinck's one-act plays, the most inventive young Russian directors—Meyerhold, Tairov, Evreinov, Komisarjevsky, Vakhtangov—all experimented with symbolism, a form that allowed them to give rein to their imaginations. Their productions exploited their research in movement, mime, design, and use of space. Russia also generated its own symbolist playwrights in Andreyev and Blok. In Germany, the naturalist Gerhart Hauptmann became at least a partial convert to symbolism with his *Assumption of Hannele* and *The Sunken Bell*, while Hugo von Hofmannsthal's writings echoed parts of the symbolist creed. As in Russia, advances in directorial practice with the concomitant emergence of the star director brought symbolist theatre a larger audience. Credit is most due to Max Reinhardt, the leading German director of the early twentieth century. Strands of influence crossed and recrossed national borders. Reinhardt gave the Swedish Strindberg's dream plays, inspired by the Belgian Maeterlinck's early static dramas, their most realized productions to date. With their gloomy sets, chanted speech, atmospheric lighting, and supernatural air, they were reminiscent of Lugné-Poe's work, albeit more sophisticated.[9] Reinhardt's stylized productions of Strindberg helped open the door to German expressionism.

Just as Saint-Denis was coming into contact with the French theatre, the international stage made its presence known in Paris. Among the factors that would contribute to the broadening of the French theatre was Jacques Rouché's book, *Modern Theatre Art* (1910), which depicted avant-garde developments in Russia and Germany, as well as Adophe Appia's and Gordon Craig's scenographic theories. Another was the cross-fertilization provided by the Paris tours of the European reformers. Still another may have been Sadayakko, the Japanese actress-manager, who brought to Paris her modernized, but still movement-based, version of kabuki in 1900 and 1908. The Paris seasons of the Ballets Russes (beginning in 1909), whose principles evolved out of Russian symbolism, stirred the French imagination. Its themes, choreography, colorful settings, and costumes presented exotic worlds—a reinterpreted Classical Greece, an amorphous East, and a romanticized primitivism—within the framework of a carefully synthesized production. Its free and sometimes erotic choreography, influenced in part by the American modern dancer Isadora Duncan, introduced a new language of the body to ballet. In 1913, four months before the opening of the Vieux-Colombier, Meyerhold directed the symbolist *La Pisanelle ou la Mort parfumée* (The girl from Pisa or the perfumed death) by Gabriele D'Annunzio in Paris. Although, for numerous reasons, the production fell short of Meyerhold's conceptualization, it was essentially a carefully composed movement piece that used the actor's body as metaphor. In many ways it extended the Ballets Russes' innovations into the spoken drama. Also in 1913, Paris audiences were given the opportunity to witness Reinhardt's production of the symbolist mime drama *Sumurûn*. This wordless piece, with musical accompaniment, depended almost completely on movement and gesture to tell its story.

However, for the most part, Paris offered audiences only the banality of the commercial theatre, the stultifying naturalism of the more serious theatre, and the dead classicism of the Comédie-Française. Antoine and Lugné-Poe's reforms notwithstanding, *fin de siècle* bravura acting still reigned; the player not the play was the thing. Aging stars attracted crowds prompting dramatists to create vehicles for them. Commercial theatre's emphasis on extravagant scenery and spectacle were poor compensations for stale work. Alongside the theatre of the middle and upper classes was a theatre aimed at the working class that staged vulgarized imitations of the commercial Boulevard offerings, mostly farce and melodrama, played in a broad style.

This was the theatre that Copeau inveighed against and Michel learned to despise. Copeau's columns excoriated those he considered to be the enemy of the theatre: money-hungry producers, retrograde directors, and ham actors or "*cabotins*," as he called them. He became a critic with a mission that he approached with quasi-religious zeal: the renewal of the French theatre. But he was not alone in his ambitions. Jacques Rouché, having studied the Russian and German experimentalists, embarked on his own program of reform and opened the short-lived Théâtre des Arts (1910–13). There, Copeau tested the dramatic waters with his adaptation of *The Brothers Karamazov*. Heartened by its success, he spent the next two years devising his ideal theatre. His prescriptions were remarkably similar to those arrived at by various European reformers—all, with the exception of Stanislavsky, anti-illusionists. As did others, he found much of his theatre of the future in the past. He proposed to recapture the meaning of theatre, through an examination of the most noteworthy eras of Western theatre: fifth-century BCE Greece, the Middle Ages, the English Renaissance, the commedia dell'arte, seventeenth-century French theatre. A revival of old forms, albeit in new dress, presupposed a return to old cultural values, to the eventual restoration of a theatre central to its audience's lives, which fulfilled a civic and communal role as in ancient Athens or medieval Europe.

Although Copeau is considered an avant-gardist, his agenda was conservative. Through his exploration of the past he hoped to revitalize the classics by finding relevant production styles. In his search for the appropriate style for a given play, Copeau resembles Meyerhold and Reinhardt. However, his scope was more limited, more academic. And despite his commitment to creating a viable theatrical climate that would attract major writers to the theatre, he showed little interest in the latest innovations. He ignored, perhaps feared, the movements that surfaced during and after World War I: Dada, surrealism, futurism, and expressionism played no role in either his theatre or aesthetic. Doubtless, these movements troubled him because of their rejection of a past he revered and their revolutionary political component. New works that Copeau mounted were generally composed by his culturally conservative and classicist colleagues at the *Nouvelle Revue Française*, most of whom were unable to make a successful transition to writing drama. Setting himself in opposition to Antoine and Lugné-Poe, Copeau refused to foster a specific dramaturgical style. It is noteworthy that he never offered his Parisian audiences productions of the seminal playwrights of modern drama—Ibsen, Strindberg, and Chekhov—perhaps because of his need to distinguish himself from his two predecessors. At the same time, despite his objections to Antoine and Lugné-Poe's reforms, he adopted elements for his own theatre. The Vieux-Colombier was a small playhouse, operated on a subscription basis, rotated its repertory frequently, and like the Théâtre de l'Oeuvre, targeted an audience of intellectuals, artists, and students. And like the symbolists, Copeau favored presentational acting.

In the spirit of the age, he conceived the function of the reformist director as educative and set out to reshape all aspects of theatre, aware that the transformation would be incremental. The initial step was the establishment of a company in 1913; the second, after World War I, was his establishing a school. In forming the company Copeau did not look for experience but rather idealists motivated by a love of the theatre and a desire to learn. The troupe consisted of six men and four women, including himself; he had decided not only to direct each production, but also to act. Among them were two actors who would make notable contributions to French theatre as directors, Charles Dullin and Louis Jouvet. Jouvet would become a renowned actor, but was then more valuable as a designer, technician, and stage manager.

In preparation for their opening season, Copeau, deliberately patterning himself after Stanislavsky, trained the actors at his country house over a ten-week period. The actors rehearsed, improvised, studied texts, and practiced gymnastic exercises. Copeau was following his intuition, since he had little practical experience. He had yet to learn how to mold actors to attain the desired results. Finding Copeau's approach too cerebral and literary, Dullin provided him with useful directorial insights.[10]

On October 13, 1913, the Vieux-Colombier premiered with a double bill, Thomas Heywood's *A Woman Killed with Kindness* and Molière's *L'Amour médecin* (The love doctor). Copeau's staging of an unfamiliar work by an Elizabethan playwright and an obscure farce, mounted in an unconventional style, using platforms, steps, and screens instead of two-dimensional painted scenery, puzzled critics and audiences. Audaciously, or perhaps foolishly, Copeau chose this maiden venture as his acting début. By his own reckoning, as well as that of the critics, Copeau was less than brilliant. Michel Saint-Denis later characterized the self-trained Copeau as an actor of limited range, excellent in roles that called for irony, but "self-conscious" and insufficiently involved in those that made lyrical or emotional demands.[11]

During 1913–14 the Vieux-Colombier presented thirteen plays, which received mixed critical and audience response. Since he was training a public as well as a company, Copeau was not unprepared for this reaction. Whatever hesitancies, fears, and doubts were his, the triumph of their final production, *La Nuit des rois* (*Twelfth Night*), vindicated his aspirations. Even the perennially dissatisfied Copeau could regard the season as "progress." He had imposed his vision and conquered the indifferent Parisians.

Watching from the wings, making himself useful in whatever way he could, was the sixteen-year-old Michel. His tasks included running errands, cuing actors, and taking notes for Copeau. Each evening when his uncle took his five-o'clock stroll Michel would accompany him, and Copeau would discuss their future. In the boy's own eyes he was one of the elect: Copeau, in an almost spiritual sense, had dedicated him to the theatre. Consumed by the theatre Michel, frequently played truant to watch rehearsals. He turned to playwriting and wrote a drama about adolescent rebellion, *La Douleur d'un enfant* (A child's pain), neglecting his approaching baccalaureate examinations, as had Copeau in his own youth.[12] His worried mother confided in Copeau and in the summer of 1914 a recalcitrant Michel was sent to his aunt's country house to study,[13] but to no avail: Michel failed just as Copeau did eighteen years earlier.

Despite promises to concentrate on his studies, Michel wrote another play entitled *Jeunesse* (Youth). Impatient to see his work realized, he assembled a cast of admiring friends and mounted it. The autobiographical and somewhat risqué nature of the play caused a scandal in Michel's neighborhood, church, and lycée.[14] Under pressure, he abandoned the project that he melodramatically confided to Copeau, was his "life."[15] Copeau brought the boy to live with him where he studied under his uncle's tutelage and finally passed his exams. While he was preparing for them, Germany declared war on France. Michel's ambitions and Copeau's plans were put on hold and their two lives diverged.

In 1916, upon receiving his baccalaureate, Michel began his four years of military service, much of it at the front in the trenches (see figure 2.2). The war marked him profoundly. He was awarded the Croix de Guerre for courage on the battlefield, although he rarely alluded to that honor. He learned to assume responsibility and to exert authority as he rose through the ranks from private to lieutenant. Saint-Denis would recall his war experiences as "exceptionally rich in human terms"; nonetheless, the theatre was never far from his mind.[16] The army gave him his first performing opportunity in a variety show popular with the troops.[17] But his vital link with the theatre was Copeau, to whom he wrote often and saw whenever possible on leave. In his letters he assured his uncle of his dedication to the task that lay ahead—the implementation of Copeau's dramatic renovation, beginning with the reopening of the Vieux-Colombier:

> You never told me about the series of experiences and indignities that led you to conceive this magnificent work. . . . I too should like to feel the spirit of the work itself, not in its development, but in the abstract, and to share in this spirit. Raise me up to as complete an understanding as possible. Since I possess the faith and the élan, what more do I need? Am I not worthy of receiving your confidence? Teach me, little by little. Give me the orientation that I need. Let me be the dough in your hands.[18]

Saint-Denis encountered combat in 1917 at Chemin des Dames, the scene of some of the fiercest fighting. When hostilities on the French front ended in November 1918, he was not released from active duty. The French government, threatened by the rise of socialism within its own borders, was anxious to put

FIGURE 2.2   *Michel Saint-Denis, home on leave, and his sister Suzanne, 1916.*

down communism. Once the Russian Communists signed a separate peace treaty with Germany, an opening was created for the Allied troops to aid the White Russian government. In an attempt to contain the perceived Bolshevik menace, Saint-Denis's division was sent to fight against the Red army, engaged in civil war. Its intervention was fruitless. Yet it enlarged Saint-Denis's perspective considerably, giving him his first glimpse of the world beyond the borders of France. His division passed through Italy, Greece, and Turkey by way of the Bosphorous and the Black Sea, en route to Moldova where they confronted Russian troops.

In Paris, the war had major effects on the Vieux-Colombier's development. Most of the male actors were inducted into the army and the theatre closed. Copeau, exempted for health reasons, used the time to visit Italy and Switzerland to confer with Gordon Craig, Adolphe Appia, and Émile Jaques-Dalcroze. He was motivated by the desire to find practical solutions for theoretical questions concerning the theatre of the future, few of which were forthcoming. Inspired by Craig's directorial vision, abstract set designs, nonrepresentational co-production of *Hamlet* at the Moscow Art Theatre (1912), and his theatre school, Copeau found himself baffled by the man. When he met with Appia for the first time, Copeau was dismissive, feeling that Appia had nothing new to teach him.[19] (He had utilized Appia's scenic ideas during the 1913–14 season.) Neither Craig nor Appia shared Copeau's belief in the primacy of the text. More illuminating were his observations of Jaques-Dalcroze's classes in eurhythmics, some of which he would apply in his teaching program. Devised as a means of training musicians, Jaques-Dalcroze's rhythmic exercises had the potential of teaching the actor how to control his or her physicality and develop a more expressive body, an aspect of acting that Copeau wanted to pursue.

In 1917, as a contribution to the war effort, Copeau gave a series of lectures in the United States to promote French culture. Otto Kahn, an American patron of the arts, offered to back Copeau if he would transfer the Vieux-Colombier's base of operations to New York for the war's duration. Accepting this offer allowed Copeau to perform a patriotic service, to test his recent research, and to reassemble the company because his actors would be released from military duty. It was a decision Copeau regretted. The two-year stay in New York was a period of relentless work, broken promises, and an uncomprehending and sometimes nonexistent audience. Especially painful was the fact that he felt compelled to compromise his values in order to attract a public he disdained. Even more difficult was the personal loss of respect from his company, which was upset by the repertory of popular French hits that Copeau imposed on them. The situation worsened after Dullin rejoined the company in New York.

The reality of trying to keep the Vieux-Colombier afloat had drained Copeau, whose demands became ever more stringent. When he dedicated the exhausted actors' summer break to a daily twelve-hour training and rehearsal schedule, resentments increased. In order to maintain this punishing schedule, Copeau handed some rehearsals over to Dullin, others to Jouvet. Dullin, restive in this subservient role, apparently came to believe that he could replace Copeau.[20] He was ambitious and talented and wanted to direct.

Copeau was caught between the reality of survival and the ideal of realizing his principles. Dullin felt that Copeau had lost sight of the vision they once shared, and that it was incumbent upon him to uphold it. Copeau's view of the theatre was hierarchical: actors, designers, and technicians were subordinate to the director. And there was room in the company for only *one* director.

On the point of collapse, Copeau left the company for two week's rest, during which time Dullin rehearsed the actors in several upcoming productions. Copeau found Dullin's work inadequate, while Dullin's journal records that Copeau "demolished" his staging only to return to the same concept later. Ultimately, Copeau fired the actor. Dullin's dismissal was the first of a pattern of such incidents. Driven by an image of perfection that even he realized was unattainable, Copeau was unable to collaborate with others on an equal footing. When associates showed independence of thought and/or action, they were repudiated.

When the war ended Copeau returned to Paris to reopen the Vieux-

Colombier. In preparation, Copeau and Jouvet created the first presentational stage in modern theatre, designed to focus on the actor's performance and the text. As Copeau later acknowledged, Appia's ideas figured prominently in the theatre's renovation, particularly its permanent architectural setting. The stage extended out into the audience from which it was separated by three sets of steps. The acting area encompassed a variety of levels that allowed a multiplicity of staging possibilities. Most startling was the stage's cement floor on which traditional settings were impossible to erect.

The reopening of the Vieux-Colombier in February 1920 marked the beginning of Saint-Denis's theatrical career. He was now formally part of the Vieux-Colombier, although not in the capacity he had fantasized. Before his uncle departed for New York, Michel revealed that he wanted to be an actor; Copeau advised him to study shorthand. Michel would not perform with the Vieux-Colombier until 1922 when he played Curio in a revival of *Twelfth Night*. Warning his nephew that he would test his commitment by assigning him the humblest tasks, Copeau made him general-secretary of the Vieux-Colombier.[21] Saint-Denis met the challenge, realizing the benefits of learning the profession from the ground up. His conscientiousness, maturity, and "excellent work" were remarked early on.[22] His duties expanded to include running the box office, public relations, administrative tasks, and eventually, stage managing and rehearsal assistant. The job of general-secretary moved Saint-Denis from the periphery of the Vieux-Colombier to the center and made him essential to Copeau. In this capacity it was natural to serve his mentor as a confidant.

After his American disappointments Copeau turned to Michel for emotional security, acknowledging that he was counting on his absolute devotion.[23] On his return to France Copeau had vowed that he would have no collaborators, but only assistants, and Michel was thrilled to fill that role. Copeau's distrust of equals served Saint-Denis's career. Having gained his uncle's confidence, he gradually assumed Jouvet's role at the Vieux-Colombier. As Copeau rewarded Saint-Denis's diligence with additional responsibility, he undermined Jouvet's authority by eliminating certain of his duties. In 1921, his directing ambitions thwarted by Copeau, Jouvet left to establish his own troupe. But it has also been said that Jouvet's leaving was hastened by his jealousy of Saint-Denis who, he felt, had usurped his place as Copeau's trusted friend and associate.[24]

Although Copeau recognized that the renewal of the theatre could not be achieved by one man in a single generation, his unwillingness to relinquish control was proving an obstruction to achieving his goals. His solution was to establish the Vieux-Colombier School, which could serve three indispensable functions. The first was the creation of a generation of disciples imbued with Copeau's ideals. Second, it would guarantee a laboratory for his research. And third, it would develop the new breed of actor he required. Since the school was to have major consequences for Saint-Denis's professional life, a description of the program is in order here. Although never formally a student, as the theatre's general-secretary Saint-Denis was involved and attended classes on a regular basis—watching, learning, absorbing.

Three divisions were proposed: classes for the general public; classes for theatre professionals; and a three-year course for apprentices. It was for this last group, made up of twelve students, that the school really functioned, and it is the only aspect discussed here. Engulfed by his responsibilities at the theatre, Copeau did not participate in the school as fully as he might have wished. Most of his teaching took the form of *causeries* or informal lectures on theatre history and practice. Suzanne Bing, Copeau's trusted assistant, lover, and actress in the company, was put in charge of the day-to-day running of the apprentice program. Acceding to Copeau's wishes, she allowed her acting career to become secondary to her involvement in the school. Committed, painstaking, and pedagogically inventive, she was nevertheless ill-suited to teach. Students found her cold and stern.[25]

The Vieux-Colombier School was a radical departure from traditional schools such as the Conservatoire National d'Art Dramatique, Paris's prestigious academy, where imitation not innovation was the training method. There, students learned to perform classical roles in the manner of great French actors of the past. In contrast, Copeau's strategy, inspired by Jaques-Dalcroze, was to make the school student-centered rather than teacher-dominated. The emphasis was less on formal instruction than on "a search for the truth, in which master and pupils shared."[26] Research was open-ended, empirical, and not oriented towards a preconceived result. Another unusual aspect of the school was its insistence on the education of the "whole" student. Not only were the young actors' skills developed, but their intellects and even their souls were cultivated as well. There was a moral component to everything Jacques Copeau essayed. He felt an almost paternal responsibility towards his students, and, in turn, exacted filial respect.

The school operated for three years, during which the curriculum and administrative structure were modified; nonetheless, the governing principles remained the same. On the academic side of the program there were courses in general culture, theatre history, and theory. For students such as Jean Dasté, whose formal education was deficient, a remedial French course including instruction in grammar and spelling was mandatory. Theoretical courses alternated with the practical, which included diction and singing, both standard elements of theatre training.

Other aspects of the students' education were less conventional. Copeau wanted to produce an actor who had similar skills to those in the theatres whose principles he wished to emulate—the Greek, the commedia dell'arte, and the Asian. Noting the essential role that dance and movement played in those theatres, plus the contemporary actor's poverty of expression, he had decided that intense physical training was needed. Thus students engaged in all types of movement, from ballet to gymnastics to circus techniques. Although frequently a part of the curriculum in today's drama schools, in 1919, teaching circus techniques to future actors was innovative. Its rationale was Copeau's belief that the circus clown was heir to the commedia players. He engaged the Fratellini Brothers, a famous clown act, to teach tumbling, juggling, pratfalls, and slapstick comedy.

Improvisation shared equal emphasis with physical training. Copeau hypothesized that improvisation would encourage the students' creativity and discourage stereotypical acting. To avoid those clichés, the students were not allowed to attempt dramatic roles until the last year of study. Vocal technique was the stepchild of the curriculum. Obviously, Copeau was aware of the necessity of training the actor to speak. He himself was vocally adept, his play readings being considered remarkable. However, reacting against the traditional French method of actor training that emphasized speech to the detriment of other aspects of acting, Copeau went to the opposite extreme. Although there were classes in diction, poetic technique, play reading, and singing, they never assumed the importance of movement. The students were not taught vocal projection or an approach to text. In later years, according to Jean Dasté, the actors found themselves unprepared for the demands of the professional theatre.

Throughout their training, it was *theatrical* and never *naturalistic* truth they sought, even in enacting improvisational scenes based on everyday reality. In the initial stages, improvisations were silent as they concentrated on simple routine actions, either alone or in groups. During the second stage they began working on characterization, concentrating on outlining their personae in bold strokes. At this point, sounds they called "*grummelotage*" were added. It was an invented language made up of cries, murmurs, and chanting, which expressed the emotion of the moment.[27]

During the most advanced phase of improvisation, masks were introduced. Originally, Copeau merely covered the students' features with a stocking to eradicate their dependence on facial expression. From this early exercise, a neutral mask devoid of any emotional context evolved. Wearing the mask eliminated self-consciousness, allowing the student to become more physically expressive and daring. At the Vieux-Colombier School, only its "noble" aspect was explored; comic masks would come later.

It should be stressed that students responded to their unorthodox theatrical education with pleasure. For these student-actors not far removed from childhood, their training felt like play. At the same time being thoroughly indoctrinated with Copeau's ideas, they believed they were creating the theatre of the future. Jean Dasté expressed these sentiments in an interview: "We really had the impression that when we did our improvisational and mask research that we were in the same state as children playing cowboys and Indians or cops and robbers, but obviously in a professional way."[28]

Their joy came partly from a sense of freedom. Their mask and improvisational work was done with little supervision, which permitted the students to experience a profound sense of discovery and even autonomy. They developed their improvisations together and criticized one another's work. Copeau's daughter Maiène functioned as group leader. Periodically, Copeau viewed the students' works-in-progress, which he often found fresh and exciting. Improvisation had a purpose beyond actor training, however. Since one of Copeau's primary objectives was the creation of a dramaturgy "capable of treating great subjects, where the action would be more important than detailed psychology," universal themes were assigned to develop.[29] It was hoped that these improvisations would eventually create the foundation of new dramatic forms.

The school attracted a great deal of interest and comment, both positive and negative. If critics such as Henri Bidou believed that the Vieux-Colombier School was "the only real drama school in France," others shook their heads in consternation at Copeau's experiments.[30] In order to address the criticism and to provide the students performing practice, presentations of their work were given for a select audience at year's end. One such student production, *Amahl ou la lettre du roi* (Amahl or the king's letter), earned Michel his first directing credits. As the three-year program drew to an end, Copeau and Suzanne Bing hit on the idea of presenting a Noh drama. Although a dress rehearsal accident prevented the project from reaching production, Copeau was stirred by its quality. He saw in the student-actors' work the means through which he could fulfill his ambitions.

Precipitously, at least in the minds of his public, he closed the Vieux-Colombier to devote himself to training his band of young followers and relocated to the Burgundian countryside. Accompanying them was Michel Saint-Denis, arguably Copeau's most faithful disciple. The move would prove to be Michel's stepping stone to an independent career.

NOTES

1. Michel Saint-Denis, letter to Jacques Copeau, 10 October 1914.

2. Clément Borgal, *Metteurs en scène* (Paris: Fernand Lanore, 1963), 57.

3. This account of Saint-Denis's early life is drawn from the following sources: an unpublished and untitled article by Georges Lerminier; Saint-Denis's correspondence and personal papers; and interviews with Suzanne Maistre Saint-Denis and Marie-Hélène Dasté.

4. Suzanne Maistre Saint-Denis, personal interview, 14 March 1996.

5. Michel Saint-Denis, *Training for the Theatre: Premises and Promises*, ed. Suria Saint-Denis (New York: Theatre Arts Books, 1982), 25.

6. Although Antoine's name is synonymous with naturalism, his directing career was far more eclectic.

7. He reopened it in 1912 and continued to direct it until 1929.

8. Eric Bentley, *In Search of Theatre* (New York: Alfred A. Knopf, 1953), 386.

9. J. L. Styan, *Max Reinhardt* (Cambridge: Cambridge University Press, 1982), 38.

10. Jacques Copeau, *Registres VI, L'Ecole du Vieux-Colombier,* ed. Claude Sicard (Paris: Gallimard, 2000), 41.

11. Michel Saint-Denis, "Jacques Copeau: Metteur en scène et comédien," in Jacques Copeau, *Notes sur le métier du comédien* (Paris: Michel Brient, 1955), 11.

12. A state-run exam French students take on completion of their secondary-school education.

13. Michel Saint-Denis, letter to Jacques Copeau, 12 October 1914.

14. ———, letter to Jacques Copeau, 20 April 1915.

15. Ibid.

16. Lerminier.

17. Michel Saint-Denis, letter to Jacques Copeau, 29 August 1917.

18. Quoted in John Rudlin and Norman Paul, eds. and trans., *Copeau: Texts on Theatre* (London: Routledge, 1990), 230.

19. Ibid., 97.

20. Valentine Tessier, quoted in Jacques Copeau, *Registres IV, America,* ed. Marie-Hélène Dasté (Paris: Gallimard, 1984), 302. Tessier, an actress in the New York company, was witness to the crisis.

21. Copeau, undated letter to Michel Saint-Denis, *Registres IV,* 356.

22. Jean Schlumberger, quoted in *Registres IV,* 356.

23. Copeau, undated letter to Michel Saint-Denis, *Registres IV,* 356.

24. Jeanne Laurent, personal interview, 28 August 1988.

25. Jean Villard Gilles, *Mon demi-siècle* (Lausanne: Payot, 1954), 114.

26. Michel Saint-Denis, "Introduction to Noah," in André Obey, *Noah: A Play in Five Scenes* (London: William Heinemann Ltd., 1949), ix–x.

27. In contemporary times, Dario Fo has made effective use of a similar technique.

28. Unpublished interview with Michel Saint-Denis, July 1958.

29. Michel Saint-Denis, "Mes années au Vieux-Colombier," trans. Kathy Koerner, *Europe* (April–May 1961), 69.

30. Clément Borgal, *Jacques Copeau* (Paris: L'Arche, 1960), 89.

chapter three

Burgundy: Working with Actors

I N OCTOBER OF 1924 the members of Copeau's community arrived at their quarters, the château of Morteuil, in Burgundy. Hopes were high, expectations kindled. The participants believed they were taking part in a brave experiment whose outcome would be the rebirth of a re-energized and retheatricalized theatre. While the goal was clear, the means to achieve it were less obvious, and the group was not as unified as it appeared.

Indeed, Copeau's adherents comprised three overlapping groups. In addition to the teachers, Jacques Copeau, Suzanne Bing, and Georges Chennevière, the staff included Michel Saint-Denis who retained his administrative responsibilities, Alexandre Janvier, the Vieux-Colombier's technical director, and Léon Chancerel, the archivist. Chancerel kept a log of the community's activities (*Le Journal de bord*), a charge executed by Suzanne Bing after his departure.[1] Ten gifted students accompanied them: Marie-Hélène Copeau, Marie-Madeleine Gautier, Michette Bossu, Marguerite Cavadaski, Yvonne Galli, Clarita Stoessel, Jean Dasté, Jean Dorcy, Étienne Decroux, and Aman Maistre. The four male students would make significant contributions to the French theatre. Besides Suzanne Bing, Copeau invited three Vieux-Colombier actors to participate: Auguste Boverio, Jean Villard, and François Vibert. Each participant, excluding the "*Patron*" (boss), as Copeau was always called, assumed a student role, researching new dramatic forms through practice.

The Burgundy experiment marked a new phase in Saint-Denis's apprenticeship. At the Vieux-Colombier he was always in Copeau's shadow, eager to learn and help but not yet a personality in his own right. As general-secretary he had demonstrated his loyalty, diligence, and administrative proficiency, but had little opportunity to exercise his artistic abilities. Albeit still burdened with managerial tasks, this venture permitted him the luxury of developing his creativity. It was in Burgundy that he "learned the craft of acting and began to direct."[2] Ultimately, he achieved autonomy, assuming the creative leadership of the group. Ironically, his artistic independence would evolve out of this, his most intimate work experience with Copeau.

In its entirety the community numbered thirty-five. Some members, like Copeau and Saint-Denis, had spouses and families who accompanied them. A year earlier Saint-Denis had married Marie Mroczkowski-Ostroga (Miko), whom he met through the Copeau family. A son, Jérôme, was born before their departure for Burgundy. With the exception of Léon Chancerel and his family and Michel's sister Suzanne Maistre (Copeau's private secretary) and her husband Aman, everyone lived at the château.

This was Copeau's third attempt to establish a communal living-training-work situation, a "family" of artists. In the latter part of the twentieth century the concept became something of a theatrical cliché, but for Copeau the vision was fresh (and even literal, given that several members were his relatives). The difference between this and his prior communities was that the majority of the group consisted of students infused with Copeau's ideals, rather than professional actors.[3] Theatrical innocents, untouched by the commercial theatre he held in contempt, they "were young, carefree, and confident in the wisdom of their leader."[4] After three years of unorthodox training they were poised to make discoveries. Jean Dasté was not alone in his conviction that their research was leading them into "the realm of sacred drama."[5] Impassioned by their task, the students felt that their vocation was to reinvent dramatic art. Essential to them was the fact that they would no longer be competing with the Vieux-Colombier company for Copeau's attention.

Nevertheless, Copeau's motives in bringing them to Burgundy were not as simple as the students imagined. This experiment was a gamble—his last, perhaps best chance for achieving his cherished aims. At the same time, he had other reasons for closing his theatre and taking up residence in the countryside. He was exhausted, his health strained by years of work and disappointments. Possibly in reaction, he had recently undergone a religious crisis that resulted in his embracing Catholicism. He was disgusted with Paris, whose atmosphere he judged to be incompatible with a life of dedication to the theatre and spiritual matters.

After ten years Copeau had made few discoveries, drawing most of his repertory from the classics. But he had literary ambitions. It was his conviction that the greatest playwrights had also been actors and directors. His models were Aeschylus, Shakespeare, and Molière. Although aware that he was not their equal, Copeau thought it incumbent upon himself to attempt what they had accomplished. He spent twenty-three years writing his autobiographical and psychologically realistic drama. When *La Maison natale* reached the stage in 1923, critics lambasted it. According to Saint-Denis, "Copeau knew that it belonged to an older aesthetic than to the promise of the future which he had never ceased to hold up to his disciples and students; he felt he had betrayed himself."[6]

Having failed in his attempt to write and to foster noteworthy dramatists, he turned his attention more fully to the actor. Away from the distracting, corrupting, and commercial influence of Paris, the group could be forged into a unified community of artists, that he called a "chorus." On the one hand, it would resemble the modern idea of an ensemble of players and, on the other, a less-defined notion of a collective character. His inspiration was the ancient Greek chorus, commedia dell'arte, and clown acts. These forms shared a collective aesthetic of performing that he sought to reintroduce into the theatre.

The foundation of his new theatre lay in a recreation of the commedia dell'arte, which he titled the "*comédie nouvelle*" (new comedy). Copeau had long admired the commedia: its comedy was physical, it required ensemble work, and it had influenced his favorite playwright, Molière. He envisaged a company made up of ten character types, much as the commedia had its stock characters. Contemporary archetypes would replace Pantalone, the Dottore, and the Capitano. As in the Italian comedy, the actors would develop and continually refine their own characters. Everyone was excited about this aspect of the work that would take their improvisational studies to another level.

Copeau's perhaps misguided view (held by other early twentieth-century directors) that popular entertainment could be imposed from the top down was elitist and idealized. He had an agenda for the *comédie nouvelle*—the promotion of his own artistic values. New comedy would be the ground on which popular and high culture would meet and marry, as they had in the works of Molière and Shakespeare. Ironically, Copeau's new comedy concept with its fixed characters anticipated in ways he could not have foreseen that television staple, the sitcom (especially of the 1950s and '60s), a genre he would have scorned. Still, there are obvious parallels. Through its easily recognizable characters, frequently embodying national as well as more generalized traits, the sitcom achieves a kind of cultural unity through laughter. And even when the characters criticize society, they typically affirm its values.

A number of potential pitfalls stood in the way of Copeau's and the community's aspirations. Among them were the difficult living arrangements. Copeau had leased the Château of Morteuil because of its reasonable rent and size. Its shortcomings were not apparent when first he saw the property on a beautiful September day. The "château," a grandiose term for the old house, was surrounded by a grove of trees; close by was a stream. When the group moved in, the house was dilapidated, filthy, and inadequate to accommodate so many. The autumn rains turned the grounds into a swamp. Within, it was damp and cold, heated by malfunctioning stoves. Illness was rampant. Thirty-two people uncomfortably huddled together made friction inevitable. Copeau's two families, legitimate and illegitimate, were inhabiting the same household: Madame Copeau was there with her three children, along with Suzanne Bing and Bernard Bing, her son by Copeau, and a daughter from her former marriage. At the very least, awkwardness must have prevailed.

Flirtations and affairs flourished among the adolescent students, often accompanied by high drama. Many were free from parental supervision for the first time. If, however, they thought themselves emancipated, they were about to be disappointed. Copeau instituted an almost monastic rule whose precepts he set down upon his arrival. He had always shown a messianic zeal; previously, the theatre had served as his religion. Now, after his recent conversion, he conflated the two creeds. His opening address announced that their purpose was "perfection of the work and human dignity." Since no one had been forced to join the community, he presumed that its members accepted the sacrifices their project entailed.

He assumed the role of an aloof but autocratic leader, establishing strict regulations and enforcing them through intermediaries. Students were forbidden to leave the grounds without permission. With permission, they had a 10 P.M. curfew. Girls had additional rules: cafés were off-limits without special authorization, smoking and drinking prohibited. Copeau assigned the community members all their duties—domestic, educational, and artistic.

Copeau appointed as lieutenants his nephew and daughter. Michel was in charge of general order, Maiène of the students. Both acted as intermediaries between the group and the *Patron*, a function Saint-Denis had filled at the Vieux-Colombier. Copeau spent much of his time writing, meditating, and worrying in his office in the château's tower. The students resumed their classes that differed from the Vieux-Colombier model in key ways. At Maiène's urging, they began developing their exercises into scenarios. Persuaded that the mask was a rich domain they had scarcely tapped in Paris, they modeled comic masks and combined them with character exploration.[7] Working with the actors for the first time as a peer, Saint-Denis became a vital member of the group. Although lacking the formal training of his collaborators, he showed an exceptional talent for improvisation and mask.

Saint-Denis's ability as an improviser despite his inexperience accentuated an enigma that was never resolved: none of the women ever created a fully developed masked character. In the early stages, Maiène worked on a princess—hardly a comic type. The *Journal de bord* makes no mention of the other women's endeavors. Jean Dasté's sexist hypothesis was that the improviser enters "a kind of delirium which demands great strength, perhaps surpassing women's physical limitations."[8] A more plausible scenario was supplied by Suzanne Maistre who recalled that the women were so busy fabricating costumes, they lacked the necessary time.[9] But perhaps the answer lies in the lack of role models: farce, particularly masked farce, was a traditionally male domain. Commedia dell'arte had a paucity of female comic characters. Moreover, the troupe's principal teachers of comedy had been the Fratellini Brothers, and clowning was an area off-limits to women. Among the men, Dasté, Villard, and Maistre each created a usable character, but only Saint-Denis was able to generate more than one.

Unknown to the group, lack of money plagued Copeau. They left Paris with no means of support, having placed their faith in the *Patron*. He, in turn, had put his hopes on the vague promises of a group of admiring businessmen in Lille. When the money was not forthcoming, Copeau arranged a sort of backers' audition. He confided to the community: "I am going to do what Molière would have done, appeal directly to those who hold power nowadays, that is to say, the wealthy industrialists."[10] It was a disaster. On January 24, 1925 the group presented two plays, hastily thrown together by Copeau. *L'Objet ou le contretemps* (The object or the mishap) was a "comedy-ballet" that drew on their improvisations. The play lived up to its name when its leading actor Auguste Boverio collapsed onstage. Michel Saint-Denis acquitted himself commendably, performing a sizable part in *L'Impôt* (The tax). This latter, as a thinly disguised entreaty for money, offended its audience.

With no resources in sight, Copeau returned to Paris vainly seeking help from his friends. Discouraged by the turn of affairs and depressed by the recent deaths of his mother and friend Jacques Rivière, he decided to dissolve the troupe. On February 19, 1925 Copeau sent Saint-Denis instructions not only to disband, but to explain the reasons to the company. Admitting that "this is a painful task I am giving you," Copeau advised his nephew to "fill it as if the director were no more and you had to take his place." Ironically, Saint-Denis was to take Copeau at his word.

Although the group was aware of the purpose of Copeau's trip, the decision was a shock. One wonders what this news meant to Suzanne Bing, who had sacrificed her acting career for the school. Most of the group spent the next several days packing. Saint-Denis and a half-dozen other participants rallied and began to discuss their future and that of the *comédie nouvelle*, now linked in their minds. Progress had been made, characters conceived, and those most involved were loath to abandon the work.

A joint decision was taken to form a producing company. Saint-Denis was appointed artistic director because of his experience running rehearsals during Copeau's absences, managerial skills, and unmistakable leadership ability. The decision to become professional was rooted in their belief that there was an untapped regional audience and that performance venues existed. These expectations were borne out when an adjacent village offered them the use of their community center and brass band for the initial show. The undertaking was an opportunity to test out their theatrical experiments before live audiences. They would continue developing character archetypes, using them as the foundation for new works—farces based on physical comedy. Thus they would "depart from the beaten path and put to use mask, mime, chorus, song."[11] Copeau was free to devote himself to his religious quest and personal research.

Les Copiaus ("Copeau's children" in the local dialect), the name given the company by the neighboring peasants, expected to become financially independent, but start-up funds were needed. Jean Villard raised money from friends in his native Switzerland. Prompted by a sense of duty, Copeau loaned them props and costumes. They began work immediately on the first production, set to open in mid-May, meeting in Saint-Denis's new office for discussion. Saint-Denis and the company were alert to the fact that this production was an audience-building endeavor. Consequently, they set out to develop material with which their theatrically inexperienced public could identify. Simplicity, comprehensibility, and familiarity were requisites. Their program was a mélange of short comic and musical pieces, most company created, and an eighteenth-century farce *Parade*, whose characters bore similarities to those they had been shaping.

In Copeau's absence the group became more democratic. Everyone pitched in on production work. Besides acting as director, Saint-Denis elected to share administrative tasks with Boverio. And with growing confidence, Saint-Denis returned to writing, creating a regional character for whom he wrote a prologue titled "*Jean Bourguignon et les Copiaus*" that set the tone for their future work. *Bourguignon* was a wine-growing peasant, designed to create audience recognition. Jean Villard composed music and lyrics. Maiène Copeau and Madeleine Gautier took charge of costumes and sets. Alexandre Janvier supervised lighting and props.

Rehearsals began as planned at the end of March. However, their independence was impinged upon as Copeau made his presence felt at rehearsals. At this juncture, the Copiaus do not appear to have resented his attendance and comments. When the program fell a half-hour short, they appealed to Copeau who promised to write and perform a one-act play.

The first reading of Copeau's drama *Le Veuf* (The widower) disquieted the Copiaus. A recent neighborhood incident, the grotesque suicide of an alcoholic peasant, furnished the subject. Copeau played the principal role; two small parts, the grave digger and the neighbor, were executed by Michel Saint-Denis and Suzanne Bing, respectively. This lugubrious melodrama was at odds with the rest of the performance. The Copiaus's mission was "to make people laugh and rid them of their cares."[12] Personifying the festive mood, Michel Saint-Denis, costumed and carrying the Copiaus's banner, led the marching band down the main street prior to the performance. Imagine then the villager's discomfiture when they saw Copeau's detailed, naturalistic impersonation of their unfortunate neighbor. According to Jean Villard, Copeau "put together in his play and performance everything that he had struggled against for ten years in his writings and actions."[13] Worried that their public would disappear, the Copiaus advised Copeau to withdraw the play. *Mirandoline*, an adaptation of Goldoni's *The Mistress of the Inn*, replaced the ill-fated work.

Over the next month the company toured the immediate region, winning audiences and gaining a reputation by word-of-mouth. As they savored their growing success Copeau decided to reassume control of the troupe. They resisted, but were forced to capitulate when he threatened to take back not only his theatrical material, but his daughter and Madeleine Gautier as well. Apparently, as with Dullin and Jouvet, the Copiaus's desire for creative independence threatened him. His possessiveness could not tolerate their succeeding without his strict supervision. Although Copeau was reinstated as director, resentment permeated the company. Regardless of Saint-Denis's affection and respect for his uncle, he was chagrined at surrendering his directorial position. While losing his creative function, he retained his administrative duties. Years later, he recalled the emotional atmosphere. "There was a state of tension between Copeau and the group of students who had become the Copiaus. It was never an open regime."[14] Following the takeover, Copeau added Molière's *The Doctor in Spite of Himself* and *The School for Husbands* to the repertoire, a counterproductive move. Producing Molière's plays drew the Copiaus away from research. Copeau himself had stated that the essential element of their research was "to keep the dramatic imagination working" in pursuit of the new comedy.[15]

More to the point was the Copiaus-created work, *La Célébration du vin et de la vigne* (Celebration of wine and vine), designed to exploit their research in mime, gymnastics, and music. Unity was provided by the event's theme; partially improvised, partially scripted, its structure was analogous to a variety show. Copeau wrote part of the text and Saint-Denis the rest in the form of poems; Villard composed the music; and Jean Dasté modeled the masks. Since the play was linked to the lives of the region's inhabitants, Saint-Denis and Villard gathered background material, interviewing farmhands and observing them at work. Incorporating the workers' chores into a fully developed performance was the logical and practical outcome of the task-oriented mimes practiced as exercises. At times, the mimes were accompanied by songs; at others, the movement became dance through the strength of the rhythms.

The production in November of 1925 coincided with the wine harvest, a connection to the Dionysian festivals of Greece that was not lost on the company who had spent a year studying the origins of Western theatre. How to adapt Dionysian revels and make them relevant for a twentieth-century rural French audience? One element was the use of choral odes in a cheerleading-like format that made complimentary references to the region's wine. The performance opened with the Copiaus chanting "Pindarics" honoring the beauty queens selected to preside over the celebration. At the play's end, the characters performed a spirited dance, chanting the name of the vineyard of the town they were in.

La Célébration du vin et de la vigne featured their farcical local stock characters, most in an embryonic stage. By contrast, Saint-Denis's Jean Bourguignon had evolved from a figure giving the prologue to the principal character. Here he appeared as "a Harlequin type of clever and foolish winegrower."[16] Jean Bourguignon's continuing appearances fostered an attachment to him in the audience.

Soon after, in December 1925, the company moved to the tiny village (population 100) of Pernand-Vergelesses, a change that ameliorated living and working conditions. Located in the Burgundy hills, Pernand's climate was drier. Communal living arrangements were almost entirely abandoned. Copeau purchased a beautiful eighteenth-century house where he resided with his family. Suzanne Bing and her children lived in a rented house next door. Saint-Denis, his wife, son, and new baby Christine stayed with the Copeaus for three months before moving to their own quarters close at hand. Other company members rented rooms nearby. A restaurant supplied meals, liberating the women from kitchen duty. Although no longer living together, the company continued to take meals in common until their shared existence became too restrictive. The Copiaus enjoyed closer contact with the local inhabitants than in Morteuil where they had been isolated. Here, they worked at creating goodwill and, after initial distrust, people took a friendly and proprietary interest in them. Thus it was natural that the company performed at regional festivities.

In Pernand, the company took up their established work pattern: classes, physical training, research exercises, and rehearsal. They had, however, lost two of their stalwarts: Boverio left to resume his Paris career, Chancerel because of a falling-out with Copeau. Two students were added, the first of a number drawn to the group because of its growing reputation. Among the instructors were Michel Saint-Denis, who taught improvisation and mask modeling, Maiène Copeau, responsible for mime, Jean Dasté, mask, and Villard, singing.

An unused *cuverie* (wine storehouse) was rented to provide work and rehearsal space. The long (35 meters) stone building was converted; a stage, rudimentary lighting equipment, portable steps, and a cement floor were added. Company members shared their expertise. Days typically began at 7:30 A.M. with Jean Dasté leading them in gymnastics, followed by mime exercises.[17] Jean Villard worked with them on choral song and rhythmics. After lunch, the company performed various tasks such as making costumes, composing music, and modeling masks. If they were developing a production, they rehearsed weekday evenings in preparation for the weekend performances. The farmers' rare leisure time determined their performance schedule. When not rehearsing, they improvised topics, singly and collectively, that might lead to performance pieces. They were seeking ways of representing large themes, relying completely on mime, rhythm, noise, and music. Themes were occasionally suggested by Copeau, but more often devised by the Copiaus.

During this period Saint-Denis introduced his second stock character, the half-comic, half-tragic Oscar Knie. It is instructive to detail Knie's evolution to understand the intricate procedure. Saint-Denis's exploration began externally with several costume pieces, a pair of baggy, filthy trousers, and a cane. An old piece of carpet that he rolled up and gesticulated with endowed the character "with an air of authority."[18] To these he added an equally dirty swallow-tailed coat, vest, and shirt fastened at the neck with a frayed string. The still incomplete costume and props allowed his imagination to take wing. At this stage Oscar Knie was only "a silhouette," since "the birth of a character is a very slow process."[19] It was also an intuitive one. Wearing his costume pieces and manipulating his props, Saint-Denis tried out different walks, movements, gestures, allowing the inanimate objects to provide him with images. He moved to observation, studying the behavior of actual people—a popular politician, a night watchman, and, drawing from memory, his father. As he made his discoveries Saint-Denis brought Oscar into his life, performing daily activities in character. At this point he created a mask dominated by round, exaggeratedly opened eyes and quizzically lifted brows that covered three-quarters of his face, leaving only the mouth and chin bare. Atop a short, dark wig he wore a peasant straw hat. Saint-Denis continued improvising until at last the full-blown Oscar Knie sprang forth, a study in opposites: "naïve, vain, sentimental, weak (but imperious when successful), carried to extremes, quick to anger and despair, often drunk, a great talker, full-blooded and, sometimes, obscene."[20] This character, developed without the help of Copeau, was an exemplar of the *Patron*'s vision of the *comédie nouvelle*. Jean Dasté brought forth his complementary César at approximately the same time, although it was never as finished a character. While Knie represented a twentieth-century Sancho Panza, César was a modern Don Quixote. Improvising together, the two found that Oscar hated César, an echo and exaggeration of the real-life rivalry between Saint-Denis and Dasté.

The company toured area villages playing in town halls, setting up a tent in a field, or a booth at a fairground, using the trestle stage of itinerant actors of old (see figure 3.1). Playing at wine festivals and local fairs, they competed for customers with carnival rides and shooting galleries, sometimes giving four shows a day. Borrowing fairground techniques, Saint-Denis, Villard, and Maistre acted as barkers working the crowds, entertaining them with their antics. For the Copiaus, these performances recalled the theatre's roots in popular entertainment. Audiences were enthusiastic, the bond strong between the actors and public. Saint-Denis commented on the unusual rapport: "Because there was never a barrier between players and audiences, the spectators sensed how much they influenced the actors, how they could affect their performances, indeed, how at times they could lift the actors to a rare degree of exhilaration."[21]

In spite of his repossession of the company, Copeau remained withdrawn, closeted in his office, conferring only with Michel.[22] According to Villard, they rarely saw him except at performances. As years passed, many of the actors became restless and dissatisfied. Devoting so much of their time to pure research with few results in the way of productions was wearing on them. They had sacrificed their youth and career ambitions for what more and more seemed a dead end. Their life was hard, with few material comforts. Married actors were paid a small salary; the others received pocket money. Discipline was breaking down, the actors spending much of their time complaining, socializing, and drinking in cafés.

FIGURE 3.1   *The Copiaus on tour. Aman Maistre and Michel Saint-Denis.*

Copeau responded by writing *L'Illusion*, influenced by Corneille's *L'Illusion comique* and de Rojas's *Celestina*. As in the Copiaus-generated works, the production was an entertainment or theatre game (*jeu*) rather than a full-fledged play. During the summer of 1926 the company jointly worked on the play. Copeau finished the scenario, Villard again composed the music, and Maïène Copeau designed and constructed the costumes, assisted in their dyeing and sewing by the actresses. The actors choreographed the mimed and danced sections. Concurrently, they created masks drawn from Copeau's suggestions (see figure 3.2). The play delighted actors and audiences alike. Even the critical Jean Villard admitted that Copeau "had rediscovered the secret of his art." In October, the Copiaus toured the play to Switzerland, where they were introduced to more sophisticated urban audiences. Their success surpassed all expectations. In Lausanne, Adolphe Appia, who followed their work with interest, applauded the production.

Instead of capitalizing on their accomplishment, Copeau left the Copiaus in Pernand for six months, going first to Paris, then on to New York to stage *The Brothers Karamazov*. Although money from *The Brothers Karamazov* was used to support the community, the company felt abandoned. Unsure of their future, they continued their classes and their discussions, but did not perform. Finally, the ambiguity of their situation drove Jean Villard to write to Copeau, elucidating their concerns. Without understanding where they stood vis-à-vis Copeau, they did not know how to proceed. Copeau's reply, while vague, encouraged the

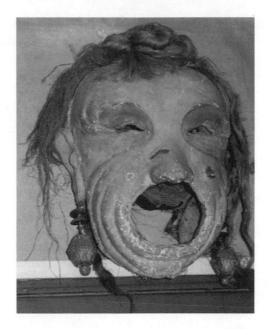

FIGURE 3.2   *Mask made by Marie-Hélène Dasté and worn by Suzanne Bing in the
Copiaus's production of* L'Illusion.

company. "Redouble your efforts," he wrote, "in order to give me, upon my
return, the profound joy, the greatest that I can know, that of being satisfied by
you and to admire you."[23] Revitalized, the Copiaus began developing two performance pieces, *Le Printemps* (Spring) and *La Guerre* (War).

Upon his return, the *Patron* pronounced himself pleased with the results.
But the familiar pattern ensued: reimposition of control, followed by disengage-
ment. In order to keep the Copiaus in line, he issued memos, accompanied by
exhortations and homilies. Acting as the Copiaus's delegate, Saint-Denis remon-
strated with his uncle. Copeau's function was to facilitate creation and, failing
that, he should resign. Furious, Copeau attacked Michel as a traitor: "You were
for a long time my so dear and faithful young companion. You have ceased to
be."[24] As far as resigning, Copeau recognized the "responsibility I took on in setting all of you on a certain path, not to withdraw my support brutally. But I
wish that it could become less and less necessary, and that I could detach myself
from you more and more in order not to suffer and exhaust myself in sorrow."[25]
Copeau's high-handedness and personal attacks fed Saint-Denis's increasing
frustration and resentment.

Copeau did adapt a play for them, Ruzzante's *L'Anconitaine*, a bawdy commedia farce, the only new addition to their repertory. In November of 1927 the
Copiaus embarked on an even more successful tour whose itinerary included

Switzerland, Luxembourg, Holland, and Belgium. Upon their return, Copeau departed for a round of dramatic readings. Emboldened by their triumph, the Copiaus began to create another collective piece, *La Danse de la Ville et des Champs*, which they intended to tour. It was a completely autonomous effort, composed and directed by Saint-Denis and Villard. To ensure it remained so, they requested that Copeau not attend rehearsals. The program listed the troupe as the Copiaus rather than the Vieux-Colombier Company, announcing their independence to the world.

A theatrical piece in the manner of *L'Illusion*, *La Danse* brought together mime, mask, dance, choral speech, improvisation, song, and music. The prologue, in which all the members of the company appeared and displayed their tricks and props, underscored the theatricality. Saint-Denis's Oscar Knie made his début, playing a major part. Despite Saint-Denis's earlier portrayal of Jean Bourguignon, the Copiaus regarded his more complex Oscar Knie as a breakthrough.[26] The deliberately naïve plot contrasted the values of town and country. François, a peasant, tempted by the vice-ridden town, discovers that happiness lies in the land. François's polar opposite was Oscar Knie, here a city slicker experimenting with rural life. Although much of the acting took the form of a mime drama, Oscar's role relied on improvised farce. His foil César was integrated into the production only after hard work on Dasté's part. The performance emphasized the company ideal of the chorus: nine cast members played everything, including the scenic effects. Adapting sound-and-movement exercises, actors created the contrasting atmosphere of city and country: sun and wind, changing seasons, fields, storms, urban sights and noises. A spectator left a record of her impressions:

> The adventures of the youth, who was a type, were shown in a series of scenes made by the grouping, miming, and dancing of the other actors. I have a vivid recollection of how they presented machinery in mime to symbolize industrialism. Then the coming of the storm over the vegetation, the havoc wrought and the subsequent joy of life reviving were all beautifully symbolized in gesture and attitude.[27]

Not until the première on March 4, 1928 did Copeau see the production. The house was full, the spectators enchanted. Sitting among them was Copeau, "laughing, touched, applauding like a child."[28] The actors anticipated Copeau's response eagerly. Instead of the constructive criticism they were expecting, "it was a total, absolute demolition":[29] they had mixed genres, their costumes were inappropriate, their characterizations unclear, their diction deficient, Oscar Knie had not worked. As he exited the room leaving the actors aghast, Copeau hurled his final condemnation at them: "Dust!"[30] In striking contrast was Léon Chancerel's article, expressing the belief that in this production the Copiaus brought to fruition Copeau's theatrical ideals.[31]

Copeau's assault notwithstanding, the troupe departed on another foreign tour, usually playing to packed houses. The company log reports laudatory press accounts.[32] Rhapsodic, but typical, was the review in the *Comoedia*, excerpted here: "An analysis cannot—any case—give an idea of the movement, the rhythm of the play, of the precision, the grace of the dances, the words of the text of another poet, indisputably Monsieur Saint-Denis who—like his friend and collaborator, J. Villard—dances, acts, mimes, sings delightfully."[33] Yet such was the impact of Copeau's criticism that the company's fragile self-confidence was devastated by a Geneva reviewer who would send them back to school.[34]

Saint-Denis's faith in the company remained strong. Still, if they were to survive, they had to evolve. The key, he believed, was collaboration with a professional writer sensitive to their needs, who would provide new direction. In principle, Copeau's primary function was to guide the actors in developing a repertory grounded in their acting exercises. But as we have seen, Copeau's withdrawal meant that the writing had been assumed by Saint-Denis and Villard. Over time, they grew dissatisfied with their efforts. In June 1928, Saint-Denis entered into an agreement with C. F. Ramuz that seemed to be the solution. A Swiss writer of folk tales, his literary interests and style paralleled the Copiaus's. Ramuz's novels, a blend of realism, folklore, and fantasy, treat the lives of Alpine people. He was impressed by the Copiaus, having seen a performance of *La Danse de la Ville et des Champs* in Lausanne. Nonetheless, he lacked dramaturgical experience; the closest he had come to writing for the stage was in composing the text for Stravinsky's *L'Histoire d'un soldat*.

Although intrigued by the collaboration, Ramuz sensed that Copeau was "going to be put into a cruel situation" and "would do nothing without his approval."[35] Certainly, there was the danger that Copeau might view Ramuz's relationship with the Copiaus as a usurpation of his own role. Ramuz's letters make clear that by this point Saint-Denis envisaged the company breaking with Copeau. Reassured about Copeau's position, Ramuz agreed to work on an idea suggested by Saint-Denis and Villard, to develop a script based on the Biblical story of Noah. Concerned that the project was not progressing fast enough, Saint-Denis and Villard spent a month working with Ramuz on the scenario. They left thinking that "a remarkable script" was forthcoming.[36] But Ramuz's anxieties prevented him from finishing. Chief among them were his fear of failure—producing a monumental case of writer's block—and Copeau's on-again, off-again involvement with the troupe. Copeau's interference—he was demanding to see the material as soon as it was written—denied Ramuz sufficient independence. In November 1928 Ramuz bowed out, delaying the implementation of Saint-Denis's plans.

Saint-Denis and the company remained active during this period, rehearsing Molière's *George Dandin*, touring, and developing a new offering, *Les Jeunes Gens et l'Araignée ou La Tragédie Imaginaire* (The kids and the spider or the imaginary tragedy), devised once again by Saint-Denis and Villard. Their last work premiered in Beaune on April 27, 1929, before touring. In Lausanne, the Comoedia reviewer continued to support their efforts: "After *L'Illusion* and *La Danse de la Ville et des Champs* a new show, *Les Jeunes Gens et l'Araignée*, vouches for the prodigious strength of vitality, verve, imagination and harmony which this young and enthusiastic troupe attains more and more with each new creation."[37] The same critic found Saint-Denis a perfect caricature of "the grand style of human sincerity." He urged the company to bring their work to Paris.

A month later Copeau dissolved the Copiaus. Typically, he did so when the company was away on summer vacation. His official reason was an invitation to submit his candidature for the directorship of the Comédie-Française. Paradoxically, as Copeau retired more and more into the contemplative religious life, he was seduced by worldly ambition. In 1928 he actively campaigned for the position, but was rejected.[38] However, a contributing cause to Copeau's disbanding the company may have been declining health; unknown to the company, he was suffering from arteriosclerosis.

Certainly, the friction between the *Patron* and the troupe was a major factor. From Copeau's perspective, the Copiaus's creations were not fulfilling his long-term goals. Saint-Denis and the actors, accustomed to working by themselves and developing their own ideas, wanted more autonomy. But, Copeau's need for control led him to reject all forms of collaboration. Again, he turned his back on the past and walked away.

As for the company, Copeau's shattering criticism, combined with his protracted absences and reassertion of power, demoralized them. Factionalism and power struggles, which were to prove destructive to the Compagnie des Quinze, had their beginnings here. Marie-Hélène Copeau and her new husband Jean Dasté felt pressured by the older, more dominant Saint-Denis and Villard.[39] Their interest in professionalizing the company seemed at odds with Copeau's vision. The Dastés believed that Saint-Denis and Villard were exploiting research material for their own ends. According to Mme Dasté, Suzanne Bing, having designed much of the school curriculum, resented Saint-Denis and Villard's appropriation of the exercises for productions. But Copeau's refusal to provide the consistent guidance the young actors desired created a leadership gap, filled first by Saint-Denis and Villard. Over time, Villard ceded the directorship to Saint-Denis, who put his own stamp on the work.

A year later Michel Saint-Denis made his definitive bid for independence. He reassembled the Copiaus and launched his own troupe, the Compagnie des Quinze. The strong directorial role he played with the Copiaus gave him confidence. Saint-Denis was convinced that the talented, avant-garde ensemble would conquer Paris.

NOTES

1. The *Journal de bord* is the most valuable source of the community's activities.

2. Michel Saint-Denis, quoted in unpublished and untitled article by Georges Lerminier.

3. Jean Villard, "Leon Chancerel, le Vieux-Colombier, et les Copiaus," *Revue d'histoire*, vol. 1, no. 2 (1968): 155.

4. Ibid.

5. "Dialogues avec Jean Dasté," unpublished interview, July 1958.

6. Michel Saint-Denis, "Mes années au Vieux-Colombier," trans. Kathy Koerner, *Europe* (April–May 1961), 68.

7. Suzanne Maistre, personal interview, 15 March 1996. At the Vieux-Colombier School, only neutral masks were used.

8. Barbara-Anne Kusler, "Jacques Copeau's Theatre School: L'Ecole du Vieux-Colombier, 1920–29," Ph.D. dissertation, University of Wisconsin (1974), 195.

9. Maistre, interview.

10. Denis Gontard, *La Décentralisation théâtrale en France 1895–1952* (Paris: Société d'Edition d'Enseignement Supérieur, 1973), 68.

11. Jean Villard, *Mon demi-siècle* (Lausanne: Payot, 1954), 117.

12. Jacques Copeau, "Fragments d'une célébration du vin et de la vigne," *Jeux, tréteaux, personnages* 19 (15 April 1932), 75.

13. Villard, *Mon demi-siècle*, 119.

14. Quoted in Gontard, 71.

15. Jacques Prénat, "Visite à Copeau," *Latinité* (December 1930), 382.

16. Kusler, 182.

17. Denis Gontard, *Le Journal de bord des Copiaus 1924–1929* (Paris: Éditions Seghers, 1974), 107–8.

18. Michel Saint-Denis, *Training for the Theatre: Premises and Promises*, ed. Suria Saint-Denis (New York: Theatre Arts Books, 1982), 177.

19. Ibid., 178.

20. Ibid., 179.

21. Ibid.

22. Villard, *Mon demi-siècle*, 126. Over time, Saint-Denis became the sole intermediary between Copeau and the company.

23. Unpublished letter from Jacques Copeau to Michel Saint-Denis, 22 July 1927.

24. Ibid.

25. Ibid.

26. Gontard, *Le Journal de bord des Copiaus 1924–1929*, 125.

27. Phyllis Aykroyd, *The Dramatic Art of La Compagnie des Quinze* (London: Eric Partridge, 1935), 142.

28. Villard, *Mon demi-siècle*, 142.

29. Ibid.

30. Ibid.

31. Léon Chancerel, "Les Copiaus," *Jeux, Tréteaux et Personnages*, no. 1 (15 October 1930).

32. Gontard, *Le Journal de bord des Copiaus 1924–1929*, 139.

33. Vincent, *Comoedia* (18 June 1928).

34. Villard, *Mon demi-siècle,* 144.

35. Unpublished correspondence from C. F. Ramuz to Michel Saint-Denis, 28 June 1928 and 30 June 1928.

36. Villard, *Mon demi-siècle,* 154.

37. Vincent, *Comoedia,* Lausanne (12 May 1929).

38. His candidacy was opposed by many of the *sociétaires* (influential actors in the company) who feared the changes Copeau would implement. He later served as the company's director during the 1940–41 season.

39. M.-H. Dasté, personal interview, 16 June 1989.

◆ chapter four ◆

The Compagnie des Quinze and the Emergence of Michel Saint-Denis the Director

I N 1930 THE COMPAGNIE DES QUINZE was created in Paris under the direction of Michel Saint-Denis.[1] This experimental troupe of fifteen actors, a progenitor of modern avant-garde theatre companies, survived a scant five years, but during that period it laid the foundations for major twentieth-century theatrical reforms. Their productions were presentations of "total theatre" long before the term was coined.

For Michel Saint-Denis, thirty-three years old, the creation of the Compagnie des Quinze was a coming of age. When in 1929 Copeau, having formally dissolved the Copiaus, sent André Obey as a parting gift, Saint-Denis seized the opportunity. Obey, a young playwright dissatisfied with the contemporary stage, went to Lyon to attend the Copiaus's production of *L'Illusion*, on Copeau's recommendation. Enchanted, Obey saw in the troupe the means to explore his own theatrical ideas. As for Saint-Denis, he recognized in Obey the potential to fulfill his goal of creating a professional company. Obey agreed to write exclusively for the company.[2]

Notwithstanding the fact that both sides pronounced themselves satisfied with the collaboration, adjustment was required. Obey was an outsider; most of the troupe had worked together as an ensemble for almost ten years. Saint-Denis described them as "a chorus with a few personalities sticking out rather than actors ready to act the usual repertory . . ."[3] (To insure its growth, six apprentices were added to the troupe and given classes by company members.) But Obey was willing to accept their mode of work—improvisation—and function as a collaborator. As Saint-Denis explained:

> The story of the Compagnie des Quinze concerns an exceptional experience: that of a creative theatre ensemble, devoted to physical expression which came to feel the need of an author. With us, casting, staging, and planning the sets and costumes were undertaken at the same time as the writing of a play. It was essential that the author become a member of our ensemble and adhere to its orientation.[4]

In practical terms, this meant that Saint-Denis and the company proposed the subject-matter, the characters grew out of the actors' imaginative and physical skills, and Saint-Denis's *mise en scène* illuminated the text. However, such a strict division of responsibilities was not always adhered to and contributions at times overlapped.

Obey also held an authoritative position in the company since, besides generating material, he brought a benefactress, Marcelle Gompel, a wealthy widow devoted to his interests.[5] Thanks to her generosity, an elaborate rehearsal studio was built to Saint-Denis's specifications in Ville d'Avray, a Paris suburb. In addition to the stage (a replica of the Vieux-Colombier's), it contained dressing rooms, workshops, storerooms, even a shower.[6]

Upon the studio's completion, the company began developing two plays concurrently, *Noé* (Noah) and *Le Viol de Lucrèce* (The rape of Lucretia). The actors shared the technical responsibilities: Marie-Hélène Dasté designed the costumes and assisted her husband Jean and Madeleine Gautier in creating the masks; Madeleine Gautier also worked with the set designer André Barsacq; Aman Maistre was in charge of administration; the apprentices lent a hand wherever they could.[7]

Noé, a contemporary mystery play, was based on the idea originally suggested to Ramuz by Saint-Denis and Villard. *Lucrèce* owed its inspiration in part to Shakespeare, in part to the Japanese Noh. As in each play Obey wrote with and for them, *Noé* has symbolist elements. Drawn from Greek tragedy as well as medieval theatre, the drama is presentational, depicting the mythic world of the Old Testament patriarch. It contains two choruses, one made up of Noah's children and their wives, the other, of the animals. Only Noah and two lesser characters, his wife and the Man, a representation of evil, are individuated.

The actors' pleasure was short-lived; an unanticipated casting decision created dissent. Pierre Fresnay, a leading actor and admirer of Copeau, came to the Quinze to enhance his technique. Trained at the Conservatoire and a former *sociétaire* with the Comédie-Française, Fresnay would appear to be an unlikely candidate for the Compagnie des Quinze. Yet Saint-Denis and Obey concluded that Fresnay would be a drawing card, a hypothesis that ran counter to the Quinze beliefs.[8]

In casting Pierre Fresnay as Noé, Saint-Denis and Obey overruled the rest of the troupe, threatening its unity. Having recently freed themselves from the tyranny of Copeau, the group was wary of unilateral decision-making.[9] In theory, the Quinze was a company of equals, a cooperative in which decisions were taken collectively. In actuality, company members brought rivalries and power struggles, dating back to Burgundy, into the new troupe.[10]

The Copiaus had been divided along family lines: those closest to Copeau—his daughter Marie-Hélène Dasté, her husband Jean Dasté, Suzanne Bing, Michel Saint-Denis, and sometimes Aman Maistre, Saint-Denis's brother-in-law—constituted the dominant contingent.[11] Within the Quinze, an even tighter inner circle emerged, made up of Saint-Denis, Obey, and Marie-Hélène Dasté. At times the trio expanded to include Boverio and Aman Maistre. This inner circle would make plans without consulting the others.[12]

The seeds of dissension sown by the Fresnay occurrence grew. Mistrust and jealousy eventually undermined the troupe.[13] Ascribing the Copiaus's collapse to Copeau's need for total control, they were reluctant to entrust Michel with much authority. Little personal hostility was directed against him; generally, he elicited affection and respect. Nonetheless, a large faction believed the choice of plays, casting, and even directing decisions should be a communal responsibility.[14] Saint-Denis, conversely, believed he had earned his position through his long apprenticeship as Copeau's general factotum and director of several Copiaus productions.

Above all, the Quinze's actors viewed themselves as a tightly-knit ensemble where no one person should predominate. In many ways the troupe functioned as a well-oiled machine whose parts were finely attuned to one another. In Burgundy, it had been their custom to introduce the shows with a prologue in which the actors did a turn, presented their masks and props, and proudly announced that there were no stars among them.[15] They felt Fresnay's assumption of the leading role sent the message to the public that they were incapable of playing demanding parts.[16] The role of Noah, contested the actors, belonged to Auguste Boverio, one of their strongest players. Because of the company's beliefs, Boverio was put in the untenable position of being unable to fight for himself.

The decision underscores a change in Saint-Denis who, having risen from the ranks, now had to establish directorial control. Above all, Saint-Denis the director viewed the actor as the medium through which the playwright speaks. A major aspect of his approach was to thwart any attempt by actors to find their inspiration in subjective emotional reactions. It was only through "active submission to the text" that an actor could realize a valid interpretation.[17] Truthful characterization could be achieved solely by intensive study of the manuscript to bring to light the dramatist's intentions.

Throughout his career, Saint-Denis strongly advocated improvisation as an instrument for training the actor. Improvisation had played an important role in his own development as an artist. Yet, in directing, he rarely made use of the technique, relying heavily on detailed preproduction plans.[18] Even working with the Quinze, competent and experienced improvisers, Saint-Denis allowed improvisation only a specific function. In the early rehearsal phase, the actors developed prospective themes and characters. The dramatist then took the rough material, gave it shape, and returned it to the director. No longer creators, the actors became, under their director's guidance, faithful interpreters of the text. Saint-Denis's methods did not differ appreciably in working with the Quinze actors from the way he later worked with actors on conventionally developed scripts.

Also notable is the fact that, although Saint-Denis's writings stress the importance of props and costumes in helping the actor achieve transformation, the Compagnie des Quinze rehearsed without either. During the early stages of rehearsals, the actors, dressed in bathing suits, mimed their props.[19] But, as an actor in Burgundy, he had discovered that "the mask or the prop or the clothing will induce in the actor a state of being-in-action, a kind of intoxication, from which a character may emerge."[20]

He brought to *Noé* the meticulous preparation and attention to detail that would become the hallmark of his direction. Rehearsals began with Saint-Denis reading the text, followed by a lengthy exegesis. Next, the actors familiarized themselves with the script through successive read-throughs. The pace of rehearsals was kept deliberately slow to encourage them to delve deeply into the material. Saint-Denis then blocked the play, having prepared an intricate production plan delineating the set, entrances, exits, the actors' movements, pacing, rhythm, and pauses. In later years, some actors would find Saint-Denis's precision fussy and constraining.[21] The Compagnie des Quinze, accustomed to this directing scheme, found it compatible. In spite of the contretemps involving Fresnay, a communal spirit still reigned and rehearsals were fun. Pierre Alder, a student-apprentice, left a description of the enthusiasm felt by so many players in performing under Saint-Denis: "Rehearsing is pleasant, interesting, fascinating work, above all, when it is directed by a man who knows what he wants to achieve, when you are a member of a team where you are not thinking about yourself, but about the group, the production you love and have to create."[22]

In part, the actors' excitement derived from the belief that their lengthy and difficult apprenticeship would finally be rewarded. Their Burgundian experience had transformed them into "an ensemble with a fertile imagination and the technical means to represent in [their] work many aspects and facets of the world."[23] And now Obey had given them a voice. Having achieved success with their rural audiences, they were anxious to test themselves against the sophisticated Parisian public.

Although neither Saint-Denis nor the company ever disavowed their debt to Copeau, they wanted to be accepted on their own merits. With this in mind, Saint-Denis considered renting the Salle Wagram, a boxing arena, to perform there on a bare platform surrounded by the audience. Had they done so, it might have minimized the Copeau/Compagnie des Quinze connection. When this proved impractical, they moved into the Vieux-Colombier at great expense several weeks before their debut. The theatre, long since converted into a cinema, was remodeled by André Barsacq under Saint-Denis's guidance. More radical than their master, Saint-Denis and the Quinze judged Copeau's fixed setting a half-way measure. Their rebuilt stage, with its permanent columns and visible sources of light in the ceiling and walls, emphasized the company's disdain for theatrical illusion. Their aesthetic was apparent, for example, in their exploitation of the columns. Sometimes they represented the trees of a forest; at others, the walls of Lucrèce's bedroom; at others, they delineated the space of the open sea.

Jacques Copeau launched the company with a talk at the premiere on January 7, 1931. His presence legitimized the enterprise, while simultaneously denying the Quinze their autonomy. Critics and public alike perceived the troupe as adjuncts of Copeau. As for Copeau, he experienced the ambivalence of a parent whose children were asserting their independence. Instead of serving as instruments disclosing the revelations he yearned to discover, they had become a company of dedicated, gifted actors more interested in performing than in abstract research.

Saint-Denis and the Quinze were disappointed by the mixed response to *Noé*. Judging by the extent of the divergent reactions, it appears the critical community was confused by the company's intentions. Some critics looked for political content where there was none; others, such as Benjamin Crémieux, were alienated by their theatricalist approach.[24] Still, the actors took bitter satisfaction in Crémieux's unfavorable critique.[25] Writing for the *Nouvelle Revue Française*, Crémieux concluded that Fresnay destroyed the troupe's homogeneity. The company was "above all misrepresented by the presence in the midst of them of M. Pierre Fresnay who, in the extravagant monologue of Noah, to which the play is reduced, overwhelms his supporting players."[26] On the positive side, Pierre Brisson, the powerful critic of the *Figaro*, praised their freshness, sincerity, and strong ensemble, but credited Copeau with their training.[27] For Philippe L'Amour, writing on the state of the French theatre in 1931, the Quinze were the first step towards a theatrical renaissance.

Doubtless, Saint-Denis experienced conflicting emotions in reading these laudatory comments. On the one hand, there was critical appreciation; on the other, misinterpretation of Copeau's role. Nowhere does Michel receive the recognition that was his due. Under the leadership of Saint-Denis, the Quinze had cut the umbilical cord. It had been Saint-Denis's ideas, persistence, energy, and talent that had given new form to the Copiaus. Yet the perception remained that the troupe was Copeau's. And strangely, their new form—collective creation—was ignored by the critics. At the Vieux-Colombier Copeau had mounted traditional pre-existing scripts, giving them innovative productions.

Although the theory that underlay collective creation was Copeau's, he had never put it into practice in Paris.

Within the artistic and intellectual community many wholeheartedly supported the new troupe. Charles Dullin offered to house them for several performances at the Atelier with the possibility of a long-term stay at a later date.[28] The general public was less responsive. Blasé audiences manifested a "show me" attitude the company found unnerving. Having captivated rural audiences, the Copiaus considered themselves a popular theatre. In Paris, the Quinze were surprised to find they were the darlings of an elite. Consequently, full houses were frequently followed by sparse ones. Fresnay did not prove to be the attraction Obey and Saint-Denis had anticipated.[29]

Alternating in repertory with *Noé* was *Le Viol de Lucrèce*, a four-act adaptation of Shakespeare's poem, which opened on March 21, 1931. Saint-Denis's inventiveness lay in combining distinct styles: medieval, Renaissance, Greek tragedy, and the Noh. The idea of the Greek chorus and likely symbolist productions led Saint-Denis to use an incantatory delivery. These myriad influences, particularly the Noh, which had fascinated Saint-Denis since the Vieux-Colombier School's aborted production of *Kantan*, functioned as a springboard for the creation of an original work. For the Noh aspects he turned to Arthur Waley's *No Plays of Japan* (1922) and Noël Péri's *Cinq Nô: drames lyriques japonais* (1921), whose translations contain rudimentary stage directions. The woodcuts in Péri's book seem to have motivated some of Saint-Denis's stage pictures. The Quinze's permanent architectural setting shared similarities with the Noh stage, which too is roofed over and supported by columns.

Waley's encapsulation of the Noh was adopted by Saint-Denis and Obey: "At its simplest, the *Nô* play consists of a dance preceded by a dialogue which explains the significance of the dance or introduces circumstances which lead naturally to the dancing of it."[30] *Le Viol de Lucrèce* is more narrative than dramatic and, as in the Noh, its plot is simple and drawn from a literary source. *Lucrèce* depends heavily upon movement for its theatrical effectiveness. The dance and movement of the Noh is a stylized language of gesture, known to the audience. The Quinze, however, were not playing to an audience of initiates. In creating an imagistic language for *Lucrèce*, they were faced with problems of intelligibility and cultural relevance. Their solution was drawn in part from the adaptations of the Noh, in part from the then new phenomenon of the radio sportscaster.[31]

The Noh is essentially a two-character play made up of the principal actor (the *shite*) who dances and a subordinate role (the *waki*) who supplies the exposition and leads the main character toward the climactic moment of the dance. But it is the chorus, sitting motionless at the side of the stage, who narrates the dance to the accompaniment of music.

Similarly, *Lucrèce* makes use of narrative devices, two *récitants*, and a chorus.

FIGURE 4.1   Le Viol de Lucrèce *(1931) at the Théâtre du Vieux-Colombier. Suzanne Bing (Récitante) at left, Marie-Hélène Dasté (Lucrèce) at right. (Source: Département des Arts du Spectacle, Bibliothèque Nationale de France.)*

The musical element was not incorporated. While the Noh has only one main character, *Lucrèce* has two, the eponymous heroine and the rapist Tarquin. The company's most vocally proficient performers, Suzanne Bing and Auguste Boverio, recounted the story, while the actors mimed the action. The female narrator spoke for Lucrèce (Marie-Hélène Dasté) (see figure 4.1), the male for Tarquin (Aman Maistre). Like the *waki* and the announcer, they furnished the exposition and set the scene for events to come. In the Noh theatre the *waki* never portrays a female role.

To underscore their archetypal godlike quality as observers of human folly and suffering, the narrators alone were masked. For the sake of vocal clarity they wore half-masks, bronze in color. This was a reversal of the Noh convention where a mask is worn only by the *shite*. His mask is a distinguishing feature that sets him apart from the other actors, as it did for the narrators of *Lucrèce*. Costumed similarly in long robes and flowing hair, the narrators' gender differences were minimized. After the introductory scenes, which they performed downstage, the narrators sat on either side of the set on immense thrones placed before the pillars, seldom leaving their places. Each throne was reached by a step as though it were a pulpit.

The *waki*, after his introductory scene, remains seated at the side of the stage at his pillar. By contrast, the *shite* is always center stage. Lucrèce too played almost all her scenes center stage, most often on a raised platform. In her first scene, Lucrèce was found upstage center, surrounded by her maids, spinning. Her slow, deliberate movements owed their inspiration to the Noh. But critics were struck by the resemblance of a medieval tapestry come to life. From all reports, Saint-Denis staged the play as a series of *tableaux vivants*, whose images long remained with the audience.

Lucrèce employs two choruses from the Western tradition, one representing the military, and the other, Lucrèce's female servants. The role of the male chorus is slight and expository. The women, on the other hand, enhance the play; they furnish atmosphere and reflect, through gesture and pantomime, Lucrèce's virtuous qualities. The play's crucial scene is, of course, the rape, the whole of Act II. It was akin to the dance of the *shite*, but with significant differences. Unlike the Noh, *Lucrèce* was not drawing on centuries-old gestural and movement patterns. *Lucrèce's* movement was far more depictive. While no music was used, discreetly chosen sounds contributed to the emotional impact.

Here, Saint-Denis again adapted the dreamlike tempo of the Noh. But, although the scene began very slowly, it built to an overwhelming crescendo. When the curtain rose, Lucrèce lay asleep in a large canopied-covered bed on a raised platform. All was still, then "a bell of delicate timbre struck twelve." The female narrator entered from up right, carrying a large book, walking soundlessly. The only sound was the tinkling of keys at her belt. Crossing to her throne, the *Récitante* paused by the bed, listening to Lucrèce's breathing. She was joined by the male narrator who entered from the opposite side and moved to his chair. He described the lustful thoughts of Tarquin, while the actor mimed his journey through the sinuous passages of the palace, reached the bedroom, forced open an invisible door, entered, opened the hangings surrounding the bed, reached out and caressed her breast, as she awoke with frightened moans. The two *Récitants* withdrew keening and Tarquin gave a cry of triumph as he forced Lucrèce to submit.

This poetic stylization of violence was remarked on by most reviewers. Norman Marshall, the British critic, left this description:

> The actor was never more than a few feet away from the bed as he mimed his journey . . ., yet so completely had we been induced to forget the conventions of the realistic theatre that the bed, instead of being an incongruous distraction, became the symbol of Tarquin's desire; we saw it not as a tangible object but as the image burning in Tarquin's brain, drawing him irresistibly towards his crime.[32]

The scene's erotic qualities were also commented upon and compared by at least one critic to Nijinsky's *Afternoon of a Faun*, almost twenty years before:

Such perfect boldness, such pure realism, where had we seen this before? A memory rose to the surface, clung to me, an old memory. The faun Nijinsky having managed to obtain from the desired nymph only the veil fallen from her shoulder, stretched out on it and mimed the act of love. There was all the beauty of the world, stylized by an artist of genius, in the figure of the eternal gesture.[33]

Neither critics nor audience perceived the Noh influences on the production. The exception was Arthur Waley who visited Saint-Denis's dressing room and introduced himself saying, "I am glad to see that my work on the Japanese Noh plays has not been wasted."[34]

Lucrèce found greater favor with Paris's audiences than *Noé*. And again, the avant-garde theatrical community rallied round. Playwright Henri Ghéon wanted to collaborate with the group; Dullin, completely won over, reiterated his offer. Copeau, always hypercritical, told the anxious actors that the performance was a respectable first attempt. Trying to soothe their wounded feelings, Saint-Denis reminded the company that this was just another "*numéro Copeau*."[35] Possibly rancor towards the project underlay Copeau's attitude; Saint-Denis and Obey had accomplished one of his major aspirations.

Their Paris season lasted three months before Jean Tedesco, owner of the Vieux-Colombier, reclaimed his cinema.[36] An assessment of the season reveals that the company was neither the success it had hoped to be nor a failure. The renovation of the theatre had been costly and box-office receipts insufficient. Although Pierre Fresnay had been a creditable Noah, the experiment had harmed the company's morale without producing the expected financial benefits. After Fresnay's departure, Boverio and Michel alternated playing the demanding role of Noah and harmony was restored.[37] Whereas Boverio had vocal power that Saint-Denis lacked, Michel brought an authentic peasant quality to the part.

The lack of a permanent home was a perennial problem for the Quinze. Since Dullin's theatre was not yet ready to receive them, Saint-Denis arranged a Swiss tour. More significantly for Michel's career and the British theatre, an invitation to play in London had been extended to them.

The actors' arduous schedule is typified by this tour. They played nine cities in eleven days in Switzerland, followed by two Paris performances, before departing for England. Fortunately, the production style of the Quinze lent itself to this mode of performance. They traveled with a lightweight, twentieth-century version of the trestle stage. The stage was collapsible and could be reassembled into three or four separate platforms if necessary. Surrounding the stage on three sides was a tent-like structure suspended from the flies by a ring. Its sides could be rolled up or draped to provide entrances. Practicable, adaptable, and deceptively simple, the company's settings conjured up images of itinerant commedia dell'arte troupes.

In London, they were booked into the Arts Theatre Club, a private playhouse, where they discovered a stage so minuscule there was barely space for Noah's ark. Opening night in London found the company highly agitated. How would they be received? How much would the audience comprehend? Prepared for the worst, the Quinze were amazed to discover they had triumphed. The reception they had hoped for in Paris was given them in London. At the play's end the audience was on its feet cheering as the cast took countless curtain calls.[38] The next day's reviews confirmed their conquest.

Unlike the majority of Parisian critics and playgoers for whom the style and repertoire of the Quinze were too esoteric, British audiences were enchanted. The actors' youth, verve, and grace all contributed to a startlingly new concept of theatre. A Quinze production was, wrote Tyrone Guthrie, "like a delightful ballet, only that it had fifty times more content than any ballet ever had."[39] Balletic and stylized it may have been, but English reviewers singled out the actors' movement for its spontaneous and natural appearance.

Held over an extra week at the Arts Theatre Club, the Quinze were in the unaccustomed position of turning away people. Every evening after the performance, theatre practitioners came backstage anxious to extend their congratulations. Among them was Bronson Albery who offered the Quinze a week's engagement at the Ambassador Theatre. Because of packed houses, the run was extended another six at the New Theatre.[40] During this period Saint-Denis made contacts that proved invaluable. The troupe left London with an invitation to revisit, which it did annually until disbanding four years later.

In July of 1931 the Quinze returned to France to rehearse their second season, having negotiated another contract with the supportive Jean Tedesco. Accompanied by their families, the company gathered in a village in Touraine. Plans had called for them to rehearse at Madame Gompel's neighboring estate, but Obey's latest play was not ready. The ensuing period of forced inactivity gave rise to new strains. Creditors were threatening; the company's their material situation was worsening. Despite the London conquest, funds were inadequate to pay off debts incurred at the Vieux-Colombier. The troupe was told Madame Gompel's patronage had definite limits and to prepare themselves to make sacrifices.[41] Remembering their impoverished years in Burgundy, the actors were reluctant to take on further burdens.[42] As an authority figure, Saint-Denis was under attack. A rebellion was launched, led by Villard and supported by Maistre, Boverio, and Marguerite Cavadaski, to restrict his authority.[43]

The resumption of work temporarily ended the revolt. Saint-Denis convinced Obey to dramatize the World War I battle of the Marne, a scenario the Copiaus had begun developing in Burgundy. While it was a historical event, the characters and plot were generalized to represent the suffering, violence, heroism, loss, and death of all war. Brecht was unknown to them, but the style of play and production was epic.

As in the previous year, Saint-Denis intended to mount two presentations to be shown in repertory. Too short to sustain an evening, *La Bataille de la Marne* was preceded by a curtain raiser, *La Vie en rose*, a charming evocation of the *belle époque*. This bit of fluff contained numerous personages, necessitating the actors to double and even triple roles. Saint-Denis's other production was a comedy by Jean Variot adapted from Plautus's *Menaechmi*. *La Mauvaise conduite* (Bad behavior) offered the Quinze the opportunity to display their farcical skills and to portray the kind of broad comic characters they had developed in Burgundy. In the program Saint-Denis explained that the company was attracted by the play's "frank and vulgar tone" as well as the opportunities it presented for "comic invention."[44]

Since Roman comedy was the influence for the production style, the actors wore full masks. Unfortunately, the masks were not completed until the première, which caused considerable apprehension. Rehearsing without the masks, it was impossible to know whether the actors' speech would be understandable. And their use was essential for character development, since a masked character is established from externals. But whether a more ideal rehearsal situation would have resulted in a better production, thereby modifying critical and audience reaction, is moot.

La Mauvaise conduite opened the season on November 5, 1931 and played to moderately good houses, although some Paris audiences were put off by those very qualities that had attracted the company to it, finding the characters grotesque and crude. Certain critics again criticized the Quinze for their excesses. For example, the *Comoedia* critic complained that he was "bothered by the masks worn by the interpreters in imitation of the classical theatre."[45] Nevertheless, the same reviewer praised the strong ensemble and Saint-Denis's direction. Popular success continued to elude the Quinze in Paris. *La Bataille de la Marne* was awarded the prestigious Prix Brieux, but it too encountered mixed reactions, in part because of its theme. Several reviews reflected their authors' political positions, and in 1931, Obey's point of view was too chauvinistic for a number of critics. Obey and the Quinze found themselves in the uncomfortable position of being championed by conservatives.

Benjamin Crémieux, observing the company's work for the first time in a year, felt they showed considerable growth:

> One is in the presence of a flexible, yet homogeneous troupe whose common style does not curb individual abilities. . . . Already, Monsieur Saint-Denis has asserted himself as a strong ensemble actor, Madame Marie-Hélène Dasté as a young leading lady, capable of expressing both ardor and purity, while remaining very much a sensual woman.[46]

He had specific reservations about the play whose style he found at once sensationalist and medieval. A strong supporter emerged in Antoine who, in an article written for *L'Information*, conferred on the Quinze the task of saving the theatre.[47]

Their three-month engagement at the Vieux-Colombier terminated, the troupe left on tour for Lyon, Belgium, and England. The second season had been more profitable than the first, and had not Tedesco's film season been arranged in advance, business would have warranted a continuation. They returned to London hailed as celebrities. Albery booked them into the New Theatre, where they performed their stock of plays in repertory. The London season was successful, but less remunerative than the previous one. Audiences were sizeable, but the Quinze were no longer turning away patrons. *La Bataille de la Marne*, a drama celebrating the courage and sufferings of the French populace during World War I, was not a subject designed to appeal to British audiences. Perhaps the novelty of the Quinze had begun to wane for the general public. If so, they still remained the toast of the theatrical and critical professions.

The reviewers' unstinting praise presents a contrast to the begrudging approval of the French critics for whom the Quinze were more rarefied than a rarity. In *Time and Tide*, Rebecca West reported that *La Bataille de la Marne* was electrifying and "as beautiful and pure as a Romanesque church."[48] James Agate's description of the opening of *La Bataille de la Marne* evokes the imaginative anti-illusionistic style of the Quinze that enthralled audiences:

> On the stage nothing save a few dun hangings veiling the bare theatre walls, and the floor artificially raked to enable the actors to move on different planes. Off the stage an immense distance away a military band is playing, and in the wings armies of France go by. We see them through the eyes of five or six peasant women clothed in black and grouped as you may see them in the fields of France or the canvases of Millet. . . . The whole cast played with a perfection of understanding and a mastery of ensemble beyond praise. This is great, perhaps the greatest acting, since on a bare stage the actors recreated not the passion of one or two, but the agony of a nation.[49]

After every performance the actors' dressing rooms were filled with visitors.[50] Invitations to parties and country weekends abounded—invitations they were unable to reciprocate. They were celebrities living in penury. Their financial situation continued to deteriorate, resulting in further disaffection.

Madame Gompel had lost much of her fortune because of the Depression and had to reduce her patronage.[51] The Quinze's expenditures, however, continued to mount. Forced to tour, the company had constant transport expenses for the personnel, sets, and materiel. A bill for £150 from the British tax office took Saint-Denis by surprise. Unable to raise the money, he was obliged to borrow, not knowing how he would repay the loan.[52] Holding the company together was becoming increasingly difficult and he feared its dissolution.

Jean Villard and Aman Maistre decided to take a different professional path. In England, the Quinze had been invited to a gala where representatives of the company were to entertain. Only Villard and Maistre, having retained several songs from the Copiaus days, were able to get up an act on short notice. On the strength of the audience's response, the two men left the company for a prosperous singing career as Gilles and Julien.[53]

By now, Saint-Denis's leadership was continually challenged. Obey and Michel's relationship had been undermined by the defection of a number of the actors.[54] Their admiration for Obey's work had developed into adulation for the man. Flattered, Obey allowed himself to be convinced that he was capable of directing a company.[55] A new troupe was assembled; Marie-Hélène and Jean Dasté and two student-apprentices left for Madame Gompel's château. Those loyal to Saint-Denis comprised Madeleine Gautier (who had become his lover), Auguste Boverio, Marguerite Cavadaski, Pierre Assy, and Pierre Alder. Michel had been dealt numerous hard blows: the depletion of the troupe, the loss of the company playwright, and, with his disappearance, an end to subsidy.

The existence of the Quinze was predicated on a working collaboration between actors and playwright. Neither Saint-Denis nor the actors seem to have considered producing any but original works. Their rejection of the established repertory created various problems. Audiences were not always receptive to new plays. Obey, as house dramatist, was under constant pressure to create. It became obvious that one playwright was insufficient. Because playwriting was viewed as a joint venture, much of the company's time was spent developing material. And, since they were slowly building a repertory, their offerings remained limited.

Despite the reversals, Saint-Denis, who had always provided the momentum for the Quinze, refused to abandon his unfinished task and set about rebuilding. His immediate problems were the replenishment of the company, developing material, and, of course, funding. Although the growing artistic reputation of the Quinze with its commitment to revitalizing the theatre had begun attracting young actors "frustrated in their aspirations by the existing commercial theatre," the reconstruction of the company proved difficult.[56] As Saint-Denis pointed out: "The kind of actor I wanted was not to be found ready made."[57] Many of the young disciples such as Marius Goring and Vera Poliakoff were foreign, reflecting the appeal Saint-Denis's work had abroad.

After six months' struggle, Saint-Denis succeeded in adding seven newcomers to the company, reached an agreement with Charles Dullin whereby the two troupes would share the Atelier for a period, and discovered Jean Giono.[58] Giono, a well-known novelist, was inspired to write his first play *Lanceurs de graines* (Sowers of the grain) after watching the Quinze rehearse. Following a brief Swiss tour, his play opened at the Atelier, where the troupe was warmly welcomed by Dullin, on November 8, 1932. *Lanceurs de graines* met with disfavor and disappeared from the Quinze's repertory. The actors thought it unplayable, which was evidently not Saint-Denis's opinion, since he revived it later in translation in London. In the absence of Marie-Hélène Dasté, Madeleine Gautier designed the costumes.

By December, Obey and Marie-Hélène Dasté had rejoined the troupe; Obey, who lacked Saint-Denis's directing talent and persuasiveness, had been unable to work with the refractory actors. His return temporarily alleviated Michel's financial worries, since Madame Gompel's money was again at the Quinze's disposal. In the interim, Saint-Denis had been working hard to resolve the company's precarious fiscal situation that had been aggravated by the Swiss tour. Capitalizing on his prestige abroad, he gave a series of lectures in Brussels, Amsterdam, and London while trying to find engagements for the company.

Dullin's proposal to share the Atelier with Saint-Denis's troupe had been prompted by several factors. Admiration of the Quinze was clearly one; his theatre practice had much in common with that of Saint-Denis's troupe. The Atelier enjoyed a prestigious reputation yet was chronically threatened by irate creditors, partly because of Dullin's frequent refusal to extend the engagements of his successful productions.[59] In spite of critical acclaim, Dullin was feeling the need to reformulate his ideas. Joining forces with the Quinze would allow him more time because he would have fewer plays to direct, and perhaps their presence would help pay the bills. Given the Quinze's history, Dullin's hopes seem unrealistically optimistic.

The benefits for the Quinze were obvious. Extending their Paris season would limit the time they would have to spend on the road, while their association with the Atelier could only raise their standing in the theatrical profession. The two companies intended to alternate performances for at least six months and share expenses and box-office receipts, with each maintaining its artistic independence. Saint-Denis and Dullin outlined their plans:

> We are uniting our efforts, not merging them. United materially, united by a commonality of artistic views, we remain independent. Each of us has his troupe, his repertory, his own means of production. Through this union, we hope not only to increase the number of productions, but to add variety. Let the public benefit from this friendly rivalry between the Atelier, an experienced company concerned with renewal, and the Quinze, a new company, which should, sheltered by its senior, strengthen its growing renown.[60]

The rivalry between the two companies was, however, less than amicable. Despite Dullin's goodwill toward the Quinze, his company regarded them as interlopers. Both companies were members of the same theatrical family, but competition led to jealousy.[61] With the return of Obey, *Le Viol de Lucrèce* reentered the troupe's repertory accompanied by his new curtain-raiser, *Vénus et Adonis*. The two works attracted sizeable audiences, arousing the envy of the Atelier company, which was undergoing a bad season.

On the advice of Saint-Denis, Dullin produced an adaptation of Aristophanes' *Peace*, the season's triumph. *Lucrèce* brought financial benefits to the Atelier, but the Quinze scarcely profited from the success of *Peace*. Disturbed by the hostility of the Atelier actors, Saint-Denis dissolved the contract at the end of two months.[62]

Nevertheless, the Quinze were able to defer the resumption of their nomadic life; the box-office receipts from Obey's play allowed them to remain in Paris for the rest of the season. Saint-Denis rented the Studio des Champs-Elysées and thence transferred *Lucrèce*, but the Right Bank theatre was not an appropriate venue. Despite the auditorium's small size, it was seldom filled. And a segment of the public who did attend was drawn to the theatre because of the play's title. Patrons arrived hoping to be titillated and left disappointed, its erotica evidently too poetic and symbolic.

March of 1933 found the troupe back at the Vieux-Colombier for the last time. They presented two new works, Henri Ghéon's *Violante* and Obey's *Loire*. *Violante*, inspired by a work of Tirso de Molina, was conceived with the intent of exploiting the company's clowning skills. The play received respectable, if not superlative, reviews. Notable in the later reviews of critics who followed their work was the growing appreciation of their style.

Loire, the fifth of six plays Obey wrote for the Quinze, was the last the company performed in Paris. At the season's end they left for a tour of Spain, where Saint-Denis met the like-minded dramatist Lorca. Lorca's theatrical aims were similar and his touring company, La Barraca, was reminiscent of the Copiaus. By now, the company of fifteen had shrunk to four—three of the original actors and Saint-Denis.[63] The problems that had plagued the troupe from the beginning had not abated.[64] In the midst of the Depression their financial plight was unlikely to improve; no new patron had stepped forward and Madame Gompel's assistance was contingent upon Obey's involvement. The absence of a permanent home would continue to compel constant touring, and, given the lack of interest in Paris of any but a coterie of followers, it was doubtful that the troupe would ever attain a playhouse.

It was a crucial period for Saint-Denis, who "understood that the energy was fast disappearing and, if any enthusiasm was to be regenerated, our initial task already at an end, the means to a new beginning would have to be through a school."[65] As the actors drifted away, Michel tried to replace them. However, it had taken years of training to create the original ensemble of the Compagnie des Quinze. Saint-Denis felt that perhaps the company could be recreated in another, more peaceful environment. With the encouragement of Jean Giono, the composer Darius Milhaud, and friends in Aix-en-Provence, Michel brought his small group of actors and students to Beaumanoir on the outskirts of Aix. Saint-Denis chose this location because Aix had a fair-sized English population that he hoped would be supportive. He set up shop in a large country house that was to serve as a drama center. Plans for the new center were similar to those drawn up for the Quinze in Ville d'Avray.[66] Accommodations at Beaumanoir, however, were Spartan, more reminiscent of Pernand-Vergelesses than Ville d'Avray.[67] The facility would be used for rehearsals and training young actors. Classes would also be held for summer-school students in order to raise sorely needed funds. The company would spend eight months a year in Beaumanoir rehearsing for four months and performing outdoors for another four. The rest of the year would be spent touring.[68] Autumn of 1934 found Michel and the reorganized Quinze back on the road.[69]

The Beaumanoir experiment survived less than a year. Pressures of communal living, compounded by economic woes, exacerbated tensions. In desperation, Michel left for London in the hopes of raising funds from his British enthusiasts in order to keep the company afloat.[70] By December 1935, Saint-Denis's pilgrimage having proved futile, the company, without sufficient funds to pay their bills or even for subsistence, disbanded.[71]

The question remains: Why was a troupe that inspired such enthusiasm abroad unable to put down its roots at home? The Compagnie des Quinze was allowed to vanish from the French theatrical world, with few to mourn its passing. But did it disappear? From its demise came new growth; its ideals and teachings reemerged and strongly influenced the post-war theatre in France. Many of its members played a significant role in the French theatre's decentralization, most notably Saint-Denis and Jean Dasté. Dasté's company, the Comédie de Saint-Etienne, was created in the spirit of the Quinze. It is a spirit that continues even today. Ariane Mnouchkine's Théâtre du Soleil embodies the philosophy and practices of Michel Saint-Denis's troupe.

But what of Saint-Denis? In France he had been one of several directors working in the Copeau tradition, but was more closely identified with his uncle than the others. Louis Jouvet and Charles Dullin, the best known of Copeau's disciples, broke their formal ties with him early in their careers and remained in Paris, whereas Saint-Denis's most formative years were spent far from the capital. The Burgundy experience, while invaluable to his artistic development, was a liability in terms of recognition.

Frustrated and exhausted by his struggles to establish the Quinze, Michel reluctantly decided to leave France for the more hospitable climate of England. He was then thirty-seven years old; he had ambitions of his own that he wished to realize, a professional autonomy to create. "If I grabbed at the opportunities offered me in London, it was above all because there, I knew, I would be totally alone, a million miles from my friends, a million miles from my master Copeau."[72]

If the French did not mourn their loss, the British rejoiced at their gain. Timing worked against Saint-Denis in France, but in his favor in England. The British theatre was at a turning point, the commercial theatre lackluster, an avant-garde struggling to be born. To its emerging practitioners, the Quinze represented a model of discipline, creativity, and ensemble. They looked to its director Michel Saint-Denis to provide artistic leadership.

NOTES

1. The dates of the birth and death of the Compagnie des Quinze are somewhat arbitrary, since the troupe evolved from the Copiaus. Its first production opened on January 7, 1931; its last performance was in the autumn of 1934. Saint-Denis struggled to keep it going until December 1935.

2. André Obey, "Introduction à *Noé*," *Théâtre I* (Paris: Gallimard, 1948), 9.

3. Michel Saint-Denis, *Theatre: The Rediscovery of Style* (New York: Theatre Arts Books, 1960), 43.

4. Michel Saint-Denis, *Training for the Theatre: Premises and Promises,* ed. Suria Saint-Denis (New York: Theatre Arts Books, 1982), 33.

5. Pierre Alder (stage name of Pierre Rieschmann), unpublished autobiography (undated), 278.

6. Jean Villard, *Mon demi-siècle* (Lausanne: Payot, 1954), 153.

7. Alder, 298.

8. Marie-Hélène Dasté, personal interview, 18 June 1989.

9. Blaise Gautier, personal interview, Paris, 27 June 1989.

10. Villard, *Mon demi-siècle,* 153.

11. Dasté, interview.

12. Alder, 337.

13. Michel Saint-Denis, diary notes (undated).

14. Alder, 338–39.

15. Phyllis Aykroyd, *The Dramatic Art of the Compagnie des Quinze* (London: Eric Partridge, 1935), 20–21.

16. Villard, *Mon demi-siècle,* 154.

17. Saint-Denis, *Training for the Theatre,* 186.

18. Pierre Lefèvre, personal interviews, New York, 13 January 1989, and Strasbourg, 20 June 1989.

19. Alder, 294.

20. Saint-Denis, *Training for the Theatre,* 182.

21. Marius Goring, personal interview, London, 14 January 1991.

22. Alder, 295.

23. Saint-Denis, *Training for the Theatre,* 27.

24. Quoted in Louise Delpit, "Les derniers épigones de Jacques Copeau: la Compagnie des Quinze et le Théâtre des Quatre Saisons," *Smith College Studies in Modern Languages,* vol. 21 (October 1939–July 1940), 48.

25. Alder, 306.

26. Quoted in Delpit, "Les derniers épigones de Jacques Copeau," 48.

27. Pierre Brisson, *Le Théâtre des années folles* (Geneva: Editions du Milieu du Monde, 1943), 62.

28. Paul-Louis Mignon, *Charles Dullin* (Lyon: La Manufacture, 1990), 28.

29. Villard, *Mon demi-siècle,* 134.

30. Arthur Waley, *The Nô Plays of Japan* (New York: Grove Press, 1922), 17.

31. In collaboration with the company, Obey conceived the idea for the play but was unable to proceed. Michel Saint-Denis visited Obey frequently to entreat him to finish. During one visit, a radio was broadcasting the Davis Cup matches when suddenly both men realized that the passion and tone of the voice was what *Lucrèce* required.

32. Norman Marshall, *The Producer and the Play* (London: MacDonald, 1957), 63.

33. *Latinité* (April 1931), 81.

34. Michel Saint-Denis, "Naturalism in the Theatre," *The Listener* (4 December 1952), 929.

35. Alder, 317.

36. Marie-Françoise Christout, Noëlle Guibert, and Danièle Pauly, *Théâtre du Vieux-Colombier* (Paris: Institut Français d'Architecture, 1993), 117.

37. Villard, *Mon demi-siècle,* 155.

38. Suzanne Maistre Saint-Denis, personal interview, Paris, 14 June 1989.

39. Tyrone Guthrie, *A Life in the Theatre* (New York: McGraw-Hill, 1959), 93.

40. Michel Saint-Denis, "The English Theatre in Gallic Eyes," trans. J. F. M. Stephens, Jr. *Texas Quarterly* 4 (autumn 1961), 30.

41. Ibid., 161.

42. Dasté, interview.

43. Alder, 338.

44. Quoted in Alder, 342.

45. Delpit, "Les derniers épigones de Jacques Copeau," 50.

46. Benjamin Crémieux, quoted in Delpit, "Les derniers épigones de Jacques Copeau," 51.

47. André Antoine, *L'Information* (8 December, 1931), supplement.

48. Ibid.

49. James Agate, quoted in Marshall, *The Producer and the Play,* 64.

50. Saint-Denis, interview.

51. Alder, 359.

52. Letter from Ian Black to Michel Saint-Denis, 18 January 1932.

53. Villard, *Mon demi-siècle,* 162.

54. Alder, 373.

55. Villard, *Mon demi-siècle,* 161.

56. Alder, 367.

57. Saint-Denis, *Theatre,* 43.

58. Saint-Denis, diary notes.

59. France Anders, *Jacques Copeau et le Cartel des Quatre* (Paris: A. G. Nizet, 1959), 200.

60. Michel Saint-Denis and Charles Dullin, *Comoedia,* December 23, 1932. Quoted in Delpit, "Les derniers épigones de Jacques Copeau," 53.

61. Alder, 393.

62. Ibid., 400.

63. Irving Wardle, *The Theatres of George Devine* (London: Eyre Methuen, 1978), 47.

64. Saint-Denis, diary notes.

65. Ibid.

66. Letter from Michel Saint-Denis to Beatrice Straight, 9 July 1934.

67. Wardle, *The Theatres of George Devine,* 47.

68. Saint-Denis, "The English Theatre in Gallic Eyes," 29–30.

69. Wardle, *The Theatres of George Devine,* 47.

70. Letter from Marius Goring to Suria Magito Saint-Denis, 12 June 1976.

71. Letter from Pierre Alder to Michel Saint-Denis (undated).

72. Saint-Denis, diary notes.

◆ chapter five ◆

Linking Theatrical Cultures: The London Theatre Studio

THE QUINZE'S DISSOLUTION USHERED IN the international phase of Saint-Denis's career during which he became an agent of theatrical change. His work was to have its most profound impact in England. In the early 1930s British theatre seemed stuck in the doldrums, awaiting reform to bring it into the twentieth century. The West End mainly offered a diet of light comedies, musicals, farces, thrillers, and revues. Serious drama was represented by the largely forgotten plays of J. B. Priestly, Emlyn Williams, and James Bridie. Scripts were chosen for commercial appeal and popular stars engaged for the run of the play. During the period following World War I, leading actors no longer tested their talents in classical theatre. The dominant acting mode had become subdued; understatement was the vogue, a style that did not lend itself to heroic roles. Permanent companies headed by actor-managers virtually disappeared. Producers, usually businessmen attracted by a quick profit, dominated the West End. The director as a theatrical force was yet to appear. The theatre outside London was in similar straits; touring companies brought last year's hits to the provinces whose theatres also served as venues for plays trying out for the West End. While permanent provincial companies still existed, the majority drew their repertory from London's commercial successes.

Although the early twentieth century was a period of experimentation on the continent, the English theatre, with few exceptions, remained focused inward. Struggling against the prevailing aesthetic complacency were a few idealists whose ambition was to provide a theatrical alternative. Their most important contribution was in the presentation of modern foreign works rather than in the realm of stagecraft. The eclectic repertoire provided the training ground for artists, including many of the future leading figures in British theatre, seeking to learn their craft. These practitioners became the mainstay of Saint-Denis's work in England as teachers, designers, and performers. Looking at their early careers, one is struck by the intertwining of their professional lives. Saint-Denis's most important first contacts were John Gielgud, Tyrone Guthrie, and George Devine.

When Saint-Denis met him, Gielgud had spent approximately a decade acting in both commercial and alternative theatre. Interested in broadening his range, he crossed over from the West End to work in art theatres, despite the financial sacrifice. He appeared in productions directed by J. B. Fagan at the Oxford Playhouse, by Nigel Playfair at the Lyric Theatre, Hammersmith, and by Theodore Komisarjevsky at the Barnes. Fagan had an eye for developing talent; among those who began their careers at his theatre were Glen Byam Shaw and Tyrone Guthrie. The Oxford Playhouse (1923–29) was emblematic of many ambitious, but ill-funded little theatres. Established in the hope of attracting a university audience, the playhouse offered a wide-ranging repertory. After six years of struggle, it succumbed to the community's lack of interest. The Lyric Theatre, Hammersmith (1918–32) provided tutelage for Edith Evans as well as Gielgud. Playfair's directorial forte was as a stylist, his interest the revival of Restoration and eighteenth-century comedy. His productions' strength lay in their elegance; their weakness, a tendency to stress decorative elements, sometimes to the detriment of meaning. Nonetheless, Playfair's emphasis on style helped prepare the way for Saint-Denis. Even Laurence Olivier, whose early career was primarily fixed on commercial success, got his start at an art theatre, Barry Jackson's Birmingham Repertory Theatre (1913–35).[1] Among those who passed through this noted company was Peggy Ashcroft, who also worked under Playfair and Komisarjevsky.

But it was the Old Vic, dedicated to Shakespeare's works, that would play a key role in Michel Saint-Denis's English career. In 1935, when Saint-Denis took up residence in England, Tyrone Guthrie had recently resigned as artistic director after struggling to raise production standards. The Old Vic was under the management of the redoubtable Lilian Baylis whose parsimony was legendary. The theatre, however, furnished excellent on-the-job training for classical actors such as Gielgud, Ashcroft, Olivier, Alec Guinness, Michael Redgrave, and Marius Goring, all of whom became part of the Saint-Denis team.

The arrival of the Compagnie des Quinze in 1931—exploring possibilities as yet undreamed of by the English—had been a revelation to the London theatre world. Here was the frankly theatrical with its emphasis on mime, mask, song, and dance. It was this theatricality, combined with a strong ensemble performance, that attracted the young actors of the time who were searching for something fresh. Pierre Lefèvre, then a law student, remembers "how hallucinatingly novel it was with beautiful performances."[2] Michael Redgrave, still a French instructor, was so moved he determined to become an actor. British actors came backstage after the shows eager to talk to Michel Saint-Denis.

Gielgud wrote: "Like many of my confrères in the theatre, I was enormously impressed with these remarkable productions and the small but brilliant team of actors who appeared in them."[3] He was so impressed that he requested Saint-Denis to direct him in an English production of *Noé*, a courageous act on Gielgud's part, since he was an unlikely Noah.

Gielgud's urge to play the role coincided with the collapse of the Quinze. Saint-Denis had returned to London to raise money to continue his work in France. The Quinze were now three: Saint-Denis, his common-law wife Madeleine Gautier (whose relationship with Saint-Denis dated from the collapse of the Copiaus), and Pierre Alder, whom he had left in Aix to deal with the deteriorating situation.[4] Because of the contacts Saint-Denis had made during his tours he knew a number of people, but was not yet integrated into the theatrical network.

Alone in London, cut off from friends, family, colleagues, country, and language, Saint-Denis needed to connect with the English theatre world. His intermediary was Marius Goring, late of the Quinze, who introduced him to his future collaborators George Devine and Glen Byam Shaw at Motley's studio. Motley was the professional name of a trio of stage designers—Margaret Harris, her sister Sophia, and Elizabeth Montgomery—who were to work with Saint-Denis from 1935 to 1952. They were just beginning to establish their reputation, having designed several Gielgud productions. Their studio was the gathering place for emerging practitioners. In spite of his rudimentary English, Saint-Denis experienced an immediate bond with its denizens. In his own words, he "had found my milieu, in this atmosphere where technique, invention, and freedom blended."[5] What Motley and their friends shared was a commitment to a new, as yet undefined, theatre. Brought together by common convictions, a core group made up of Gielgud, Devine, and Guthrie rallied around Michel. They held meetings in which they discussed their similarities, differences, plans, and "professional considerations which might tempt" them.[6] One possibility proposed by the English was that Saint-Denis remain in Britain to work with them.

Saint-Denis was neither the first nor only European reformer to attract a following in England, but he was the most resolute, unique in building a stable long-term professional life in London. Unlike his contemporaries Theodore Komisarjevsky and Michael Chekhov, he galvanized a group of professional practitioners, gave form to their inchoate vision, and transformed disciples into collaborators. Komisarjevsky was something of a gadfly. He had talent and magnetism but was inconsistent; his capriciousness was as legendary as his brilliance. More importantly, he was not an organization-builder. Saint-Denis, on the other hand, was able to establish and maintain a theatrical home through his schools for more than ten years. Michael Chekhov's ambitions resembled Saint-Denis's, but in the rarefied air of Dartington Hall in Devon where he briefly established a studio he was unable to realize them.

Saint-Denis was willing to take on a leadership role, with all the responsibility and commitment that the position demanded. Yet, if he had much to teach English theatre practitioners, he, in turn, learned from his contact with them. Saint-Denis's career differed from that of many émigré artists in that he did not view his task as trying to implant the theory and practice of his native country in foreign soil. His theories continually evolved in response to the cultural context, influencing both his practice and the growth of theatre in countries where he worked.

In his favor too was the fact that he was not dependent on a foreign reputation. His productions had been seen and evaluated by the artists with whom he would work. Fortuitously, the world he entered was peopled with talented, energetic, ambitious professionals committed to transforming their theatre. As he later wrote, "Without realizing it, I was consorting with those who were to shape the English theatre for the next thirty years."[7]

Still mulling over possibilities, Saint-Denis accepted Gielgud's offer to direct *Noah* (produced by Bronson Albery). Rehearsals were difficult for Saint-Denis even though cast members—Marius Goring, Jessica Tandy, Alec Guinness, George Devine—were drawn from the Motley inner circle. Accustomed to a long exploratory period with an ensemble of physically trained actors, Saint-Denis was dismayed by having only three weeks of rehearsal. Unable to express himself adequately, he was often obliged to mime his directions. Because of time and language constraints he decided to repeat the Quinze production—a frustrating experience. Some actors felt straitjacketed by his insistence on dictating every blocking detail; Saint-Denis was nonplussed by the actors' lack of agility. Nevertheless, he was, as Margaret Harris, who with her colleagues designed the production, remembers, "tremendously dominant. He was strong in what he wanted, and insisted on getting it."[8]

Impressed with their previous work, Saint-Denis engaged Motley to create the decor for *Noah*, but feared they would be unable to achieve the abstract yet realistic style he wanted for the masks and costumes. He considered jobbing in the original designer Marie-Hélène Dasté, but Motley convinced him otherwise. However, Saint-Denis rejected some of their designs as sentimentalized and naturalistic. To help execute the masks and keep Motley on track, Marie-Madeleine Gautier joined Saint-Denis in London, bringing their son Blaise (1930–92).[9]

The production was favorably received and ran for ten weeks. Ivor Brown of *The Observer*, in the critical vocabulary of the era, wrote that "the play has been most skillfully handled by M. Saint-Denis; the acting owns strength of style and not a minimy, pinimy pretense of it (the obvious danger when the modern flirts with medievalism), and the decoration has power with humour."[10] This version, nonetheless, fell short of the original. Tyrone Guthrie, who had been enchanted by the "style of the Quinze, the elegance and simplicity of the setting, the choreography, the music of the speech, and especially by the complete break with naturalism," felt the magic was gone.[11] In retrospect, it would seem absurd to expect the London production to recapture the quality of the original. Unsurprisingly, Gielgud was unable to depict Noah's peasant earthiness. All the actors lacked the requisite skills and training. Literally and figuratively, Saint-Denis did not have a language with which to communicate to his actors.

One happy consequence of *Noah* was the friendship forged between Saint-Denis and George Devine. Devine had not found his niche. As his biographer Irving Wardle points out, it was "clear that he needed someone else to give him a lead and turn his general dissatisfaction toward some specific purpose."[12] Saint-Denis, for his part, welcomed the younger man's energy, enthusiasm, and admiration as well as his ribald sense of humor. Both men wanted to continue their working relationship.

The experience with *Noah* confirmed Saint-Denis's belief that transient enterprises were not for him. His goal remained the creation of a school with a view to forming a company. George Devine and Marius Goring urged him to establish that troupe in London. A permanent company under Saint-Denis's direction would find support among the young idealistic theatre practitioners in England. As Saint-Denis had discovered, a similar institution, the Group Theatre, whose models were the Vieux-Colombier and his own Compagnie des Quinze, had been launched by the dancer Rupert Doone. Organized after the Quinze's first visit to London, the Group Theatre consciously pursued similar aims: theatricalist production and a permanent ensemble of physically trained actors. Though the company never materialized, the Group Theatre held classes.

Guthrie had long-standing reasons for supporting the Saint-Denis project. Involved with the Group Theatre at its inception, Guthrie had dreamed of making it the English equivalent of the Compagnie des Quinze with himself at its artistic helm. However, the Group Theatre remained under Rupert Doone's authority. Moreover, it soon became obvious that Saint-Denis's ambitions for what would be known as the London Theatre Studio (LTS) were closer to those championed by Guthrie. Several years earlier, he had written of the importance of just such an institution in revitalizing the theatre.[13] The Quinze was instrumental in leading him to that conclusion.

But Michel Saint-Denis was reluctant to leave France permanently and give up the hope of resuscitating the Compagnie des Quinze. In the end, unable to find the necessary funding, he allowed himself to be persuaded to remain in England. The deciding factor was the money given by Guthrie with the proviso that it be used to establish a London school. According to Saint-Denis, Guthrie wrote to him that "he had deeply reflected on the school that I had spoken to him about, that he approved of the idea, and that he was ready to put the sum of £1,300 at my disposal if I considered it possible to set up this school in London."[14]

Others followed Guthrie's lead. Help was forthcoming from Laurence

Olivier, John Gielgud, and Charles Laughton, who had helped finance the Quinze's last production shown in England. A committee to provide practical guidance (and later a governing board) was formed consisting of Gielgud, Bronson Albery, and the banker Ian Black. After several months Guthrie left the board, replaced by Laurence Olivier. In this governing board Saint-Denis had a group of well-connected and powerful men who supported his intentions.

George Devine and Michel Saint-Denis, with advice from Marius Goring and Vera Poliakoff, spent six months planning the school. It was called the London Theatre Studio to emphasize its commitment to process and development. Saint-Denis envisaged LTS as a "self-contained theatrical organisation" made up of a permanent company, an acting school, and a group of artists and technicians in residence.[15] To this end, the students targeted were professional actors seeking advanced and alternative training, young, inexperienced actors, and prospective technicians and designers. Saint-Denis hoped to build his company from the best of the students. He intended to "equip our young acting students with all the means of expression we used at the Compagnie des Quinze, but we wanted to extend the imaginative, the creative basis of the Quinze's training."[16] It had been apparent to Saint-Denis that the strength of the Quinze actors lay in their physical skills, the weakness in their vocal capability. Vocally demanding parts were usually played by Suzanne Bing and Auguste Boverio, who had undergone training before their exposure to Copeau's methods. When Saint-Denis assumed the role of Noah, he discovered that his own training left him insufficiently prepared to tackle the play's long monologues. Saint-Denis proposed to remedy this deficiency through building a strong speech and voice department.

When LTS opened in January of 1936 it had not found a permanent home because of unresolved financial difficulties. Initially, it was housed in cramped quarters in Diaghilev's former dance studio, classes held in a practice room. Because of space limitations, course offerings were reduced and classes began in early morning and continued long into the night. Overcrowding was alleviated in the second term when the school rented the Old Vic's rehearsal studios during the company's summer vacation. At about the same time, a small, unused Methodist chapel was discovered in Islington. To render it serviceable, the interior needed to be rebuilt at an estimated cost of £6,500, but Saint-Denis was able to raise only half that amount. A generous contribution of £3,500 from Laura Dyas, a student in the production course, saved the project.

Renovations began in July of 1936 and were completed by the autumn. Working with Saint-Denis was the architect Marcel Breuer, a disciple of Gropius. Functional and beautiful, combining classical and modernist properties, the remodeled building showed the Bauhaus influence. In order to save space, Breuer designed plywood nesting chairs, the first to be seen in England. The interior contained a stage, rehearsal rooms, workshops, and a raised light-and-sound booth at the back of the auditorium, which was a recent innovation. Its most notable feature was a modernized Georgian stage, the apron a playing space bordered by two doors on either side. Above each door was a balcony, another potential acting area. Although the auditorium was small and narrow, seating fewer than two hundred, the stage had a proscenium opening thirty-two feet wide and a depth of twenty-two feet, without any wing space. Its size was an indication of Saint-Denis's expectations: the stage built to the specifications of a commercial theatre would facilitate LTS's productions being "transferred complete with play to a West End theatre."[17]

Saint-Denis was LTS's managing director, and George Devine, a superb organizer, was the assistant director. The faculty was impressive. Saint-Denis, Devine, and Goring taught acting; Suria Magito, Saint-Denis's future wife, was in charge of movement. On the advice of Darius Milhaud, Saint-Denis saw Magito perform in Paris and promptly hired her. Her work, "which combined mime, the use of splendid original No masks, speech, chanting and dance," approached the technique of the Compagnie des Quinze.[18] Acrobatics were taught by Frank Duncan, fencing for the male students by Gabriel Toyne. Iris Warren headed the voice department. Choral speech, a class reminiscent of the Vieux-Colombier School and the Quinze's work in that domain, was given by Mona Swann. John Gielgud graciously came in several times a quarter and taught Shakespearean verse.

Voice and movement differed from the equivalent classes given later at the Old Vic School. Voice tended towards the traditional; Magito's movement classes resembled interpretive dance with a dramatic component.[19] In it, she used themes based on legend or paintings with a narrative composition—Goya's "Shooting of the Rebels of May 3," for instance. Students built their characters and developed a plot with their teacher's help. These dance/movement compositions were rehearsed intensively, music composed, and costumes made. The most promising were performed at the end-of-term show.

In addition to the professional and student acting classes, there was a French acting section for students with speaking proficiency. The rationale was that performing in another language would improve their English diction. The course, taught by Saint-Denis, was divided into two parts: practice in French verse and prose, and production of French plays. Because of limited enrollment the professionals and beginners overlapped. Hence, a novice such as Chattie Salaman found herself working with former Quinze member Vera Poliakoff. Saint-Denis and George Devine, who spoke some French, occasionally performed in the school's French plays, an experience Michel relished. These productions were the only outlet for his acting talents, since his heavy accent cut him off from the English stage. Salaman recalled how much fun he and Devine had playing comic old men in *La Première famille* by Jules Supervielle and in a French farce adapted from a La Fontaine fable.[20]

There were three technical sections. Saint-Denis led a theoretical and practical production course for designers, technicians, and stage managers. Practitioners gave lectures on text, acting, design, costuming, lighting, theatrical architecture, and theatre history. The students worked on all phases of production, building, painting, sewing, lighting, and stage managing. LTS was the first drama school in England to offer a design course (given by Motley), normally the province of art academies. Margaret Harris taught scene design, Sophia Harris, costume, and Elizabeth Montgomery, scene painting. John Burrell, whose career would again intersect with Saint-Denis's at the Old Vic Theatre Centre, worked closely with Motley and also directed school shows. Richard Southern taught the history of scene design and technical drawing and building. Theatre history and textual study were mandatory for acting and technical students.

Thus the school came close to realizing Saint-Denis's goal of a self-contained organization. It was more of a totality than any previous English drama school. Lacking were courses in directing and playwriting, and, of course, the company. At the school's inception, Saint-Denis was optimistic that the company would materialize within two years.[21] His optimism seemed warranted. Within a period of months he had received a new lease on his professional life, created and built a school to his specifications, and become a person to be reckoned with in the London theatre world. The rising theatrical elite was observing classes at the school; offers to direct were coming in.

But there were hard realities confronting him. The school had to be self-supporting; subsidies were nonexistent and salaries low. In order to keep LTS operating, Saint-Denis supplemented its income by giving evening lectures and public readings of French plays. Finding a sufficient number of talented students was problematic. Saint-Denis was esteemed by his peers, but his name was hardly a household word. Despite the efforts of the school publicist, initially, places at LTS were not in great demand. Publicity was oftentimes more detrimental than helpful, such as the article in *Picture Post*, a popular weekly, which poked fun at the classes.[22] During the first term there were twenty-four beginning students, sixteen professional actors, eighteen technical students, and six French course students. The professional actors took specific classes or coaching. Alec Guinness studied under Saint-Denis; Laurence Olivier joined an acrobatics class.[23]

A few students like Pierre Lefèvre were invited to join. Saint-Denis met Lefèvre (who ultimately taught at all of Saint-Denis's schools) while directing an amateur production of Cocteau's *Antigone* at the French Institute. Impressed by Lefèvre's handling of the Messenger, Saint-Denis suggested that he consider becoming an actor. Chattie and Merula Salaman knew about the school through their older sister Susan, who stage managed for the Quinze in France. Peter Ustinov was brought to LTS by his mother, a friend of Saint-Denis's. Undoubtedly the school had some gifted students, but Chattie Salaman wondered how "some of those people got in."[24] Contrary to student rumors, there were indeed criteria that Saint-Denis refined over time. Standards became easier to implement as the talent pool grew larger. Saint-Denis's preferred candidate was between the ages of seventeen and twenty-three, since the optimal training period was adolescence when the student still retained "something of the naïve and open attitude which naturally belongs to children."[25] He looked for a flair, marking the individual as distinctive, that piqued his curiosity. This attitude, combined with his social conscience, led him to accept atypical applicants in reaction to England's class-consciousness of the period: "people with impossible accents," foreigners, the socially disadvantaged.[26] At the audition, candidates presented prepared monologues; an interview with the judges followed. If the judges deemed that the candidate showed promise, they would suggest a theme for the applicant to improvise. Their decision was usually reached at that juncture.

At the end of the two-year course, the students presented their work to a paying public. Since LTS began in January 1936, the first class had not completed its full two years when its production took place during the spring of 1937. (A different show was presented later in the summer.) The initiatory production was given for four evenings; as the public came to know its quality, the performance schedule was extended to two weeks. Though faculty directed, all other production aspects were in student hands. Advanced technical students designed and executed scenery and costumes; the best first-year technical students served as stage managers. In keeping with Saint-Denis's broad vision of the role of theatre practitioners, actors served on production crews, and designers and technicians played small parts or walked on. He insisted that every student understand theoretically and practically how the theatre functions.

The first show set the model for the future. The performance was divided into four sections, each representing a theatrical style, each exploiting an aspect of the training. There was a classical selection (Greek, Renaissance, or Restoration), an original experimental work, a modern play, and a short farce based on physical comedy. None of the literary dramas was performed in its entirety; either one act or a significant body of scenes was culled from the text. The first year, Saint-Denis directed *Judith*, which he adapted from the Apocryhpha with Carl Wildman, choreographed by Suria Magito.[27] It was a piece in the mode of the Compagnie des Quinze. Exploring the relationship among music, choral expression, and movement, it featured a chorus that interacted with Judith, the play's only character. The dance-like movement of the solo performer contrasted vividly with the motionless Chorus that spoke and sang its dialogue to music commissioned for the play. Like the Quinze productions, *Judith* used a neutral stage, moving the action from the "wailing city of the Hebrews to the Assyrian camp" through "imaginative use of lighting and clever grouping."[28] Included in the evening was the first act of *Three Sisters*, also directed by Saint-Denis, scenes from *A Midsummer Night's Dream* mounted by Marius Goring, and *The Fair*, a short commedia-like piece arranged by Suria Magito and George Devine. Since Magito, Devine, and Goring were new to directing, Saint-Denis supervised them closely. *The Fair* showcased the students' comic and acrobatic skills. It was replete with carnival characters, musicians, jugglers, funambulists, and a Harlequin character (Pierre Lefèvre) who leapt out a window at the end.

It is a measure of the interest Saint-Denis's work generated in the theatrical profession that critics of prestigious newspapers and magazines attended the performances. *Judith* was the hit of the show. Desmond MacCarthy of the *New Statesman* and Nation was "self-forgetful and moved" by the quality of the acting and directing, writing that "no one has understood so well as M. Saint-Denis the dramatic power of the chorus."[29] The *London Daily Telegraph* considered "the most striking thing of the evening was the Apocryhpha play."[30] John Gielgud was so taken by *Judith* that he telephoned Saint-Denis to ask to transfer it to the West End. Saint-Denis rejected the move as premature.[31] Less sophisticated spectators were bewildered. Yvonne Mitchell recounts her father's "dismay, even disappointment" at her end-of-term show. LTS's experiments "seemed to bear no resemblance to what they expected us to be learning."[32] In fairness, it should be added that in *The Fair*, Mitchell played a Siamese twin, sharing the same costume as her other half, the two perched "to somersault, locked together, over the back of two clowns."[33]

Because of their familiarity, a fresh approach was *de rigueur* for the classical works. For the Shakespearean scenes, Marius Goring used experimental techniques in vocal expression that were being developed at LTS. Critics faulted the students' verse speaking, in contrast to Saint-Denis, who found the vocal work promising.[34] The first show remained for him one of the LTS's "most exciting productions."[35] Almost certainly, the critical response derived from the unconventional approach to a traditional work. The following year, the *New Statesman* critic returned for an evening that included Farquhar's *The Beaux Strategem*, an act of Noel Coward's *Hay Fever*, and Suria Magito's movement composition. He thought the event "well worth attending"; *Hay Fever* "had points any professional production might have coveted."[36] However, he still criticized the students' vocal ability, this time in the Farquhar piece, "which bore the stamp of being a 'school' production." Sixty-five years later, it is hard to know what standards were being brought to bear. Was the vocal work inadequate because the training needed improvement? As we have seen, one of Saint-Denis's goals for LTS was the development of an effective voice and speech department capable of producing an actor "whose voice would have the wide range necessary to carry classical and modern texts, rather than one capable of only the jerky, staccato delivery usual in the stock companies of the time."[37] Evidently, he did not fully realize his ambition, since in his next school he replaced the voice and speech faculty. Or was the critic disturbed because it departed from accepted methods, as in *Midsummer Night's Dream*? What is notable was that the reviewer took exception only to the handling of English classics. Nonetheless, the critical consensus was that LTS productions surpassed their competitors'.

Much of what Saint-Denis was exploring with his students was an extension of his French work. An occasional play, such as *A Woman Killed with Kindness*, came directly from Copeau's repertory, but, in general, classical works used to train the students descended from the Vieux-Colombier School and the Copiaus. Saint-Denis expanded the previous esoteric research and lifted it out of the laboratory to test before an audience. At the Vieux-Colombier students studied theory of Greek tragedy, theatrical architecture, and improvised Greek myths in their acting classes. But there was no attempt to stage any of the plays. As a result of the Vieux-Colombier research, Saint-Denis was well-grounded in the background and sought to give what he knew a theatrical context. At LTS, Saint-Denis directed Sophocles' *Electra* and Euripides' *Alcestis*. Later, he applied what he had learned from staging the student performances to his professional productions of *Oedipus* in 1945 and *Electra* in 1951.

After *Judith*, the movement dramas were directed by Suria Magito. Drawing upon the Quinze's explorations of the Noh with Saint-Denis as her guide, Magito conceived and performed her rendition, wearing an authentic Japanese Noh mask of a witch, accompanied by an ensemble composed of percussion instruments.[38] In 1938, Magito presented the school's response to the horrors of the Spanish Civil War, a "dramatic ballet" based on Goya's *Disasters of War*. Inspired by the Quinze, Monica Swann, the choral speech teacher, created her own Spanish-sounding version of *grummelotage*.

The four years of the London Theatre Studio's existence were very productive for Saint-Denis. Deeply involved in the school, he also directed for the professional theatre. While in the preliminary planning stages of LTS, he was asked by the Group Theatre to stage *Sowers of the Grain* (Lanceurs de graines). Given the convergence of aspirations between Saint-Denis and the Group, *Sowers of the Grain* might have led to mutually beneficial collaborations. As it was, the October 1935 production with Marius Goring and the celebrated Irish actress Sara Allgood earned respectable notices, but attracted comparatively little attention.

More crucial to Saint-Denis's career was Tyrone Guthrie's invitation to direct *The Witch of Edmonton* at the Old Vic. The offer was appealing on a number of counts. In undertaking a British classic, albeit a seldom produced one, Saint-Denis broke with his French past. With *The Witch of Edmonton*, not only would he direct an English drama in English, for the first time professionally he would stage a play not tailored to him. If Saint-Denis wanted to be accepted as something more than an exotic specialist, then he would have to work with the established repertory. However, *The Witch of Edmonton* was not part of that repertory. It is unclear what drew Guthrie to the play. As a foreigner whose English was still less than fluent, Saint-Denis may have been unaware of its flaws. He does tell us that he "had long been attracted to this play with its Elizabethan surreal-

FIGURE 5.1   *Edith Evans (right) in* The Witch of Edmonton *(1936), The Old Vic. (Angus McBean Photograph, Copyright © The Harvard Theatre Collection, The Houghton Library.)*

ism."[39] Or perhaps he felt he could achieve with this little-known work the *succès d'estime* that Copeau had with the equally unfamiliar *A Maid's Tragedy*. Imbued with an appreciation of Elizabethan and Jacobean drama since his youth, Saint-Denis considered himself prepared to direct an English classic despite his French background.

Edith Evans, for whose talent Saint-Denis had enormous respect, played the witch (see figure 5.1), and Marius Goring, the juvenile lead. Appearing in small roles were Alec Guinness and Michael Redgrave. Motley designed the sets and costumes, George Devine the lighting. There is no record of the rehearsal schedule, but doubtless it was insufficient for Saint-Denis. At this stage of his career Saint-Denis's productions frequently ran into time problems. It may be that he was unwilling to cede control. At the dress rehearsal he decided a church was needed upstage to complete the picture. Opening night found Motley still building the church during the first scene.[40]

Critical opinion was lukewarm; the overall view was that the play was better consigned to obscurity. Writing for the *Times*, James Agate, nonetheless, thought Saint-Denis had directed it with "lively adroitness." Summing up, he added, "the revival was an experiment worth making, but it must be confessed that its chief value was experimental."[41] Some of the reviewers, particularly Ivor Brown, disdainfully pigeonholed the production as "arty" (as if the theatre were a stranger to art!).[42] Even the turntable designed for the production came in for its share of negative criticism—too twentieth century. Audrey Williamson, while not a fan of the play, found that "the production caught something of the grey sordidness and intolerance of sixteenth-century village life, as well as the sharp fantastic flare of contemporary daemonism."[43]

Further impressions come from Saint-Denis's students at LTS, admittedly not an unbiased group. However, their words offer a hint of the results Saint-Denis was seeking. Pierre Lefèvre stresses its originality, while for Chattie Salaman, "it was very powerful with a lot of weird magical things going on."[44] And the skeptical Tyrone Guthrie, not always a Saint-Denis admirer, was intrigued by the production.[45] Following *The Witch of Edmonton*, Olivier asked Saint-Denis to direct him in *Macbeth* at the Old Vic. Although Olivier's interest was piqued by a school course in the staging of *Macbeth* he observed at LTS, surely the production of *The Witch of Edmonton* played a role in his decision.

History has dismissed Saint-Denis's 1937 *Macbeth* as "inconclusive," "leaden-footed," and "fussy."[46] Yet interviews with Margaret Harris, audience members, and reviews indicate the production warrants a reassessment. Included in the cast were the tragedienne Judith Anderson and Andrew Cruikshank, of whom Oliver said, "I do not believe there has ever been a more perfect Banquo."[47] Once again Motley designed the scenery and costumes, and George Devine the lighting. Music was composed by Darius Milhaud, known for his eclecticism and polytonality, the simultaneous use of different keys. Saint-Denis was again caught in an artistic bind. He was blessed in his company, but did not have the conditions he required. Time and money were short. Despite, or perhaps because of, scrupulous preparation, he found it difficult to conform to the schedule.

It is apparent looking by at the reviews, both good and bad, that Saint-Denis broke with tradition in his staging. As a Frenchman, he was unfamiliar with the conventions of British theatre; as an innovator, he sought to replace outworn practice. Given that a major part of Saint-Denis's charge—at least in his sponsors' minds—was to bring contemporary continental stagecraft to the British theatre, it is hardly surprising that *Macbeth* outraged critics stuck in a Victorian mindset. There was an sanctioned way of doing Shakespeare; "wrong-headed" was the judgment applied to an original concept.[48]

The production's expressionistic aspects emphasized the macabre and the violent, as if the world of the play were a projection of Macbeth's mind. Many of the critics commented on the use of sickly greens and browns, reds of "dried-blood hue and consistency."[49] Margaret Harris explained that these tones, plus blacks and deep purples, depicted "the intensity of the characters and the brooding Scottish landscape."[50] The entire set was outsize, as were the characters. A tall column dominated the stage, a staircase running down its side. Saint-Denis used masks for the witches and Banquo. Appropriately, the witches were a terrifying sight, "hideous and more than life-size in fantastic masks" and padded cos-

FIGURE 5.2   *Laurence Olivier and Judith Anderson in* Macbeth *(1937), The Old Vic. (Angus McBean Photograph, Copyright © The Harvard Theatre Collection, The Houghton Library.)*

tumes, glowing "red as fire above their smoking cauldron."[51] Banquo's mask had a dual purpose. Aesthetically, it linked the character to the witches and the supernatural. Practically, it allowed Saint-Denis to stage the banquet scene placing several actors wearing the same disguise at varying points so that the ghost could reappear immediately in different areas. The impression was of "an image struck from Macbeth's guilt-ridden brain."[52] Consistent with the fantastical elements of the production, Olivier—the master of makeup—applied a yellowish base, donned an enormous false nose and false gums, and slanted his eyes (see figure 5.2). The lighting contributed to the dark, elemental, and phantasmagoric quality.

True to its reputation, *Macbeth* was haunted by misfortune. Saint-Denis was involved in a taxi accident before the opening, Lilian Baylis's dog was run over, the scenery was not completed by the dress rehearsal, and Olivier contracted laryngitis. Because of a combination of production problems and Olivier's voice, the premiere was postponed, a first in the Vic's history. The ailing Lilian Baylis died of a heart attack the day before the rescheduled opening. Many, Olivier among them, credited the postponement with killing Baylis. Opening night was fraught with difficulties. Actors and audience were distressed by Baylis's death, an event that may also have colored critical reaction. Anderson and Olivier were unprepared. Unknown to the director and designers, Judith Anderson was acrophobic. The blocking required her to descend Motley's steep staircase. Since Anderson had been unable to work with it during rehearsals, the effect on her performance was damaging.[53] Olivier, suffering from his cold, feared he might be incapable of completing the performance. Detecting his fatigue, J. C. Trewin noted that Olivier "appeared to be outlining a performance he would block in later."[54] James Agate was curious enough to return a second time, finding the last act the best he had ever seen, "played at white heat of both imagination and energy so that it becomes a molten whole."[55] For Agate, Olivier was "admirably aided by the production of M. Saint-Denis." Writing about the production in retrospect, Audrey Williamson recollected that Olivier's performance was "perhaps the best Macbeth before the war . . . in a blood-boltered production" alive with "the spirit of darkling imagination."[56] But for the majority of critics the production was too avant-garde. Margaret Harris attributed the negative reaction to a lack of comprehension, narrow-mindedness, even xenophobia: "His classical work had a very different approach from that of the British, an excitement and character that was unique, thrilling. And people didn't appreciate it. It was a time when people resented the fact that Michel was French."[57]

Despite the mitigating reviews, Olivier had few fond memories of his Macbeth, choosing to regard it as a youthful error for which Saint-Denis was equally responsible. Years later, he was still haunted by the memory of Noel Coward's laughter in the audience and his wife Vivien Leigh's quip: "You hear Macbeth's first line, then Larry's make-up comes on, then Banquo comes on, then Larry comes on."[58]

If, as Saint-Denis believed, Olivier had engaged him precisely to break the mold of tradition, then the actor's rancor towards him must have seemed a betrayal.[59] The pain of what he deemed a failure stayed with Saint-Denis. Without trying to exculpate himself, he sought an explanation. How much was his responsibility and how much was the result of critical incomprehension? He mildly reproached the critics for their conservatism and ignorance of European developments in the modern theatre. And like Margaret Harris, he felt that "Shakespearean interpretation in England is so bound up with the roots of English life and art that it is difficult for a foreigner to succeed with him."[60] Saint-Denis's comments might be dismissed as the result of wounded feelings, except that others corroborated his experience. Komisarjevsky directed a number of

Shakespearean plays at Stratford during the 1930s, most of which were critical failures. Although reviewers paid lip-service to his inventiveness, there was general agreement that Shakespearean production "was not to be revolutionized by a Russian émigré."[61] Only in recent years has the influence of his ground-breaking productions been recognized. Unmentioned by Saint-Denis was the production's enormous popularity, attracting the largest audience the Vic had ever known. Why was audience reaction so different from the critics? Could it be that the public was bored with seeing the same kind of production year after year? Were audiences a step ahead of the critics?

There is an epilogue to this story. Thirty years later Olivier acknowledged the help that Saint-Denis had given him. When Olivier undertook *Macbeth*, his handling of elevated language was disparaged. During rehearsals, Saint-Denis pointed out that in his attempt to create an emotionally truthful performance, Olivier was treating the poetry as prose, the result being that he butchered the language. This was astute counsel that Olivier exploited and went on to set the standard for contemporary verse-speaking, merging realism with the beauty of the language, a technique that broke with time-honored usage. It is noteworthy that Olivier's new approach was commented on favorably by at least one reviewer of *Macbeth*.[62]

In 1937, John Gielgud invited Saint-Denis to direct Chekhov's *Three Sisters*. This landmark production that redeemed Saint-Denis's reputation is discussed in chapter 6. Following its stunning success, Bronson Albery offered to back Saint-Denis in setting up a company for the season at the Phoenix Theatre in the West End. Saint-Denis immediately retained a group of actors, most of whom had appeared in *Three Sisters*. They were Peggy Ashcroft, George Devine, Marius Goring, Michael Redgrave, and Glen Byam Shaw. Other prominent actors, notably Olivier, Ralph Richardson, and Edith Evans expressed interest. The ambitious season was to include *The Cherry Orchard*, *Uncle Vanya*, *The Wild Duck*, *Twelfth Night*, Giraudoux's *The Trojan War Shall Not Take Place*, and Molière's *Le Bourgeois gentilhomme*.

Saint-Denis's students envisaged the project as the fulfillment of the pledge made at the school's inauguration when he announced that LTS's purpose was the eventual creation of a company. When Saint-Denis eventually assembled his company, its character had changed and only a few of the students were allowed to participate and only in bit parts and walk-ons. Those excluded were angered and hurt.[63]

The company did not realize its promise. Saint-Denis was not in top form. He was exhausted as a result of his duties at the school, directing, and a complicated personal life. Demands were being made on him from all sides. He was separated from his wife Miko, who was living in France with their two children. Unhappy in her relationship with Saint-Denis, Madeleine Gautier returned to France with their son. He was under constant pressure to provide for his dependents. He was also living with Vera Poliakoff who wanted to marry him and was emotionally involved with Peggy Ashcroft. As a result of all these competing demands, the season was again insufficiently prepared. It opened on June 6, 1938 with Bulgakov's *The White Guard*, chosen perhaps to capitalize on Saint-Denis's prior success with a Russian playwright, but certainly because of its relevance to the international situation. There was an obvious parallel with the Spanish Civil War.

The performance was a critical success. James Agate commented: "The production by M. Michel Saint-Denis was superb at every turn."[64] Summing up the critical analysis some years later, Eric Keown wrote: "Most critics agreed on its thinness, but nearly all were touched by its blending, in an authentically Russian way, of sadness and gaiety and Saint-Denis knew exactly how to make the most of it."[65] Nonetheless, it was not what the public wanted.

Twelfth Night, the second production, fared no better. Saint-Denis had envisioned Olivier as Malvolio, Richardson as Sir Toby, and Edith Evans as Maria. All three were unavailable, pleading other engagements. He was left with only two actors of equal caliber, Ashcroft (Viola) and Redgrave (Sir Andrew Aguecheek). In staging the play, Saint-Denis cautiously followed his uncle's *mise en scène*. Conceivably, he believed by so doing he would finally succeed with an English classic; Copeau's production had enjoyed the esteem of critics and audiences alike in Paris. Redgrave learned Jouvet's characterization and stage business and "painted a character who is not simply the butt of all around him, but an ass who knows he is an ass and takes the utmost delight in it."[66] Although Agate liked Redgrave's performance, he missed the familiar characterization of Aguecheek.[67] He resented what he perceived as trendy staging: "M. Saint-Denis produces in the now fashionable manner, suggesting that all the characters are taking part in a fancy dress ball." And again, certain notices overtly stated that a foreigner had no business directing Shakespeare. A more sympathetic view was Ashley Dukes's who felt that Saint-Denis stressed the humor to the detriment of the play's romance, but that the production would have succeeded if all the acting attained the level of Ashcroft and Redgrave's. He hastened to add, however, that the play was inherently English.[68]

The Phoenix season was terminated after the two productions; Albery was unwilling to invest further. Many in the theatre community were discouraged by the collapse of Saint-Denis's company, which contained the seeds of a promising future for British theatre. Undoubtedly, its failure deeply distressed Saint-Denis. Albery had given him the short-lived opportunity of achieving his ambition of having a company in tandem with the school. However, any West End endeavor, no matter how visionary, was dependent upon commercial success. The kind of theatre Saint-Denis was proposing would have to wait for subsidies.

In the spring of 1939 Saint-Denis directed two plays. The first, the English premiere of Lorca's *Bodas de Sangre*, translated as *Marriage of Blood*, was given a surrealistic production for the Stage Society, an alternative theatre group. The second, *Weep for the Spring*, was the only original work Saint-Denis ever mounted professionally after disbanding the Quinze. It was written by Stephen Haggard, a young actor in the Phoenix Company. Peggy Ashcroft played the female lead and Haggard, the male, in a tale of two lovers caught in the political crisis of Nazi Germany. Saint-Denis worked closely with Haggard, successfully helping him reshape the Chekhov-inspired drama. A contemporary account describes "a memorable production, full of shadows, the suggested scent of lilac, the nearness of a lake surrounded by forest, the gloom of an old order changing, heartbreak, and the fruits of 'man's inhumanity to man.'"[69] Unhappily, the production was mistimed. Worried about war with Germany, audiences were put off by the topic; the play was never brought into London.

Despite commercial failures, Saint-Denis's supporters retained their faith in his work, but any continuation was halted by the outbreak of World War II. Called up for military service, Saint-Denis returned to France, his career interrupted by war for the second time in twenty years. He encouraged his LTS colleagues to keep it afloat, but without Saint-Denis at the helm, it foundered.

In its four years of existence the London Theatre Studio made inroads into British theatre in acting, directing, and design. It was a revolutionary school that, although it owed the Vieux-Colombier School a debt, was more pragmatic, being as dedicated to producing professional actors—albeit a different kind of actor—as it was to research. Most of his students left the school infused with Saint-Denis's idealism, convinced that it was essential to do the work they believed in. Still, not every student shared his purity of vision. Saint-Denis had his detractors who resented being trained for the ideal rather than the existing theatre. Peter Ustinov claimed that LTS steered its students "into tiny temples of true art, making their own masks and coffee in chipped mugs, in the belief that, because money corrupts, poverty must therefore be equated with integrity."[70] Others found his methods too demanding.

Saint-Denis was immersed in LTS's day-to-day operation and teaching more than in his other schools. He took pride in the fact that his schools were experimental, but LTS, perhaps because it was the first, had an improvisatory quality not found elsewhere. As noted, the faculty sometimes performed with the students. Saint-Denis never discussed the rationale for the student/teacher performances. Was there a different student/teacher relationship? Was there more of a mentoring system at LTS? For whatever reason, this aspect of the training was discarded.

In London, Saint-Denis proved to himself that he could stand alone. The price of his autonomy was a rift with Copeau that never fully healed, although the two men remained in contact until Copeau's death in 1949. Copeau regarded as betrayal the modifications Saint-Denis made to his theory and practice. Saddened by his uncle's censure, Saint-Denis made intermittent attempts to gain his approval. For instance, he asked his uncle to give a series of lectures on world theatre. Copeau came, lectured, looked at the school, and left with no word of praise. Invited to *Three Sisters*, Copeau took Peggy Ashcroft aside to give her notes, infuriating Saint-Denis.[71] In some measure, Saint-Denis replaced the relationship through cultivating his own disciples, most notably George Devine. Although the war suspended the operation of LTS, the foundations remained. Saint-Denis remained hopeful that work could be resumed after the war.

NOTES

1. The Birmingham Repertory was under Jackson's authority from 1913 to 1935, when a Board of Trustees took over the playhouse's ownership, negatively impacting the company's experimentation.

2. Pierre Lefèvre, personal interview, 13 January 1989.

3. John Gielgud, J. Miller, and J. Powell, *An Actor and His Time* (London: Penguin, 1979), 103.

4. Letter from Pierre Alder to Michel Saint-Denis, 13 December 1935.

5. Michel Saint-Denis, "The English Theatre in Gallic Eyes," trans. J. F. M. Stephens, Jr. *Texas Quarterly* 4 (autumn 1961), 33.

6. Ibid., 32.

7. Ibid., 31.

8. Margaret Harris, personal interview, 5 June 1989.

9. Ibid.

10. Ivor Brown, *The Observer* (7 July 1936), 15.

11. Tyrone Guthrie, *A Life in the Theatre* (New York: McGraw-Hill, 1959), 93.

12. Irving Wardle, *The Theatres of George Devine* (London: Eyre Methuen, 1978), 35.

13. Tyrone Guthrie, *Theatre Prospect* (London: Wishart and Co., 1932), 53–55.

14. Saint-Denis, "The English Theatre in Gallic Eyes," 34.

15. London Theatre Studio Prospectus, 1935

16. Michel Saint-Denis, *Training for the Theatre: Premises and Promises,* ed. Suria Saint-Denis (New York: Theatre Arts Books, 1982), 45.

17. *News Chronicle* (21 April 1936).

18. Saint-Denis, *Training for the Theatre,* 48.

19. Margaret McCall, ed., *My Drama School* (London: Hobson Books, 1978), 86.

20. Chattie Salaman, personal interview, 8 June 1989.

21. *Manchester Guardian* (9 June 1936).

22. Salaman, interview.

23. Alec Guinness, *Blessings in Disguise* (New York: Knopf, 1985), 157; Marius Goring, personal interview, 10 January 1991.

24. Salaman, interview.

25. Michel Saint-Denis, *Theatre: The Rediscovery of Style* (New York: Theatre Arts Books, 1960), 108.

26. Lesley Retey, personal interview, 31 May 1989.

27. Michel Saint-Denis, "The English Theatre in the Thirties," BBC, November 1965.

28. George W. Bishop, *London Daily Telegraph* (2 April 1937).

29. Desmond MacCarthy, *The New Statesman and Nation* (10 April 1937), 590–91.

30. Bishop, *London Daily Telegraph.*

31. Saint-Denis, "The English Theatre in Gallic Eyes," 36.

32. Yvonne Mitchell, quoted in McCall, *My Drama School,* 88.

33. Yvonne Mitchell, *Actress* (London: Routledge & Kegan Paul, 1957), 10.

34. MacCarthy, *The New Statesman and Nation.*

35. Saint-Denis, *Training for the Theatre,* 49.

36. Ibid.

37. Ibid., 46.

38. Ibid., 49–50.

39. Saint-Denis, "The English Theatre in Gallic Eyes," 35.

40. Harris, interview.

41. James Agate, *Times* (9 December 1936), 12.

42. Ivor Brown, *Observer* (13 December 1936), 15.

43. Audrey Williamson, *Old Vic Drama* (London: Rockliff, 1948), 67–68.

44. Lefèvre, interview; Salaman, interview.

45. Guthrie, *A Life in the Theatre,* 186.

46. Wardle, *The Theatres of George Devine,* 75; Anthony Holden, *Laurence Olivier* (New York: Atheneum, 1983), 131; J. C. Trewin, *The Turbulent Thirties: A Further Decade of the Theatre* (London: MacDonald, 1960), 111.

47. Laurence Olivier, *Confessions of an Actor: An Autobiography* (Middlesex: Penguin Books, 1984), 104.

48. *News Chronicle* (February 1938).

49. James Agate, *The Amazing Theatre* (London: George G. Harrap & Co., 1939), 66.

50. Motley, *Designing and Making Costumes,* ed. M. Mullin (New York: Routledge, 1992), 41.

51. Williamson, *Old Vic Drama,* 92.

52. Ibid.

53. Harris, interview.

54. Quoted in Holden, *Laurence Olivier,* 131.

55. Agate, *The Amazing Theatre,* 67.

56. Audrey Williamson, *Theatre of Two Decades* (London: Rockliff, 1951), 271.

57. Harris, interview.

58. Holden, *Laurence Olivier,* 131.

59. Saint-Denis, "The English Theatre in Gallic Eyes," 37.

60. Ibid., 36.

61. Ralph Berry, "Komisarjevsky at Stratford-upon-Avon," *Shakespeare Survey,* no. 36 (1983).

62. Agate, *The Amazing Theatre,* 66.

63. Salaman, interview.

64. Agate, *The Amazing Theatre,* 194.

65. Eric Keown, *Peggy Ashcroft* (Bristol: Rockliff, 1955), 59.

66. Michael Redgrave, *In My Mind's I: An Actor's Autobiography* (New York: Viking Press, 1983), 115.

67. Agate, *The Amazing Theatre,* 198.

68. Ashley Dukes, "The English Scene," *Theatre Arts Monthly,* 23, no. 2 (February 1939): 99.

69. Christopher Hassall, *The Timeless Quest* (London: Arthur Barker Ltd., 1948), 124.

70. Peter Ustinov, *Dear Me* (Boston: Little, Brown, and Co., 1977), 109.

71. George Hall, letter to author, 15 December 1999.

◆ chapter six ◆

Chekhov, the Rediscovery of Realism: Saint-Denis's Productions of *Three Sisters* and *The Cherry Orchard*

DURING HIS LIFETIME MICHEL SAINT-DENIS was considered "perhaps the most perceptive interpreter of Chekhov in the theatre of the West." [1] Yet throughout his career he directed only two professional Chekhovian productions: the landmark 1938 *Three Sisters* at the Queen's Theatre in London, and the 1961 *Cherry Orchard* at the Royal Shakespeare Company (RSC). Several questions immediately come to mind. With just two plays to his credit, how did Saint-Denis acquire that reputation? Was it merited? What characterized his interpretations of Chekhov? Did he employ the same approach for both presentations?

The British had only begun to accept Chekhov as a major dramatist in the mid-1920s when the émigré director Theodore Komisarjevsky staged a season of Russian plays, including Chekhov's *Uncle Vanya*, *Three Sisters*, and *The Cherry Orchard*. Komisarjevsky's productions did much to change the British perception of Chekhov as a tedious playwright of gloom and doom. Contrary to popularly held opinion, Komisarjevsky had neither directed Chekhov in Russia nor was he a disciple of Stanislavsky. In Russia, his directorial mode was to synthesize styles developed by theatrical trailblazers of the period, a practice he continued in England. Consequently, in preparing his Chekhov productions for an English audience, Komisarjevsky, like Saint-Denis a decade later, looked in part to the Moscow Art Theatre whose performances of Chekhov he admired. The quality Komisarjevsky adapted most successfully was found in the actors' performances that expressed an internal reality, heretofore unknown in the London theatre.

While Stanislavsky served as his inspiration, Komisarjevsky brought his own innovations to the production. The most striking was his de-Russification of the plays in order to bring them nearer to the common experience of his public. He romanticized the characters, settings, and costumes, making the cuts necessary to conform to his concept. Although his upper-middle-class English audience identified with the society in transition placed before them, Komisarjevsky's changes impaired the play's meaning. As a further concession to his public he employed a brisk tempo, adding a great deal of movement and business.[2] Still, the prevailing view was that of Norman Marshall, who praised the director's atmospheric sense, the emotional truthfulness of the acting, and the musicality of these productions.[3]

SAINT-DENIS'S *THREE SISTERS*

Three Sisters was a departure for Saint-Denis, his first foray into realism in the professional theatre. At an initial glance, little in his experience would seem to have prepared him for undertaking Chekhov. From the beginnings of his artistic life he had rejected naturalism and espoused theatricalism as a production ideal. However, as head of the London Theatre Studio (LTS) he had begun to experiment with other modes, including Chekhovian realism. For Saint-Denis, realism was a genre distinct from naturalism, which he abhorred, both in its writing and concomitant production style. He associated naturalism with the excesses of the French director André Antoine. Saint-Denis maintained that naturalism depicts only the flat surface of life, that it is "the vehicle of superficial, factual little plays." Realism, he believed, is far richer than the expression of the details of people's lives, the portrayal of commonplace behavior, an account of the sordid and petty. Although set in contemporary times and presenting the stories of identifiable characters, a realistic play probes beneath the veneer to "express the nature of things, the meaning of human life, what happens behind and below appearances."[4]

Chekhov's dramas, with their light and shadow, embody those qualities Saint-Denis most prized in realism. These are plays that, while seeming to chronicle ordinary events in the lives of ordinary people, actually are "written in an impressionistic style."[5] And it was finding the appropriate manner of creating this style theatrically that Saint-Denis assumed as his principal task. No one in England, certainly not Komisarjevsky, had as yet discovered the key to playing Chekhov faithfully.

John Gielgud, who had played Baron Tusenbach in Komisarjevsky's *Three Sisters*, was very interested in Saint-Denis's Chekhovian work at LTS. An admirer of Komisarjevsky, Gielgud had, nonetheless, been baffled by the director's insistence that he play Tusenbach as a handsome young hero, a reading that went against the text.[6] He was eager to tackle the play once again. Now, at a point in his career where he could realize his ambition, Gielgud engaged a company (which included Peggy Ashcroft, Michael Redgrave, and Angela Baddley) and leased the Queen's Theatre in the West End for a season of four plays, three of which he would direct himself, reserving the Chekhov for Saint-Denis. Although Gielgud's previous experience acting under Saint-Denis had not been totally satisfactory, he valued Saint-Denis's artistic integrity and ability. As producer, Gielgud would provide Saint-Denis with almost ideal working conditions, very different from those of the hastily mounted *Noah*.

In planning the production, Saint-Denis sought ways to bring out the atmosphere, "the breath of the ephemeral" demanded by Chekhov.[7] Komisarjevsky had substituted cultural relevance for Chekhov's essence; this would not be Saint-Denis's solution. However, despite his experimentation with the LTS students, the subtlety and intimacy of Chekhovian acting still posed problems for him; until now, his professional productions had been staged in a presentational mode.

What were Saint-Denis's resources? What productions of Chekhov would he have witnessed? While he could not have seen the Barnes season, it is highly probable that he would have attended Komisarjevsky's *The Seagull* in 1936, but if so, he has not left us his opinion. He certainly would have been privy to Komisarjevsky's thoughts since John Gielgud had appeared in both *Three Sisters* and *The Seagull*, while Peggy Ashcroft, in addition to playing Nina in the same production of *The Seagull*, had briefly been Komisarjevsky's wife. Earlier in Paris, he saw George Pitoëff's 1921 *Uncle Vanya*, a production that may have served as a negative object lesson; Pitoëff and his wife dominated the drama at the expense of the ensemble.

But the single most important influence was Stanislavsky. When the Moscow Art Theatre visited Paris in 1922, Saint-Denis and a group of Vieux-Colombier students went to see *The Cherry Orchard*, prepared to mock an outdated naturalism. Their derision soon faded. The experience of seeing that company which was committed to "a passionate search for truth" profoundly modified Saint-Denis's views.[8] Several days later, introduced to Stanislavsky by Copeau, Saint-Denis pressed the Russian director for the strategies he had employed to get his results. Subsequently, in laying the groundwork for *Three Sisters*, Saint-Denis had undertaken an exhaustive study of Stanislavsky's newly translated *An Actor Prepares*. His purpose was to capture the qualities of Stanislavsky's production that most impressed him: spontaneity, emotional truth, depth of internal characterization.

Before he could begin rehearsals, a number of casting problems had to be resolved. Although a permanent company was an ideal Saint-Denis hoped to recreate in London, working with Gielgud's troupe he again confronted one of its negative aspects—a limited pool of actors, all of whom had to work together over a long period. In this situation, casting decisions can provoke jealousy, hurt feelings, and quarrels, as happened in *Three Sisters*. Initially, some of the actors were reluctant to play their assigned roles. Gielgud envisioned playing Andrei, the brother in whom the sisters have invested their hopes; instead, he was cast as Vershinin. In *Noah*, Gielgud had played against type, with questionable results. Saint-Denis, perhaps unwilling to take the same chance, opted instead to exploit Gielgud's elegance. Although Gielgud had brought Saint-Denis into the project, he was wary, ambivalent about Saint-Denis's authoritarian methods and disappointed in losing the part of Andrei. He remained on guard, reluctant to relinquish all control to Saint-Denis as he had in *Noah*.[9]

As an alternative Andrei, Gielgud suggested Michael Redgrave, a choice Saint-Denis again overrode. Redgrave had appeared Saint-Denis's *The Witch of Edmonton* and failed to impress the Frenchman.[10] Given the part of Tusenbach, Redgrave felt slighted and inadequate, "thinking that Michel obviously did not want me as Andrei and perhaps not particularly as Tusenbach."[11] Andrei went to George Devine, who had not yet made his mark as an actor. In Devine's favor was his performance as the Bear in *Noah*, in which he revealed characteristics that must have struck Saint-Denis as invaluable for Andrei—a flair for comedy, an awkwardness, a pathos—even Devine's stockiness suited the role.

Two actresses were jobbed in, the American Carol Goodner to play Masha and Gwen Ffrangcon-Davies for Olga. Ffrangcon-Davies's first reaction was to refuse, perhaps because Gielgud, an old friend, had offended her in not selecting her as the company's leading lady.[12] She accepted the role only after Saint-Denis mollified her, as he did the other disgruntled actors, through a combination of charm, persuasion, and authority.

After working with Komisarjevsky, Peggy Ashcroft, the company's Irina, was curious to see how "a Frenchman was going to handle Chekhov."[13] She was surprised to find a similar approach, although "where Komisarjevsky was a rather destructive director, Michel was incredibly creative and positive."[14] Both directors shared certain rehearsal practices, including a preference for extensive table work. But their greatest similarity resulted from their use of Stanislavsky's discoveries.

In other respects their approaches were quite different, given Komisarjevsky's predilection for playing fast and loose with Chekhov's words and Saint-Denis's faithfulness to textual authority. Saint-Denis's work on *Three Sisters* began with comprehensive analysis of the script that, in his standard fashion, he blocked before the first rehearsal. Preliminary blocking was not an arbitrary or rigid procedure; rather, Saint-Denis believed that the patterns of movement were inextricably linked to the play's style, the one determining the other. The actors in this production did not consider the fact that "every move and piece of business was prepared beforehand on paper" was a hindrance to their creative process, but they were somewhat alarmed by the length of the rehearsal period: eight weeks in Gielgud's recollection, seven according to Ashcroft's reckoning.[15] They had no idea what would be expected of them or how they would use all that time.

The rehearsal period, which began with a week of reading the play aloud in conjunction with Saint-Denis's explication, allowed director and actors the luxury to explore characterization, relationships, rhythm, milieu. Saint-Denis wove a tapestry of mood and atmosphere from an accumulation of carefully chosen features of daily life. His profound attention to detail added a depth and complexity to characterization and ensemble that were new to the British stage. This cast's performances contrasted sharply to the typical acting pattern of the period where "as each actor opens his mouth to speak the rest fall petrified into an uncanny stillness."[16] The players in *Three Sisters* remained in character throughout, reacting to situations in accordance with their personal motivations, needs, and emotions. All the actors, no matter how small their roles, created three-dimensional characters rather than playing types.

Critics remarked on the "chiaroscuro of characterization in which no one colour and no one note predominates."[17] This quality resulted from the constant shifts in rhythm and focus that provided much of the texture of the production. As the focus changed, characters playing a minor role in a scene acted as a kind of Greek chorus, but one that provided an individual commentary to the events. The following is one example from many cited by the reviewers. In the last act, Olga is an onlooker to the farewell of her sister Masha (Goodner) and Vershinin (Gielgud). As Olga, Ffrangcon-Davies's expression was suffused with embarrassment and envy as she slowly turned her back on the emotional good-byes of the two lovers.[18]

Judging by the descriptions of the production by actors, critics, and audience, it appears that Saint-Denis adapted Stanislavsky's ideas on dealing with the given circumstances, particularly those external elements that influenced the characters' actions. Peggy Ashcroft remarked that she had never seen a production in which the seasons were portrayed so vividly and provided so well the mood of each act.[19] To achieve that result, Saint-Denis gave his actors exercises analogous to those used by Stanislavsky in experimenting with sense memory. The company spent hours inventing and rehearsing details to show the effects of the weather on each character. Ashcroft recalled Ffrangcon-Davies clapping her hands to swat mosquitoes away. Although the rehearsals were a departure for most, if not all of the actors, they found it exciting, as daily they made new discoveries.[20] Saint-Denis appropriated the discoveries made in rehearsal for his teaching, and conversely, brought applicable teaching strategies to rehearsal.

Michael Redgrave also read *An Actor Prepares* and endeavored to translate his own findings into his characterization in the hope of impressing his director. Confronted with Saint-Denis's obvious disapproval, Redgrave's lack of confidence increased; as he redoubled his efforts, his portrayal grew more labored. Finally, Saint-Denis interrupted a speech to caution him to "throw away" some of it: "You speak as if the lines were important. You speak as if you wanted to make it all intelligible, as if it all made sense."[21] Redgrave followed the implicit suggestion and was amazed to discover the scene come to life. After this breakthrough Saint-Denis's attitude changed; he became encouraging and guided Redgrave more gently towards the development of Tusenbach. Still, after the opening, Saint-Denis had further criticism; the performance was too fussy. "It's beautifully done," Redgrave was told, "but you are underlining, and once you start underlining, it's not art."[22] This advice Redgrave found valuable and retained.

Saint-Denis's strategy in dealing with Redgrave is revealing of his directorial process. Employing a technique he often used with students and actors who were on the wrong track, Saint-Denis allowed Redgrave to flounder for a period, directionless in a very real sense. Desperately struggling to grasp the role, an actor often produces stereotypical results. Trying one tactic after another, the actor finds that he or she has nothing more to hide behind. At that moment, the actor may begin to move towards the truth of the character or the scene. This was the case with Michael Redgrave, who had tried a variety of approaches. However, his interpretation of realism led him to become bogged down in minutiae. But the preparation had served him well. At the point when Redgrave would most benefit, Saint-Denis intervened with a simple solution. When Redgrave followed the suggestion and began to underplay, the comic elements, key to the role, emerged. Although this process was painful for the actor, the outcome was usually worthwhile.

Despite Saint-Denis's new approach, it would be a mistake to think that in directing *Three Sisters* he rejected everything he had done earlier. As his work with Stanislavskian techniques demonstrates, he was not an ideologue. Certain aspects of *Three Sisters* drew on his experience with the Quinze. For instance, when in 1933 he directed *Loire*, the French company developed scenes of everyday village life depicted through movement and mime. Saint-Denis regarded all productions as

> a kind of choreography where the language must have its own measure to correspond with the measure of the movement in the three dimensions of space, if the interpretation of the play is to come to a concrete expression: a physical expression of both the actor's voice and body, which will be strengthened and sharpened by the shape and color of the scenery and costumes.[23]

The choreography of *Three Sisters* can be seen in its photographs: the physical work is obvious, character and mood are expressed corporeally, but subtly. Saint-Denis had moved from what Eugenio Barba terms "extra-daily" movement to freer, more "natural" movement.[24]

George Devine's Andrei is a case in point. As a teacher of comic mask, Devine was an advocate of developing a character physically. An Act I photograph from *Three Sisters* shows Devine, dressed in an ill-fitting suit, dancing oafishly with Baron Tusenbach to the amusement of all present. Another Act I photograph, showing the end of the party scene, indicates the future relationship between Andrei and his wife Natasha. The two are embracing, Natasha fastened on Andrei as if he were prey, while Andrei's arms hold her awkwardly as he sinks into a half-sitting position, as if the weight of this relationship is too much for him to bear. A photograph of a moment in Act II shows Peggy Ashcroft's exhausted Irina and Redgrave's Tusenbach asleep on a couch, side by side. Even in this intimate position their bodies reveal their psychological distance. Peggy Ashcroft, her serene face belied by her sagging body, is slumped to a side, anticipating a defeated middle age. Tusenbach, his mouth agape, his back partially turned away from her, is hugging a pillow close to his body rather than the Irina he desires.

Reviewers took favorable note of the actors' physical characterizations as in this *Time and Tide* notice: "Michael Redgrave . . . gave the best performance of his career, since his very bones seemed to shape themselves differently and his physical habits . . . to adapt themselves to the mental habits he took on with the character."[25] The critical consensus can be summed up in the following phrase: "We shall never see this production of *Three Sisters* surpassed; and we owe homage to the genius of M. Michel Saint-Denis that he has given it to us."[26] Not since the first appearance of the Compagnie des Quinze in London had Saint-Denis earned such laudatory notices. His former English-language productions, in particular the Renaissance plays, had been considered too "arty." The critics believed Saint-Denis had redeemed his promise in becoming the new Chekhovian expert. They had found a niche for him: "poetic naturalism."

Why this critical turnabout? Saint-Denis's productions of *The Witch of Edmonton* and *Macbeth* were innovative, as was *Three Sisters*. In the one case, innovation was respected and admired, in the other, rejected. Was the assessment just? I propose that in directing Elizabethan and Jacobean dramas, one of Saint-Denis difficulties stemmed from the fact that he challenged British tradition, causing many of the reviewers to pounce. Indeed, Ivor Brown stated plainly that he disliked a foreigner tampering with English classics.[27] Directing Chekhov, Saint-Denis did not put himself on the line in the same way. And the critics did not bring the same preconceptions to Chekhov. This is not to say that Saint-Denis's earlier productions were necessarily of the same quality, only that the critics were less predisposed to find fault with the 1938 production.

Then too, Saint-Denis's adjustment to England may have been more difficult than he had originally anticipated. Not only did he have to learn a new language, the theatrical culture was foreign as well. In *Three Sisters* Saint-Denis encountered a working relationship in some ways comparable to that he had enjoyed in France with the Compagnie des Quinze. The result was that *Three Sisters* shared qualities that made the Quinze productions so memorable, among them a strong ensemble, still something of a novelty in England.

The Quinze's core group of actors had performed together for more than a decade. While the cast of *Three Sisters* did not equal that record of longevity, most had collaborated before and many had been directed by Saint-Denis. They brought to the project a youthful idealism, an *esprit de corps*, and a sensitivity to one another's playing that enhanced the play's qualities. As a group they were committed to the ideal of permanent company and invested in revitalizing British theatre. They viewed Saint-Denis as an agent of change. Their attitude, combined with the intensive rehearsals and the nature of the play, inspired the actors to give a performance that is remembered as being one of "the most perfect examples of teamwork ever presented in London."[28] Still, their dedication to ensemble did not preclude the actors from developing idiosyncratic characterizations. While the production was noticeable for its unity of style, that unity grew out of the attention paid to detail.

Although the actors' performances were the foremost element in the creation of mood, the unity of style encompassed all the technical aspects of production as well. Motley's set, while realistic, captured the poetic and lyrical quality with which Saint-Denis imbued the production. George Devine, in addition to acting, designed the lighting for the play. Several critics commented on its aptness, its "diffused and faded beauty," which contributed a strong atmospheric effect, novel in 1938.[29] Saint-Denis worked long and hard to achieve the right quality, tempo, timing, and volume of sound—the sleigh bells for the winter scene, the rise and fall of conversation, the distant sound of a fire alarm, the faint echo of a shot, the final marching song as the regiment leaves at the play's end.

The participants in the production shared the positive reaction of the critics and audiences. Peggy Ashcroft, who began her long association with Saint-Denis in *Three Sisters*, spoke for the cast: "For most of us it was the most memorable production we ever had."[30] The production was memorable not only in itself, but for what it accomplished in terms of disseminating Michel Saint-Denis's core beliefs.

Three Sisters proved that artistic and commercial success were not mutually exclusive. The production moved Chekhov from his marginalized position on the fringe, a playwright who attracted only a "highbrow" audience, placed him squarely in the West End and turned him (for the moment) into a "hit" dramatist—and without sacrificing meaning or pandering to the audience. The production also had long-term effects on the actors. As we have seen, Saint-Denis functioned as an acting teacher, helping the company to explore character, situation, and relationship in ways that were a departure from typical practice. George Devine would use his newfound knowledge in his teaching; Gielgud would bring these discoveries not only to his own acting, but also to his work as a director; the other performers would provide a new model of acting.

Through this unified and integrated production Saint-Denis reinforced the changing role of the director in England, begun by Komisarjevsky. Saint-Denis was a force in establishing directorial authority, paving the way for Peter Brook, Peter Hall, and the many distinguished British directors of the latter half of the twentieth century. For his own part, Saint-Denis felt that the experience had enriched him immeasurably: "At that particular stage in my career I had discovered secrets which, in my classical French training, had been unknown to me."[31] The major discovery for Saint-Denis was, certainly, learning how to synthesize internal and external approaches to characterization. *Three Sisters* set the standard not only for Chekhovian production in England, but for his own future work.

THE CHERRY ORCHARD

The following year, hoping to capitalize on the box-office success of *Three Sisters*, Hugh (Binkie) Beaumont offered to back Saint-Denis in a production of *The Cherry Orchard*. Another extraordinary cast was assembled, with Edith Evans as Madame Ranevsky, Ralph Richardson as Lopahin, Alec Guinness as Trofimov, Peggy Ashcroft as Anya, and Cyril Cusack as Firs. For Saint-Denis, "it was too beautiful to be true."[32] And indeed, after two weeks of rehearsal, war was declared and the production canceled.

Twenty years later, when Saint-Denis's friend Peggy Ashcroft joined the RSC under the directorship of Peter Hall, she used her influence to resurrect the idea: "I knew that Michel had always wanted to direct *The Cherry Orchard*. And so Peter asked Michel over, and they met then in 1961. Peter was enormously impressed by Michel and always says that he had a great influence on him in his attitude toward the theatre and directing."[33] At their meeting it was agreed that Saint-Denis would direct *The Cherry Orchard* for the 1961–62 London season.[34] The play would be rehearsed and preview in Stratford and then transfer to the Aldwych for its run.

Again, conditions seemed perfect. Abd'el Kader Farrah, whose work had been shaped by Saint-Denis's ideas, joined him in England to design the show. Saint-Denis had at his disposal the RSC's permanent company, composed for the most part of strong actors. He was also free to go beyond the limits of the company, if needed, as was the case for Anya—Judi Dench, then appearing as Juliet at the Old Vic. The production reunited Peggy Ashcroft (Madame Ranevsky), John Gielgud (Gaev), and Saint-Denis for the first time since *Three Sisters*. Included in the cast were Dorothy Tutin as Varya, Ian Holm as Trofimov, and Patience Collier as Charlotta. George Murcell (Lopahin) would prove problematic, as would some of the other actors.

Despite seemingly ideal circumstances, the production was beset by difficulties. Unlike the *Three Sisters* company, this cast was generationally and ideologically split. The expectations of the younger generation of actors differed from those of their seniors. Saint-Denis was an almost historical figure to them; the older actors were personally acquainted with his work and admired him as a theatrical revolutionary. The Saint-Denis mystique failed to impress the younger group, some of whom balked at the discipline imposed upon them. In Peggy

FIGURE 6.1   *Rehearsal of* The Cherry Orchard *for the RSC. Michel Saint-Denis (center) giving notes to cast members. Judi Dench (Anya) is seated at the right.*

Ashcroft's words: "The younger actors were accustomed to the freer and more flexible approach of the other directors at the RSC."[35]

As always, Saint-Denis had methodically prepared before beginning rehearsals. According to his assistant director, however, his working methods in this respect had undergone change.[36] The blocking was only roughly sketched out, allowing the actors to improvise moves. Nonetheless, the younger actors found Saint-Denis's approach too meticulous, dogmatic, and oppressive. However, from his assistant's vantage point, Saint-Denis was "relatively easy to work with as far as the actors were concerned."

At the first read-through, Saint-Denis explained that in Chekhov, "the text is an important result of something else and their job was to find what that something else was."[37] The statement seems to contain a tinge of heresy coming from a director for whom the text was sacred. In fact, he was exhorting the actors to probe beneath the words, since the meaning in Chekhov's plays resides in the subtext; the dialogue only "reflects psychological states, moods [and] the general atmosphere of the moment."[38] He wanted to use the long rehearsal period to explore all the nuances of characterization and motivation (see figure 6.1).[39]

Not everyone was comfortable with the slow pacing of Saint-Denis's exploration. Judi Dench and Ian Holm especially had difficulty adjusting to Saint-

Denis's rehearsal rhythm. "They kept trying to peak too soon," while Saint-Denis "kept cutting away at the peaks because he wanted them to go deeper."[40] Above all, he wanted them to avoid sentimentality and facile solutions. Adjusting to Saint-Denis's rhythms was only one of many problems Dench encountered. Her experience was akin to Michael Redgrave's in *Three Sisters*. Having enjoyed considerable success in the theatre at a young age, Dench was baffled by her inability to achieve what Saint-Denis wanted. She felt very much "a whipping boy," unable to satisfy, try as she might.[41] Her frustration led to a breakdown of confidence. Especially painful was the moment when notes were given: "He would get to me and would just kind of throw up his hands and shrug" at what she believed was her hopelessness.[42]

Unfortunately for her, Dench was competing with Saint-Denis's memory, perhaps idealized over time, of Stanislavsky's Anya, played by Alla Tarasova. One image he cherished was Anya's Act I entrance as she leapt onto a couch laughing and in that brief moment expressed simultaneously "exhaustion, happiness, youth, and tenderness."[43] For Saint-Denis, that entrance set the mood for the act. For Dench, it was an exercise in futility as her director had her work the moment over and over, but without supplying the encouragement she craved. An entire afternoon was spent rehearsing the entrance until, disheartened, Dench says she "became completely hysterical."[44]

Like Redgrave, she persevered, stumbling through weeks of rehearsal. One day after a run-through Gielgud took her aside to say that had he been directing, "I would be delighted if you had been doing that for me."[45] The praise from the renowned actor unblocked her; Anya began to emerge and Saint-Denis became helpful. Ultimately, Dench, who won the Clarence Derwent Award for Anya, came to believe that acting under Saint-Denis was a valuable experience. So right did the interpretation of her entrance seem that when Dench played Mme Ranevsky years later, she insisted upon entering hand-in-hand with Anya and recreating the same emotional sequence that Saint-Denis had pushed her to achieve.

Peggy Ashcroft also fell victim to Saint-Denis's recollections. Still vivid for him was the moment in the Stanislavsky production when "tea is brought to Mme Ranevski [*sic*] by a servant. She holds the cup in her usual absent-minded mood. The tea is hot—she is burnt and drops the cup. It was so true, so beautifully done, so light, so realistic."[46] Ashcroft was unable to react spontaneously to the tea. Years earlier, Saint-Denis had asked Stanislavsky how he achieved such depth of truth at that moment. Now he used the Russian director's stratagem, asking Roy Dotrice (Firs) to pour real hot water on Peggy Ashcroft's hand during rehearsal. It worked.

More serious for Ashcroft than her brief difficulty with the tea was her working relationship with Saint-Denis. A veteran actress of Saint-Denis productions, she had anticipated repeating positive experiences. Still disappointed years later by *The Cherry Orchard*, she cast about for the reasons.[47] She felt that Saint-Denis's English had suffered as a result of his long absence and therefore he was no longer as articulate. She believed they no longer shared the same compatibility, which affected his direction of her. Consequently, she was dissatisfied by her own performance. But perhaps also time had idealized Ashcroft's memories. This was not the first clash between them over the interpretation of a role. Approximately a decade earlier, during rehearsals for the Old Vic production of *Electra*, Saint-Denis made emotional demands on the actress that previously she had not had to meet. Rehearsals were tense affairs, with Saint-Denis pushing Ashcroft to the point of collapse as she strained to fulfill his vision.[48]

Ashcroft felt that age and illness had taken their toll on him, affecting his ability to function as a director. But neither age nor illness had affected Saint-Denis's strongly held opinions. He had been ruminating on *The Cherry Orchard* for two decades and knew exactly what he wanted. His intention, on the one hand, was to recapture the intensity and improvisational quality of the acting in Stanislavsky's 1922 production and, on the other, to add a sociopolitical dimension through stripping the play of much of its romanticism, emphasizing the comic aspects of Gaev, Madame Ranevsky, and their household, while retaining what he termed the play's "impressionistic character."[49]

Theoretically, Saint-Denis's concept was compatible with Ashcroft's view of her role. But, strangely, they were at odds. Saint-Denis thought that much of the play's humor resided in "the contrast between the terrible state of affairs in which Madame Ranevsky finds herself as a mother and a woman of good upbringing, and her irresponsible and light-hearted behavior in her love and business affairs."[50] Ashcroft agreed that Madame Ranevsky was a "totally volatile, almost shallow character." Yet Saint-Denis demanded that she develop the tragic aspect.[51] He insisted that Ashcroft's Ranevsky was "too young," a statement that puzzled her because she was well into her fifties at the time. What he seems to have meant was that she was too coy, a quality picked up by at least one reviewer.[52] He was also trying to create balance in the characters, to prevent the actors from overdeveloping any one trait. Despite her misgivings, Ashcroft tried to conform to his judgment, since she "always felt extremely ready to accept Michel because he was a great director."[53]

If Ashcroft was always willing to accede to Saint-Denis, this was not true of the entire company. The faith in their director that had characterized the company of *Three Sisters* was lacking in this cast; consequently, morale was lower and the ensemble reportedly weaker. Compounding Saint-Denis's problems was George Murcell who, as Saint-Denis's assistant director recalls, was not up to the role of Lopahin. Halfway through rehearsals, Saint-Denis had exhausted all his resources. Recasting was out of the question. A pragmatist in many situations, Saint-Denis did not allow his ego to stand in his way. He asked John Gielgud to coach Murcell after normal rehearsal hours. For the next several weeks Gielgud spent each evening with Murcell, teaching him the role.[54] The result was a workmanlike, if uninspired, performance. Remarkably, considering the role's importance, most critics had little to say about Murcell's performance. A few had reservations; others damned him with such faint praise as "a convincing enough Lopahin."[55] One of the harshest critiques came from Kenneth Tynan, who found the character "sturdily dull. The dimension of self-torment is absent, and the climactic drunk scene in the third act goes for nothing."[56] In agreement was Caryl Brahms, who thought Murcell "inadequate, lacking in weight and not contained within the skin of the character."[57]

Unlike Ashcroft, Gielgud was happier than he had ever been before under Saint-Denis's direction. Playing Gaev was a rewarding experience—far more than Vershinin and Noah, parts he had never achieved to his satisfaction.[58] In this production he felt connected to his character and was more able to respond to Saint-Denis's directorial intentions and release his own creativity.

In contrast to the almost unanimous rave notices of *Three Sisters*, *The Cherry Orchard* opened to mixed reviews. The critics fell into three main camps, with approximately a third judging it an outstanding production. J. C. Trewin wrote: "This Aldwych presentation is the finest British performance of *The Cherry Orchard* in our time."[59] The *Daily Mail* described it as "a luminous production that almost matched the play's glittering perfection," in which Saint-Denis "achieves a rare balance of emotion, blending exquisite poignancy with the most pathetic of humor."[60] Eric Gillett found it "an entirely satisfying evening in the theatre."[61] For Kenneth Tynan—who was too young to have seen *Three Sisters*—a few hitches aside, it "was just what one had hoped of Michel Saint-Denis."[62] Paradoxically, the other two camps were divided between those critics who thought Saint-Denis had emphasized the comic elements to the detriment of the tragic, and those who thought the comedy was lost because of the director's "underlying tragic intent."[63]

Several dissatisfied critics likened the Saint-Denis *Cherry Orchard* to the Marxist production brought to England by the Moscow Art Theatre three years earlier. The Russians had presented the play as a drama of social process, which foreshadowed the downfall of the upper-middle class. Admittedly, Saint-Denis had changed the traditional interpretation of Trofimov from a pitiable, even ludicrous character to a young man to be taken seriously, who in the intensity of his convictions had something of the revolutionary about him. At the same time, in order to contrast the old order with the future, the director divested Madame Ranevsky and her family of some of their charm, their aura of decaying glamour. Yet neither his intention nor its realization was heavy-handedly political.

It would seem, in fact, that Saint-Denis was a casualty of his own success. Even as he had mythologized Stanislavsky's *Cherry Orchard*, so had his own 1938 *Three Sisters* entered the realm of legend. Saint-Denis had been the primary contributor to what had become the accepted directorial style of producing Chekhov. With *The Cherry Orchard*, he seemed to modify that style somewhat, to the chagrin of the critical profession. What the critics missed was their "sentimentalized" Chekhov permeated by atmosphere and "romantic nostalgia."[64] However, Saint-Denis's search for style was predicated upon exploring the total environment of the given work. Critics' protests to the contrary, the Russian political climate is an integral part of Chekhov's play. A sociological dimension and a traditionally poetic interpretation of *The Cherry Orchard* are not incompatible. The nostalgic quality craved by the critics is intimately connected to the transformation forced on Madame Ranevsky and her family by society. Saint-Denis often skillfully caught both aspects, sometimes in a single moment as in this example from the first act. The narcissistic Madame Ranevsky is seated after her journey, drinking coffee, charming her entourage in her self-dramatizing fashion, oblivious to the ancient and arthritic Firs on his knees massaging her foot.

A major complaint was the play's "violently anti-romantic" aspects.[65] Abd'el Kader Farrah's second act garden setting exemplified this quality. The set, devoid of "the charm that once drenched" this garden, is dominated by a telegraph pole upstage center.[66] Chekhov's stage directions do mention telegraph poles off in the distance, but they are scarcely noticed. Farrah's looming telegraph pole is emblematic of the encroachment of the modern world soon to overwhelm Madame Ranevsky, her family, and their way of life. It also makes visible and prominent Madame Ranevsky's only connection to her lover, to her world outside. A little down right of the telegraph pole is a balustrade, while to the left is a rough rail fence. Two divided societies existing side by side are represented by the fencing. Down center are two backless benches. It is a landscape that has already undergone devastation. The indoor sets, on the other hand, are realistic.

In light of the divergent critical opinions, we are fortunate in having a visual record of the production that the BBC televised in the spring of 1962.[67] The tape is valuable for its own sake, but also for what it can tell us about the 1938 *Three Sisters*. Today the reviewers' negative criticisms of an overtly political, harshly realistic, robustly comic *Cherry Orchard* do not seem relevant. Saint-Denis's directorial concept no longer startles; rather, what we see are his fundamental ideas on producing Chekhov that, in all probability, changed very little over time.

What Saint-Denis brought to the theatre of the mid-twentieth century was an appreciation of style, a directorial approach based on finding the appropriate manner of expressing the intrinsic form, meaning, and context of the play "in contemporary terms."[68] Contemporary terms meant rejecting a reconstruction of the past; it entailed making use of current techniques. At the same time, Saint-Denis repudiated what he termed "stylization," that is, an attempt to impose an external style for the sake of novelty and/or relevance. Saint-Denis's technique was by its nature conservative. Therefore, having studied Chekhov's plays both as a director and teacher and having developed a profound understanding and technique for their playing, it is unlikely that he would have fundamentally modified his approach.

Obviously, there are disadvantages to viewing the production on tape; the blocking is often lost from sight and the acting too large for the small screen. Still, there is a great deal to be learned about Saint-Denis's handling of Chekhov—what was meant by "poetic realism." In view of the critics' comments, it is surprising just how much the production is suffused in atmospheric quality. It is found in the comedy, often gentle and telling, as in the moment when Gaev, lost in thought and leaning against the bookcase, is dusted by Firs as if he too were an inanimate object. It is in the timing, the long silences of the characters, their changes of mood, the clear and sharp transitions. It is especially present in the use of multiple and varied sound effects, from carriage wheels to bird song, Epihodov's squeaky shoes, laughter, the breaking string.[69] Laughter is employed frequently, often as a means of suppressing or covering a negative feeling such as anger or fear. Judi Dench uses an automatic giggle, which is almost a tic. As in *Three Sisters*, Saint-Denis worked diligently to find the most appropriate sound effects that in Chekhov "express the poetry of everyday life."[70] It is in the romantic but moving background music that underscores moments of nostalgia and sadness. Act I contains several such instances: music is heard when Madame Ranevsky imagines she sees the ghost of her dead mother, and again when Varya rocks Anya who has fallen asleep. Indeed, the entire production has the quality of chamber music.

If the essence of Chekhov is in the collective solitudes of his characters, then Saint-Denis captured that essence. The stage is peopled with well-intentioned but self-absorbed characters who struggle, often clumsily, to make themselves understood in a world where no one can provide them with the empathy they seek. The actors' presentation of their frustration is at once comical and sad.

The individual performances are, on the whole, quite good. John Gielgud, in particular, created a complex character that, while psychologically truthful, acts as a social commentary. Peggy Ashcroft's Madame Ranevsky is shallow and emotionally labile. At least one critic protested her lack of "warmth of heart underlying her weaknesses."[71] Writing that she seemed "forbidden to exhibit" that element of character, the same critic perceptively sensed in Ashcroft's performance the conflict between director and actress. However, it is clear from the videotape that Saint-Denis made the right decision: the character works as directed. It is probable that what many of the critics missed in the performance was her customary graciousness, a personal trait that Saint-Denis forbade her to draw upon. One critic who did not find this characteristic sufficiently subdued was Kenneth Tynan, who often chided Ashcroft for excessive gentility. He wrote: "There is far more to Ranevsky than the distracted hostess Dame Peggy conjures up."[72] George Murcell's Lopahin is a little too brutish. More seriously, we do not see his admiration of and affection for Madame Ranevsky. Roy Dotrice's Firs is rather the stereotypical old man.

In the end, we are left with a production that is a bit old-fashioned but still beautiful, a period piece. And despite the contemporary comments and criticism we are struck by its ensemble, which gives us more than a suggestion of what *Three Sisters* may have been.

NOTES

1. Michel Saint-Denis, introduction to "Chekhov and the Modern Stage," *Drama Survey* 3 (spring–summer 1963): 77.

2. Robert Tracy, "Komisarjevsky's 1926 *Three Sisters*," in Patrick Miles, ed., *Chekhov on the British Stage* (Cambridge: Cambridge University Press, 1993), 72–73.

3. Norman Marshall, *The Producer and the Play* (London: MacDonald, 1957), 271.

4. Michel Saint-Denis, *Theatre: The Rediscovery of Style* (New York: Theatre Arts Books, 1960), 50.

5. Michel Saint-Denis, "Stanislavski and Shakespeare," *Tulane Drama Review*, vol. 9, no. 2 (winter 1964): 77.

6. John Gielgud, J. Miller, and J. Powell, *Gielgud: An Actor and His Time* (London: Penguin, 1979), 98.

7. Saint-Denis, "Chekhov and the Modern Stage," 79.

8. Michel Saint-Denis, "Naturalism in the Theatre," *The Listener* (4 December 1952): 928.

9. Ronald Hayman, *John Gielgud* (New York: Random House, 1971), 112.

10. Irving Wardle, *The Theatres of George Devine* (London: Eyre Methuen, 1978), 76.

11. Michael Redgrave, *In My Mind's I: An Actor's Autobiography* (New York: Viking Press, 1983), 112.

12. Hayman, 112.

13. Peggy Ashcroft, personal interview, 5 June 1989.

14. Ibid. Ashcroft's estimation of Komisarjevsky is confirmed by Gielgud.

15. Hayman, 112.

16. John Grime, *Daily Express* (29 January 1938): 15.

17. Unsigned review, *Stage* (3 February 1938).

18. Desmond MacCarthy, *New Statesman and Nation* (5 February 1938): 205–7.

19. Ashcroft, interview.

20. John Gielgud, *Stage Directions* (London: Heinemann, 1963), 91.

21. Redgrave, 113.

22. Ibid.

23. Michel Saint-Denis, "Music in the Theatre," unpublished lecture at Bryanston Music School, summer 1949.

24. Eugenio Barba and N. Savarese, *A Dictionary of Theatre Anthropology: The Secret Art of the Performer* (London: Routledge, 1991), 9.

25. P. F. G., *Time and Tide* (5 February 1938): 186.

26. Lionel Hale, *News Chronicle* (1 February 1938): 9.

27. Ivor Brown, *The Observer* (13 December 1936): 15.

28. Gielgud, *Stage Directions*, 91.

29. Hale, 9.

30. Ashcroft, interview.

31. Michel Saint-Denis, "The English Theatre in Gallic Eyes," trans. J. F. M. Stephens, Jr., *Texas Quarterly* 4 (autumn 1961): 36.

32. Ibid.

33. Ashcroft, interview.

34. John Gielgud wrote the adaptation for this production.

35. Ashcroft, interview.

36. Stephen Aaron, personal interview, 29 October 1988.

37. Ibid.

38. Michel Saint-Denis, *Training for the Theatre, Premises and Promises*, ed. Suria Saint-Denis (New York: Theatre Arts Books, 1982), 215.

39. Although lengthy rehearsal periods were standard at RSC, again there is a difference of opinion as to the duration of Saint-Denis's work with the cast. Aaron, Saint-Denis's assistant, remembered twelve weeks; Peggy Ashcroft, seven; and Judi Dench, eight.

40. Aaron, interview.

41. Judi Dench, personal interview, 12 June 1995.

42. Ibid.

43. Saint-Denis, "Naturalism in the Theatre," 928.

44. Dench, interview

45. Ibid.

46. Saint-Denis, "Naturalism in the Theatre," 927.

47. Ashcroft, interview.

48. Pierre Lefèvre, personal interview, 12 January 1989.

49. Saint-Denis, "Chekhov and the Modern Stage," 80.

50. Saint-Denis, "Introduction," Anton Chekhov, *The Cherry Orchard* (trans. John Gielgud), x.

51. Ashcroft, interview.

52. Caryl Brahms, *The Rest of the Evening's My Own* (London: W. H. Allen, 1964), 116.

53. Ashcroft, interview.

54. Aaron, interview.

55. Philip Hope Wallace, *The Guardian* (15 December 1961).

56. Kenneth Tynan, *The Observer* (17 December 1961).

57. Brahms, 117.

58. Gyles Brandreth, *John Gielgud: A Celebration* (Boston: Little, Brown, 1984), 118.

59. J. C. Trewin, *Birmingham Post* (15 December 1961).

60. Robert Muller, *Daily Mail* (15 December 1961).

61. Eric Gillett, *Yorkshire Post* (15 December 1961).

62. Tynan, *The Observer*.

63. Milton Shulman, *Evening Standard* (15 December 1961).

64. T. C. Worsley, *Financial Times* (15 December 1961).

65. Ibid.

66. Ibid.

67. There is a copy of the videotape in the BBC archives in London, and another at the RSC archives in Stratford-upon-Avon.

68. Saint-Denis, *The Rediscovery of Style*, 56.

69. Epihodov's shoes were problematic. Unable to find shoes that squeaked, the technical staff gave Patrick Wymark a small noisemaker to carry in his pocket that produced the proper sound. The actor was handicapped by having to keep his hand in his pocket whenever he walked. When the play was televised the actor was still without the squeaky shoes, as can be seen in his performance.

70. Saint-Denis, "Music in the Theatre."

71. Unsigned review, *The Times* (15 December 1961).

72. Tynan, *The Observer*.

chapter seven

Michel Saint-Denis/Jacques Duchesne at the BBC

T HE OUTBREAK OF WORLD WAR II cut Saint-Denis adrift once again, his artistic and professional life severed as he was bringing his plans to fruition. Although he was returning to France to fight a war, he was obsessed by thoughts regarding his vocation. At age forty-two, he felt the mounting pressure of middle age and uncertainty about his future. How long would the war last? What effect would it have on his life? On the theatre? He could not be sure that the theatrical foundations he had laid in England would be there at war's end. Despite his success in England and fondness for its people, he was ambivalent about remaining there permanently. He had maintained theatrical connections in France and from time to time contemplated returning. But would he be welcomed? Would there be work for him? Perplexed, he toyed with the idea of writing which had always tempted him.[1]

In this frame of mind, Saint-Denis found himself in June 1939 marching to the boat train singing, "without much conviction," the *Marseillaise* in the company of fellow expatriates, mostly chefs and hairdressers.[2] Twenty years after leaving it, Saint-Denis was rejoining his former regiment, the Infanterie Coloniale, reclaiming his rank of lieutenant. But the war he was to confront was very different from that of 1914–18. Saint-Denis too was changed, his naïve, youthful enthusiasm replaced by wariness. In 1914 the French military had confidently marched off to combat, filled with the desire to defeat the Germans. Saint-Denis's attitude on the eve of his first battle in 1916 was representative: "Tomorrow with all my comrades I enter the war zone. What an atmosphere here! I am overwhelmed with emotion and joy."[3]

Although the French ultimately won World War I with the help of its allies, it was at great economic and human cost: of the 8,000,000 men mobilized, close to twenty percent were killed, another 3,000,000 maimed, a generation lost, the country bankrupted. The generational loss was the prime reason middle-aged men like Saint-Denis, fathers of dependent children, were called up in 1940. Loath to enter into another war, the French had preferred to turn a blind eye to the danger Germany represented. Nonetheless, as Germany continued to gobble up middle and eastern Europe, France and England signed a mutual-protection pact with Poland. Therefore when Germany attacked Poland on September 1, 1939, France declared war. But hostilities did not break out; eight months of military paralysis followed. The factionalized French government did not have the political will to pursue a war that the majority of its population did not want and few thought would actually take place. They were convinced that the Maginot line, a defensive fortification stretching across the Franco-German border, could repel an invader. No real preparations for combat were undertaken because none were needed. After war was declared and the army mobilized, the soldiers had no recourse but to wait, resulting in demoralization.

Saint-Denis coped with the tedium of what was termed the "phony war" by writing, visiting his family in Burgundy when he had the opportunity, and becoming reacquainted with his children. Anxious about his professional life, he made a quick trip to London on a week's leave in February 1940 for two related purposes: to try to arrange an extension of credit for the preservation of the London Theatre Studio (LTS) and to ascertain whether George Devine's new Actors Company could survive. Endeavoring to continue and build on LTS's work, George Devine had founded the company with several Saint-Denis stalwarts— Alec Guinness, Martita Hunt, and Vera Poliakoff. It produced only one play, Guinness's adaptation of *Great Expectations*. Despite the production's success, the group dissolved because of internecine feuding. Saint-Denis returned to France "much troubled by the failure of the Actors Company" and no surer of LTS's destiny.[4] Here too his only option was to wait.

On May 10, 1940 the Germans swept into France through Belgium, bypassing the Maginot line and the massed French troops. French resistance was futile, its military outmaneuvered by the superbly trained and equipped German army. Saint-Denis, newly attached to the British army as a liaison officer and interpreter, retreated with the British and was evacuated at Dunkirk. He barely escaped, crossing the channel on the last boat out. A month later Paris fell; an armistice was signed on June 22, 1940. Under its terms, France was divided into two zones. The northern, which included Paris, was occupied by the Germans; the southern, far smaller in size, was the nominally free zone, its capital Vichy. The president of the French Republic resigned, his truncated position assumed by the octogenarian Marshal Philippe Pétain, a hero of World War I. With Pétain's accession to power, democracy died.

In London, Saint-Denis, appalled by his country's humiliating capitulation, resolved to remain in England and do whatever he could to help liberate France.

The decision was difficult, since its consequences meant effectively abandoning his families for the war's duration. He considered joining the Free French under de Gaulle, but distrusted the General. As he was about to enlist in the British army the BBC engaged him to form a French radio team whose purpose would be to combat the German propaganda machine in France.[5]

Saint-Denis was not an obvious choice for the position. Prior to World War II, his politics, insofar as he had any, were vaguely liberal as can be seen from his productions. The Goya piece supported the Spanish Left in the civil war; Bulgakov's The *White Guard* humanized the Bolshevik enemy, the White Russians; Stephen Haggard's *Weep for Spring* performed a comparable function for the Germans. For Michel, art was the supreme good. With few exceptions, his life had been spent in the company of similarly apolitical artists and intellectuals.

The war changed that, casting him as the conscience, the rallying cry of his country. His mission was clear to him: "the liberation of men's minds."[6] He became "the voice of French tradition, the voice that does not deceive."[7] How did a man whose life had been spent in the arts find the common touch needed to reach an entire country? He drew upon his background, which included living among the peasants of Burgundy, the *petits bourgeois* of Versailles, the *poilus* of World War I, and his comrades in World War II. Fighting in Normandy before his evacuation, he witnessed the intimidating and corrupting effect of Nazi propaganda on his compatriots. He understood the potential power of radio in this the first war to be fought also on the airwaves. As he did for the Copiaus, Saint-Denis organized, conceptualized, wrote, directed, and performed. Although he quickly formulated a number of ideas about the program's shape, he wanted and needed to work collaboratively. The BBC envisaged a nightly half-hour show. To fulfill the production demands of the rigorous schedule, Saint-Denis required a group of diverse talents who could function as a team but were also capable of working autonomously. From the many Frenchmen living in London who vied for places, Saint-Denis chose six. While only one man had performance experience, all were attuned to public taste, since their careers were audience-oriented. Afraid that their families in France would suffer if their identities were known, several adopted pseudonyms. Befittingly, Saint-Denis selected as his Jacques Duchesne, the *vox populi* of Parisians during the French Revolution. The others included Jean Oberlé, Saint-Denis's friend of twenty years, who was an artist; Maurice van Moppès, a cartoonist; Pierre Bourdan and Jean Marin were journalists; and Jacques Borel, a poet and essayist.[8] The youngest member was Pierre Lefèvre, Saint-Denis's pupil at LTS, whose acting career was interrupted by the war.

Today, the absence of women raises a glaringly obvious question: How could a program whose intention was to speak to an entire population overlook half that population in forming a team? Nowhere is this omission addressed, a fact that demonstrates clearly that women had no public voice; men spoke *for* them as well as *to* them. Saint-Denis's team was broadcasting to a world where women were confined to conventional roles, where women's suffrage would not become a reality until the war ended in 1945.[9]

Saint-Denis's intention was to turn his BBC team into an ensemble that paralleled his theatrical ideal. Like the Quinze, this group had varied capabilities. He sought and acquired "not only indispensable editors, but dialogue and newswriters, makers of songs or slogans and even a composer."[10] Part of his task was to broaden their skills: "If journalists had good voices and expressive talents, why shouldn't they become actors, announcers, singers?"[11] Consequently, early rehearsals resembled a crash course in acting methods, which the group accepted with goodwill. Saint-Denis, however, was frustrated by awkward line readings, untrained speaking voices, or songs sung out of tune. Rehearsals were occasionally tempestuous affairs with Saint-Denis half-jokingly pursuing van Moppès, the group's *enfant terrible*, around the studio brandishing a cane, aghast at van Moppès's lack of professionalism. Realizing that they would never be polished performers, Saint-Denis capitalized on their limitations, making sincerity the hallmark of their performances.

Saint-Denis had no radio experience but was a quick study, treating "the mike as an old friend" from the beginning.[12] The challenge was to attract and maintain the attention of a demoralized people in a country where radio was tightly controlled, its main purpose the dissemination of Nazi and Vichy propaganda. Aware that straightforward propaganda wasn't going to convince anyone, Saint-Denis's innovation was to turn politics into entertainment. He employed subtlety, humor, drama, and theatrical values to make his points. In so doing, he created an original format, which combined elements of the music hall, drama, and news reporting. Borrowing a page from his Burgundy research, Saint-Denis revived the idea of the stock character. In this case, the characters were more realistic than the Copiaus commedia types, more stereotypical than archetypical—modern Frenchmen with whom their audience could identify. Variety, not only of content, but of rhythm and pacing was key to its success. A British radio writer and director summed up the views of many when he said: "Half an hour's propaganda became more exciting in his hands than any other radio programme I had heard."[13]

Saint-Denis appealed to his audience's cultural identity in a moment when it was being undermined. Both Pétainist Radio Vichy and pro-Nazi Radio Paris attacked France's republican ideals, insisting that it was these values that had brought the country to its knees. In both the occupied and unoccupied sectors, the government jammed the broadcasts; within the occupied sector, listening to the BBC was a crime. Simply tuning into the program was an act of resistance, albeit a passive one. One way Saint-Denis achieved his objective was through honest news reporting, which broadcast Allied losses as well as victories to an information-hungry populace. While propaganda and truth might seem mutually exclusive, the broadcasts' frankness reaffirmed democratic principles in the face of fascist despotism. Crucial to Saint-Denis's effectiveness was his faith in an eventual allied victory.

Those in the theatre world who had grumbled that Saint-Denis's perfectionism set him behind schedule would have been astounded by the speed with which he assembled his program. He signed his contract on July 7th and exactly a week later, with scant preparation, Jacques Duchesne and his team stepped before the microphone. Their debut was inauspicious, giving little indication of the force Duchesne's program would become. Jean Oberlé recollected the performance as mediocre.[14] Ignoring whatever qualms he may have had, Saint-Denis spent the few hours prior to that broadcast advising and encouraging his nervous group of neophytes.

Saint-Denis's function was to discuss, analyze, and clarify the political events of the day for his audience. The nightly half-hour program opened with "Reflections" in which Saint-Denis assumed the character of a prototypical Frenchman—simple, shrewd, honorable, and patriotic. In this guise he spoke to his compatriots, bolstering their spirits, and as the war progressed, encouraging them to resist, at first passively, then actively. He helped unify a France that was living under a veil of silence, one section of the country unaware of events taking place in another. Through these broadcasts the populace learned of German atrocities and French defiance, resulting in a growing solidarity. By 1941, in response to the program's suggestions, the French would gather on national holidays in silent demonstrations or protest marches. The majority of Saint-Denis's talks concerned military developments, but he also analyzed political and sociological issues, speaking familiarly as if to good acquaintances. His commentaries mark him as both chronicler and maker of French public opinion. Even his terse introductory words reflected the country's psychological barometer. At first the broadcasts began, "Today, the first (or the tenth or the fiftieth or whatever it was) day of the German Occupation. . . ." As resentment toward the invader increased, the words became: "Today, the hundredth (or ———) day of the struggle of the French people against oppression. . . ." Within a year, *Les Français parlent aux Français* found its signature, the opening four notes of Beethoven's *Fifth Symphony*—Morse code for the letter *V* symbolizing victory—followed by Saint-Denis's announcement: "Today, the two hundredth day of the struggle of the French people for their liberation. . . ." This formula was repeated every night until D-Day, June 6, 1944, the 1,444th day of the struggle. Saint-Denis also functioned as a cultural interpreter of English actions that the French found baffling, even treacherous. This last objective was particularly important in light of the ceaseless targeting of the British as the enemy of France by the press of the occupied and unoccupied zones. A news commentary by Bourdan or Marin followed "Reflections."

The third segment varied from night to night. An audience favorite was the weekly "Les trois amis" that incorporated dramatic elements of characterization and atmospheric effects, an insignia of Saint-Denis's directing. The format was a discussion of current events among three representative Frenchman, Jacques, Pierre, and Jean. Every week found them chatting in different surroundings: a restaurant, a London park, a cliff in Dover. If the scene was set outdoors, the dialogue might make allusion to a threatening storm or tormenting insects. Saint-Denis worked hard to achieve a realistic sense of place, replacing visual effects with sound. Since sound techniques were primitive, Pierre Lefèvre, their audio specialist, had constantly to improvise anew. Each character brought a distinct personality to the conversation: Bourdan, an incisive logic; Saint-Denis, rationality; while Oberlé provided comic relief as their foil, the dullard to whom everything had to be explained. But whatever the content or locale, the discussion's purpose was always to expose satirically the falsifications of fascist propaganda. Ridicule exposed the enemy's fallibility.

Another popular segment was "La petite Académie," a spoof of the Académie Française in which four professorial types revised the French dictionary with zany wartime definitions. Duchesne played the academy's archivist, Jacques Borel the president, van Moppès its secretary, Oberlé its recorder, while the "protean" Pierre Lefèvre barked and whined as the academy's pet dog. Since the humor was situation-bound, the definitions seem labored now. As an example: "*rutioning*, a noun meaning the leavings of the occupying forces." But for the inhabitants of the occupied zone, who were allowed only a meager diet, the joke was trenchant with its recognition of the difficulties of their lives.

Interspersed with other segments was another clever propaganda ploy, the use of slogans and jingles borrowed from prewar French radio. Radio was new enough that audiences regarded commercials as amusements rather than irritants. The team took existing rhyming sales-pitches, kept the same music, but modified the words to give them an anti-fascist cast, delighting audiences. It was not unusual for their listeners to hum the tunes publicly, an act of protest that, without incriminating themselves, let others know that they were partisans of the BBC. Dramatic scenes drawn from the French classics (particularly those pertaining to the country at war) or the lives of national heroes and artists, cultural episodes, and musical interludes made up the rest of the show. The music was strategically placed to give the auditors a chance to discuss the political themes that had just been delivered.

One of the most telling signs of the program's clout was Radio Paris's attempt to combat it with *Les Français de France parlent aux émigrés*, which used a similar format for contrary purposes. From Radio Vichy, no less a figure than Pétain attacked the BBC program for its "perfidious propaganda."[15] Another indication was the listeners' correspondence. In the occupied zone, the determined letter writer could find ways around the regulations prohibiting foreign correspondence. In the unoccupied zone, there was postal service with Switzerland,

Spain, and Portugal, but mail was subject to censorship. Letters sent to those countries could be forwarded by the recipients. From the occupied zone mail was smuggled across the demarcation line to the unoccupied one and then forwarded. It was more than fan mail; the information received clarified the day-to-day struggle in France and provided broadcast material. Saint-Denis often read excerpts aloud.

Saint-Denis's role placed him in a delicate situation, leaving him open to censure, despite or perhaps because of his moral integrity. His difficulties stemmed from what seemed to be divided loyalties. The title of his postwar article, "In London between Churchill and de Gaulle," sums up his predicament. Although Saint-Denis's patriotism was undeniable, he was considered an Anglophile, which, in Gaullist quarters, left his allegiance open to question. Whereas his admiration for Churchill was unwavering, his feelings for de Gaulle were conflicted. Notwithstanding Saint-Denis's respect for de Gaulle as the Resistance's standard-bearer, he distrusted the General's ambition, fearing for postwar France. He viewed de Gaulle as a divisive influence, and his followers as potential fanatics. Some of those followers were on his own team—Oberlé, Marin, and van Moppès, which created strains around program content, although none of these men were rabid Gaullists. At times, Saint-Denis exploited the tension on the air, particularly in the "Les trois amis" segment, in the form of lively, occasionally acrimonious debates.

The BBC, acknowledging de Gaulle's self-appointed role as leader of the Free French, had given him a nightly five-minute segment preceding *Les Français parlent aux Français*. From the start, he and Maurice Schumann, who served as de Gaulle's spokesperson, used *Honneur et Patrie* to denounce Pétain, "the father of defeat." Saint-Denis incurred the anger of de Gaulle, Schumann, and their entourage by his reluctance to do likewise, as well as his refusal to join the Free French. While rejecting Vichy and its collaborationist policy, Saint-Denis could not regard Pétain, whom he esteemed for his service to France in World War I, as a traitor, although he had seen the Marshal lose "his sense of human understanding."[16] At the age of twenty Saint-Denis was present at Chemin des Dames when the Marshal put down a nascent mutiny. Having ordered Saint-Denis's battalion to line up in formation in the public square, Pétain condemned three of Saint-Denis's comrades-in-arms to death and fifty others to prison.[17] As the condemned men were marched past in full sight of the battalion, Pétain promised the others better rations and rest. Saint-Denis shared the British government's belief that there was support for Pétain in France, and to condemn him or even his policies too precipitously would alienate the average French person. He was convinced that "beyond all else we had to understand the climate of opinion in France and the state of mind of her people, acting with the greatest consideration towards them until such time as Pétain, either in word or deed, provided us with the occasion for direct and justifiably violent attacks."[18] Moreover, as an employee of the BBC, Saint-Denis was subject to its regulations and needed program approval. De Gaulle tried to have Saint-Denis's program abolished.

The incident Saint-Denis needed occurred on October 24, 1940 when Pétain met with Hitler on occupied French territory. Photographs published worldwide showed them shaking hands. Pétain, a man of the nineteenth century, naïve about the power of the media, was frozen in time, his outstretched hand clasping Hitler's. In contrast to Hitler, who was a master at staging events, Pétain appeared strangely oblivious to the ways in which this gesture would be read. What appeared to be Pétain's willingness, indeed eagerness, to collaborate repulsed even some of his apologists. The meeting furnished the justification Saint-Denis sought, but the English directives against attacking the Marshal remained in effect until 1942. Working within these directives, Saint-Denis managed on air to analyze the meeting as well as Pétain's subsequent actions.

It was during this period that Saint-Denis, distressed about the events in France and the Gaullist attacks on his integrity, experienced one of the high points of his BBC tenure. Churchill chose *Les Français parlent aux Français* as the venue for his historic broadcast in French to the French people on October 21, 1940. Saint-Denis was to introduce Churchill, a task he relished because it allowed him to express publicly his esteem for the man. Saint-Denis spent the better part of a day with Churchill at 10 Downing Street in informal circumstances, helping him amend the translation of the speech as well as coaching him. As might be expected, Churchill had strong views about how to present himself. For example, he believed that his address would be more powerful if he were allowed an occasional mispronunciation. When the moment came to air the speech, Saint-Denis and Churchill descended into the bomb shelter used as Churchill's command center. The prime minister seated himself behind the only microphone, leaving no place for Saint-Denis. Observing his plight, Churchill invited him to sit on his lap to read his introduction. The incongruity tickled Saint-Denis and became an anecdote he loved to relate.

During the four years of its existence, the Duchesne team gained the French population's confidence and developed a reciprocal relationship with its listeners. As previously mentioned, their correspondence proved that the French relied on the program as its information source. Further confirmation was provided by on-air interviews with French escapees. These interviews, in turn, fostered more group identification among the listeners. Because of this mutual trust, *Les Français parlent aux Français* could play a role in the landing at Normandy on D-Day in 1944. In the weeks leading up to the invasion, the BBC team prepared the French, giving instructions, invoking their patriotism, transmitting code messages to the underground. For the invasion to succeed, cooperation was essential. Women and children were advised to leave the cities, civilians to prepare provisions, and, at the onset of the invasion, to take shelter. As the invasion date drew nearer they were told how to assist the underground army and to take their orders from them. Once the country was liberated, a provisional peacetime government, composed largely of the Free French and members of the Resistance, would be set in place so that France would not fall into administrative chaos.

On June 6th, Saint-Denis announced that the liberation of France had begun. His undeniable satisfaction was, however, tinged with regret. The majority of his team accompanied the invading armies as correspondents, leaving Saint-Denis and Oberlé, the oldest members, in London, away from the action to coordinate dispatches and encourage the French. The war of the airwaves continued: Saint-Denis sought to assuage the fears of civil war and allied bombardments raised by Radio Paris, which was attempting to retain loyalty to a regime that had long since lost it. His weapon, as always, was his sincerity, as this excerpt demonstrates: "We don't deny the ordeals of the Liberation; but what would the ordeals of France enslaved to Germany for a dozen years be? It is for the unity of France risen up against the hated invader that we work."[19]

On August 20th, Saint-Denis acknowledged that the end of *Les Français parlent aux Français* was at hand; Jean Marin had taken charge of a Breton radio station, the first to be rescued from the hands of the enemy.[20] It was Saint-Denis's intent to remain on the air "until finally from Paris the sovereign voice of France was raised once again."[21] In fact, because of the damage done to the French transmitters by the retreating German army, the program continued for several months after France's liberation. Saint-Denis's grateful country bestowed on him the Legion of Honor. England awarded him a CBE (Commander of the British Empire), and Belgium, the Order of Leopold. And from America came a tribute to the Duchesne team, "who in the dark days of June 1940 were the first to cry 'no!' to the Germans [and] whose broadcasts were for four years an iron lung for France that the enemy wanted to asphyxiate."[22]

His mission completed, Michel was free to resume his career. However, seeing his family whom the war had scattered was his first priority. When the Germans occupied Burgundy, his wife and their two children took refuge with friends in central France. His sister and mother fled Burgundy and spent the rest of the war in Versailles. Madeleine and Blaise Gautier returned to her native Algeria, where Saint-Denis visited them in the spring of 1943 while on a fact-finding mission for the BBC.[23] Since wartime restrictions made correspondence so difficult, as a favor the Canadian minister to Vichy had twice secretly transported his letters to and from France. The family, having recognized Jacques Duchesne's voice, were aware of Saint-Denis's activities. Nightly they followed his broadcasts that occasionally contained a disguised message for them.

Beyond seeing his family, Saint-Denis had other reasons for visiting France. He was no longer sure where his theatrical path lay. He had sorely missed his country during the war and dreamed of participating in rebuilding French theatre, of taking it to the next step in the evolution that Copeau began and he continued with the Quinze. Yet his circle of collaborators and theatrical reputation were in England. Pulled by conflicting ambitions, he brooded about his future, even during the midst of war. As his diary records: "I am stuck between two countries and the center of my work is in England—it's strange, for it seems impossible to me to live elsewhere than France. But, how would I be received in France, and what should I do there?"[24] What he had not reckoned with was his newfound renown. From Pernand Copeau wrote, the villagers "proud of their Jacques Duchesne had been awaiting him every day" since his return.[25] If Saint-Denis was largely unknown in France, Duchesne was a national hero. Accordingly, a variety of offers were extended to him: artistic director of the Comédie-Française, director of the English Service of Radio-Diffusion Française, a run for political office, a position as a journalist for a new periodical.

While investigating theatre opportunities he accepted the radio directorship on a provisional basis, but found it unrewarding because of "the problematic working conditions which inevitably lead to mediocrity."[26] The Comédie-Française offer, while flattering, was rejected. Saint-Denis's commitment was to the contemporary theatre and its reform. More intriguing were plans to form a company dedicated to research and training as well as production with his cousin Maiène and her husband Jean Dasté. Ultimately, he refused; he felt that for an alternative company to flourish, France had to make fundamental changes politically and socially. Otherwise, support would be lacking for the kind of radical transformation of the theatrical culture he wanted to implement. Saint-Denis was no longer willing "to drag our research from elite inner circles to elite inner circles or from barn to barn without even succeeding in earning a living."[27]

Saint-Denis's despondency arose not only from the difficulties inherent in resuming his artistic life in France. On January 27, 1945, three months before the war's end, his twenty-year-old son Jérôme was killed in Alsace while serving in the army. Tormented by his loss and confused about his prospects, he decided to leave for London to settle personal affairs and to discuss a directing possibility.

NOTES

1. Michel Saint-Denis, diary notes, 21 January 1940.

2. Quoted in Jean Oberlé, *Jean Oberlé vous parle: Souvenirs de cinq années à Londres* (Paris: La Jeune Parque, 1945), 12.

3. Jacques Copeau, *Registres IV, America*, ed. Marie-Hélène Dasté and Suzanne Maistre Saint-Denis (Paris: Gallimard, 1984), 112.

4. Saint-Denis, diary notes, 17 February 1940.

5. The BBC began planning its political programming shortly before the invasion of Poland in 1939.

6. Michel Saint-Denis, translated typescript, "In London between Churchill and de Gaulle," *Crapouillot*, no. 17 (1954).

7. Ibid.

8. Pierre Bourdan's real name was Pierre Maillaud; Jean Marin's was Yves Morvan; Jacques Borel's was Jacques Cottance.

9. The original six men, with Saint-Denis, remained the nucleus, but because of the program's success offshoots were added, all under the aegis of Duchesne. The new programs necessitated about a dozen supplementary personnel. One was a woman, Geneviève Brissot; after an apprenticeship, she administered a noontime broadcast.

10. Quoted in Hélène Eck, *La guerre des ondes: Histoire des radios de langue française pendant la Deuxième Guerre mondiale* (Paris: Armand Colin, 1985), 67.

11. Ibid.

12. Asa Briggs, *The History of Broadcasting in the United Kingdom*, vol. 3: *The War of Words* (London: Oxford University Press, 1970), 248.

13. Ibid.

14. Oberlé, 38.

15. Ibid., 110.

16. Saint-Denis, "In London between Churchill and de Gaulle."

17. Saint-Denis's experience contrasts sharply with conventional opinion. History has praised Pétain for suppressing the insurrection with minimal harshness.

18. Saint-Denis, "In London between Churchill and de Gaulle."

19. Jacques Duchesne, "Les Français parlent aux Français," 17 June 1944, *Ici Londres: Les voix de la liberté*, ed. Jean-Louis Crémieux-Brilhac, vol. 5 (Paris: La Documentation Française, 1976), 69.

20. Ibid., 191.

21. Ibid.

22. Ibid., 224–25.

23. Although they remained in contact because of Blaise, this visit ended the relationship between Madeleine Gautier and Michel. Letter from Madeleine Gautier to Saint-Denis, 8 October 1943.

24. Saint-Denis, diary notes, 22 August 1942.

25. Jacques Copeau, letter to Michel Saint-Denis, 5 December 1944.

26. Michel Saint-Denis, letter to Jacques Copeau, 29 March 1945.

27. Ibid.

chapter eight

Saint-Denis's *Oedipus*

WHILE STILL AT THE BBC, Saint-Denis had followed the London theatre scene, with particular interest in the changes taking place in the Old Vic's organizational structure. The new management's inaugural production in August of 1944 of *Peer Gynt* (starring Ralph Richardson, directed by John Burrell, with Laurence Olivier playing the cameo role of the Button Molder) coincided with Saint-Denis's announcement that his wartime mission was drawing to a close. His aspirations remained steadfast: the formation of a school and a permanent experimental company working in tandem. The new Old Vic offered his best hope for achieving that dream; an invitation to direct *Oedipus* the first step on the rung.

Prior to World War II, Saint-Denis had staged *The Witch of Edmonton* and *Macbeth* for the company. As resident director, Tyrone Guthrie had been instrumental in his mounting these two dramas. Following Lilian Bayliss's death, Guthrie took over the administration. When the Germans began bombing London, Guthrie moved the Old Vic's headquarters first to Burnley, then Liverpool. (The empty playhouse, converted into a shelter, became a casualty of the air raids in 1941.) From its provincial base, the Vic patriotically ran tours to industrial and mining towns for audiences of defense workers. So well-received were the tours—even with their heavyweight repertory of Shakespeare, Shaw, and Chekhov—that there were several road companies. In a first for England, a government agency, CEMA (Council for the Encouragement of Music and the Arts), provided financial support, permitting the Old Vic company to pay off its debts.[1]

Although CEMA's function was to build wartime morale through glorifying national culture, its existence paved the way for continuing government subsidy and revived dreams of a national theatre. The Old Vic was a contender not only because it was a repository of classical drama, but also because its tours transformed it into a national institution. Guthrie felt that the company would be more competitive if it had a wartime London venue. At his request Bronson

Albery became the Vic's joint administrator and made the New Theatre available. Ensconced in the West End, the Old Vic was competing with commercial theatre. In order to increase its profits, Laurence Olivier and Ralph Richardson were recruited to join the company in an artistic and managerial capacity. (Strings were pulled to obtain their military discharge.) More importantly, the prestigious stars would bolster the Vic's claim on the national theatre.

In 1944 Albery resigned (although the company remained at the New Theatre) and Guthrie became sole administrator. Beneath him was the triumvirate of Olivier, Richardson, and John Burrell. Burrell, a former teacher at the London Theatre Studio (LTS), lacked the glamour, force of personality, and experience of his colleagues, but was a valuable team player.

Soon after, Guthrie was forced out by the triumvirate, who wanted absolute control. The official reason for Guthrie's departure was "exhaustion."[2] Perhaps to placate him, the triumvirate suggested that he direct Olivier in *Oedipus* at the Vic. Whatever grudges Guthrie harbored, the idea attracted him on several counts: a cast that included Olivier, Sybil Thorndike, and Richardson; the Yeats translation; and the fact that it would be a departure for the Vic. Problems surfaced when Olivier took exception to Guthrie's production plans and also insisted on capping the performance with Sheridan's theatrical burlesque, *The Critic*.[3] Olivier wanted to display his virtuosity, a notion Guthrie dismissed as vulgar. Neither would yield. After consulting his associates, Olivier, who had "complete confidence in the undoubted genius of Michel Saint-Denis," offered him *Oedipus*.[4] Olivier's biographer reports that Guthrie was humiliated by the rebuff, which opened up a rift that "would have resounding consequences for them all."[5] At the time, however, the production only served to burnish further Saint-Denis and Olivier's reputations. Guthrie spent the next few years abroad where he mounted two separate productions of *Oedipus Rex*: in Tel Aviv for the Habima, and in Finland. Before leaving London he saw *Oedipus* and, unsurprisingly, faulted Saint-Denis's production.

STAGING *OEDIPUS*

Trying to reconstruct a Saint-Denis production is often frustrating because of the paucity of documentation. By and large, British mid-century critics discussed the actors' performances rather than the director's concepts or even staging. And although Saint-Denis wrote about his teaching and even his ideas on directing, he said almost nothing about his individual productions. In the case of *Oedipus*, the task is made easier through having Saint-Denis's blocking notes (drawn up before rehearsals started; see figure 8.1), a few sketches, the ground plan, and a number of production pictures. The notes especially give us the opportunity to examine the visual aspect of Saint-Denis's directorial process.

Although *Oedipus Rex* was the first Greek play Saint-Denis directed professionally, his study of Attic drama dated back to his days with Copeau. Of the

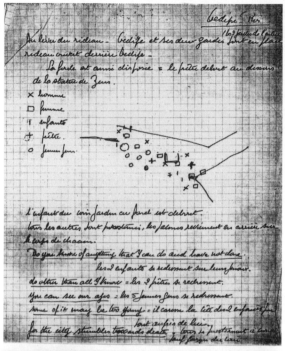

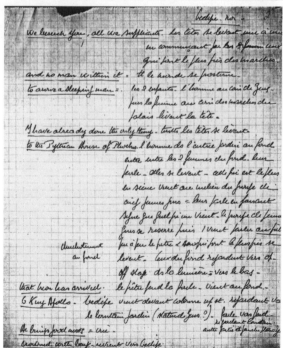

FIGURE 8.1 *Saint-Denis's pre-rehearsal blocking notes for* Oedipus. *Note that the stage directions are in French, the text in English.*

four plays he mounted at LTS, two were Greek—Sophocles' *Electra* and Euripides' *Alcestis*. Laurence Olivier's awareness of Saint-Denis's work in this domain was surely a factor in selecting him to direct *Oedipus*. A director with even this depth of experience staging Greek drama was rare in London. The notable exception was Lewis Casson, Sybil Thorndike's husband, with Euripides' *Hippolytus, The Trojan Women*, and *Medea* to his credit.

Oedipus Rex had previously received only one professional production in London. Banned because of its incestuous content until 1910, Max Reinhardt mounted the first British presentation in 1912 at Covent Garden with John Martin-Harvey as Oedipus in Gilbert Murray's poetic translation. In 1936 (at the age of 71), Martin-Harvey revived Reinhardt's theatricalist production. Considering its impact, it is more than probable that Guthrie and Saint-Denis saw this revival. With Reinhardt's rendering still vivid in the minds of the critics and public, *Oedipus* posed a challenge to Saint-Denis.

His directorial choices diverged from Reinhardt's. As always, the central issue was style. How to be true to the play, which meant the text and the author's world, and make it relevant to the audience? How to bridge the culture gap between England in 1945 and the pre-Christian Greece of 2,500 years past? What commonalities did the two cultures share? Saint-Denis's resolution was to marry classicism with modernism.

Yeats's translation suited the modern temper; the text was clear, spare, and eminently actable. At the same time, its austere language was closer to Sophocles' than Murray's "Swinburnian" verses.[6] Unlike the original, it was written in prose with the exception of rhymed choral odes. Yeats also abbreviated the choral speeches, which went unnoticed by the critics. His justification for the cuts was that this version was to be produced on the Abbey Theatre's small proscenium stage. The diminished importance of the chorus was exploited by Saint-Denis's production. He also was constrained by a proscenium stage (the venue was the New Theatre); a diminished chorus was more acceptable to a mid-century audience and also served to isolate Oedipus even further, "transforming him into a modern tragic hero."[7]

The production design demonstrated Saint-Denis's synthesis. Ending his collaboration with Motley, Saint-Denis turned to the art world and the painter John Piper.[8] Both an abstract and representational artist, Piper created a setting that fused the two styles. As was his wont, Saint-Denis was very involved in the design process; his first major step in preparing a production was to sketch his setting and costume vision. Staging problems to be resolved visually included the physical relationship between the chorus and characters and the placing of the entrances and exits for both.[9] The set for *Oedipus* was simple and uncluttered. In a departure from the standard concept for Greek tragedy that featured a central entrance with the requisite door or doors, this palace facade, flanked by two massive Doric pillars, was angled stage left, permitting unconventional stage pictures. Eighteen feet in length, it ran from center stage to the curtain line on the left. The facade was on a platform; a step running its width led to the stage level. There was a shallow playing area between and behind the pillars; draperies covered the opening above the playing area, "hiding the play's more shocking episodes."[10] Draperies, more permeable than a solid door, hinted at those episodes as well as concealing them. In addition, the speed with which they could be opened and shut served to modulate the moods of entrances and exits. Reviewers were impressed by the "momentous entrances and sudden exits."[11] On stage right, also placed at an angle were two gigantic statues, one of Artemis, the other, larger and almost center, of Apollo. As goddess of the chase, Artemis's presence points up the irony of the play because the action revolves around a hunt. The statues were approximately twelve feet apart. An upstage wall, with a central entrance leading to the wings further delimited the characters' world. While the style of the palace facade was realistic, or at least traditionally classic, the statues were at once surrealistic and archaic. They hearkened back to the art of the Archaic period in their flat and triangular planes. But even in the Archaic period proportion was an important value, and these statues were disproportionate, elongated, reminiscent of Giacometti's sculptures.

Color was used sparingly; the pillars were the chalk white of an idealized classical Greece, the gods golden. The only other note of color in the set was the sky, variously described as "lowering," "inky," "stormy." The immense set pieces, statues, and the sky evoked a threatened and threatening world in which human beings were dwarfed by powerful forces. As the performers did not interact with the statues, it is to be assumed that the characters were unconscious of them. Primordial figures with mask-like features, they loomed over the characters, lending the production a surreal quality.

For the costume designer Saint-Denis availed himself of his cousin Maiène Dasté, perhaps at the suggestion of Copeau, who relished seeing his "children" collaborating.[12] Costume was a long-standing interest of Saint-Denis who, in his Copiaus days, had collaborated with Maiène and her husband Jean in making masks. Given Saint-Denis's expertise with the mask, it would be reasonable to suppose he would employ them in this production, where he could do so legitimately. However, his vision of the play rejected stylization, militating against masks. Although several critics commented on the archaic and primitive quality of the production, the costumes represented the Hellenic era. The characters wore the everyday clothing of that period rather than an approximation of the theatrical costuming of fifth-century BCE Athens. Dasté's sources were classical Greek art and artifacts: statues, vases, pottery.

Although clearly situated in a Greek world, the chorus also suggested Old Testament prophets. The fifteen elders, all with sculpted, curly beards, were identically dressed in black-and-silver flowing robes, accented with red, over which they wore a hooded poncho-like garment decorated with geometric designs. The black and silver referenced the dark and light of the set, a reminder of the thematic oppositions of *Oedipus*: guilt and innocence, blindness and vision, ignorance and knowledge. The red foreshadowed the blood that will flow before the play is done.

Jocasta was a majestic figure in a long mauve gown, its bodice heavily jeweled and cinched at the waist with a girdle strewn with gems. Long sleeves, fastened at the wrist and elbow, were slashed to reveal her arms. Her head was covered with a large crown, a mantle was thrown over her shoulders. The costume emphasized her matronly body—Thorndike was then age sixty-three—pointing up the disparity in ages between her and the youthful Oedipus. Thorndike exploited the disparity; "more mother than wife" was one critic's characterization of her portrayal.[13]

In contrast to the other male characters, who were shrouded in long robes, Oedipus wore a brief, short-sleeved tunic that revealed muscular thighs and arms.[14] The short tunic, worn by manual laborers and warriors, depicted him as a man of action. On each wrist were heavy cuff bracelets; his feet were shod with sandals clasped at the calves. Pinned to his shoulders was a striped cloak trailing behind him on the ground. The cloak was a valuable acting tool, allowing Olivier to drape it in multiple ways that underscored Oedipus's changing moods. The costume accentuated his youth and virility. Olivier was strikingly handsome in the role—strong, lithe, graceful—and heavily made up; close to forty years of age, he looked fifteen years younger. For Olivier, makeup was an indispensable component of characterization. He customarily developed a role from an external image—his false noses were legendary in the theatre world.

A classical Apollo was the probable model for his physically idealized Oedipus that bore no resemblance to the menacing statue of the production. The likeness between Olivier's Oedipus and the sculpted god on the fifth-century frieze at the Temple of Zeus at Olympia is remarkable: the same large eyes, high-bridged "Grecian" nose, curly locks falling over the forehead, full sullen lips, and rounded chin. (Olivier, alone of the male actors in this production, was beardless, which helped point up his youth.) Oedipus as an incarnation of the god made visible to the audience the character's overweening pride for which he will be punished. This is not to say that Olivier's Oedipus was endeavoring to usurp the god's powers. Rather, he had turned away from religion, putting his faith in human reason as the means to cure society's ills. Moreover, Olivier's appearance added another layer of ambiguity and irony for which the play is celebrated, since in looking at Oedipus the audience also beheld Apollo—the idea that Oedipus is both victim and agent of his destiny being driven home. The dialogue instantiates the concept as in the following example. After Oedipus blinds himself, the chorus asks what power drove him to it? Oedipus's response: "Apollo, friends, Apollo, but it was my own hand, wretched that I am that quenched these eyes."[15]

Incidental music was commissioned from Antony Hopkins. Judging from the reviews, it was cacophonous, dissonant, effective, and served to heighten the tension. Like the setting, the music had a quality both modern and archaic. It heightened the tension and intensified the barbaric atmosphere provided by the gods. Hopkins also composed music for the chorus, who sang in addition to speaking and chanting.

It was not merely through the external elements that Saint-Denis made the production accessible to its audience. He saw a connection between the world of the play and that of postwar Europe.[16] For the Greeks, the theatre served as a forum for the discussion of ethical questions, in much the same way as Saint-Denis's *Les Français parlent aux Français*.[17] When the play opened in October of 1945, the horrors of war still lingered: the death camps had been discovered within the previous six months; millions of displaced people roamed Europe; the atomic bomb had been dropped on Japan only weeks before. Life continued to be difficult for the English despite victory; the population was malnourished, poorly housed, and ill-clad. In part, Saint-Denis's notion of style was predicated on the idea of universality. If a work of art can reach across time and space to another culture, it is because great works treat situations, desires, emotions, and ideas that repeat themselves over the centuries, albeit in different guises.

It must be stated, however, that Saint-Denis's interpretation was multifaceted. He created a world that was primal in its beliefs and contemporary in its fears. The production was not overtly political. Only the most perceptive critics grasped those implications. Alan Moorehead, in an article for the *Daily Express*, drew a parallel between the Greek sense of fate and the sense of doom pervading a world menaced by the atom bomb.[18] The *Tribune*'s reviewer made a connection between the helplessness of the individual (Oedipus) confronted with an amoral agency stronger than himself, in this case merciless gods and the evil of concentration camps. Could twentieth-century humanity believe in a beneficent god any more than could the Greeks?[19] Paramount for Desmond MacCarthy was the issue of power, the rise and fall of a tyrant and the transience of public acclaim.[20] Oedipus's downfall brought to mind Mussolini's recent murder at the hands of a mob.[21] The text in its multivalence supports all these views.

Sophocles typically constructed tragedies around an imperiled central character caught in a crucial situation seemingly not of his or her own doing. His characters experience fervent emotions with which audiences can identify. The intensity of Oedipus's emotional arc makes it one of the greatest roles in the dramatic canon and thus could not fail to appeal to Olivier, an actor Saint-Denis admiringly described as one who "draws the line at nothing and . . . loves excess."[22] In Saint-Denis, Olivier had an actor-centered director—in that the actor is the embodiment of the text—who was fascinated by character. Unlike Reinhardt's production in which theatrical effects frequently overwhelmed the acting, Saint-Denis's rendering was of a piece; the acting, setting, and staging were congruent. Reviewers remarked on Saint-Denis's realistic approach: "His direction judiciously combined imagination with realism" sums up a typical point of view.[23] While realism seems incompatible with Greek tragedy, what the critics perceived was the very human quality of the characters, particularly Oedipus. In no way naturalistic, Saint-Denis and Olivier's interpretation of Oedipus was nonetheless three-dimensional. Saint-Denis's notes to Olivier stress the character's compassion, pride, temper, and essential nobility. The result for W. A. Darlington was an Oedipus who was "no remote demigod, but a practical man of action brought low by fate."[24]

In light of comments such as these, Saint-Denis appears to have balanced his interpretation between the human and religious aspects. The production was influenced by its consultant, the Sophoclean scholar C. M. Bowra, for whom the focus of *Oedipus* was the role of the gods in human destiny. Pertinent quotations from his book *Sophoclean Tragedy* are found in Saint-Denis's notes.[25] In Bowra's judgment, Oedipus was guilty, albeit unwittingly, of horrendous crimes against the gods. The tragedy "inculcates the lesson that man must be humble before the gods and know that he is as nothing against their will."[26] But the play offers an alternative, almost existential interpretation in which the hero chooses his fate. Saint-Denis's Oedipus was more than the plaything of the gods.

Attributes of the production repeatedly cited by the critics were its *dignity* and *drive*, two seemingly incongruent terms. Dignity appears to have meant restraint and austerity. That quality is perhaps best seen if once again we use Reinhardt as a point of departure and compare the opening of Saint-Denis's play with that of the German director's mass spectacle. In the prologue, Oedipus addresses the frightened Theban people who are being ravaged by a mysterious plague. For his production, Reinhardt rebuilt the stage, adding a projecting altar over the orchestra pit, a *hanamichi* or gangway running from the altar to the back of the house, steps, and platforms.[27] As the lights dimmed, trumpets sounded, followed by a frenzied mob made up of three hundred extras surging onto the stage via the bridge and the aisles prostrating themselves, moaning and shrieking. It was a *coup de théâtre* that took the audience by storm. While not denying the scene's power, the London critics questioned its authenticity and appropriateness. What they objected to was a violation of the norms of classical decorum, although those norms were established centuries after Sophocles' death. While Saint-Denis's production was no more authentic in the sense of reproducing antiquarian conventions, it escaped similar censure because of its restraint.

Saint-Denis, the master of atmospherics, created a somber ambience at the tragedy's opening. In place of a maddened throng was a group of two dozen actors and actresses ranging from childhood to senescence, all timorous, awestruck, depressed. They scurried on in semi-darkness, producing "a mood of dread and foreboding before a word had been spoken."[28] As they took their places, they prostrated themselves with arms outstretched and palms up, beseeching before the palace steps where stood Oedipus with two guards behind him. Balancing the picture was a child who remained standing stage right observing the scene. Two priests, one in a speaking role and the other mute, were closest to the king and clutched the step in supplication. The angle of the set facilitated Saint-Denis's frieze-like composition; in this scene the characters were seen only in profile. The supplicants' bodies lying in a diagonal arrangement across the stage formed one side of a triangle, the palace platform being the other. Towering above them, facing straight out were the gods. Music and an offstage antiphonal plaint chanted and sung by male and female choruses accompanied the action—"the murmurs of prayer and lamentation" of the text.[29] The scene's rhythm was slow and measured. As was his custom, Saint-Denis methodically choreographed the movement. Each member of the group was given a phrase to raise his or her head or rise to a kneeling position during Oedipus's first monologue, which prevented the image from becoming static and also established Oedipus as a benevolent ruler trusted and respected by his people. Oedipus demonstrated his political astuteness, caressing the heads of two children during the speech, a kind of ancient Greek take on the modern baby-kissing politician. A variation of the supplicants' wave-like motion was repeated throughout the next two speeches. On the line "the city stumbles toward death" they prostrated themselves. From this position they again raised their heads on a given line, but in a different pattern, the action more compressed: first the two children, then a man close to Apollo, then a woman at the corner of the steps. Towards the end of Oedipus's second speech, "I have already done the only thing . . .," the others lifted their heads as one. Excitement began to build, some of the supplicants got up, some talked to each other, one signaled the arrival of Creon. Creon entered up right as the crowd parted—"not daring to descend further"—formed two sides of a triangle to let him through and closed on itself as he passed.[30] Creon arrived downstage left facing Oedipus. Five old men resumed their supine posture on Creon's line, "Then with your leave, I speak."[31]

During the following stichomythic dialogue with Creon, Oedipus remained on the palace platform until his line to the crowd, "come my children," when he decides to search out Laius's murderer. In an ambiguous movement that showed respect but also augured the Thebans' repudiation of Oedipus, the crowd drew back as Oedipus approached them. On the line "as God wills," Oedipus turned toward Creon and the two entered the palace. The guards closed the draperies behind them as the crowd disappeared the way they had entered, music playing underneath.

From this slow-paced beginning the production built until it reached one of the most celebrated climaxes in the annals of theatre history, Olivier's cry of agony on discovering that *he* is the pollution. His search for the means to produce that sound, somewhere between a moan and a howl, bears repeating here. Like Saint-Denis, Olivier was deliberate and meticulous, beginning his study well before the onset of rehearsals. As with his physical characterization, Olivier's point of departure was exterior; in this instance, he experimented with vowel sounds until he fixed on "er," which was more agonized and original than the "oh, oh" found in most texts.[32] Having discovered the shape of the sound, Olivier moved to the emotional level. Needed was an image to help him reach the degree of pain he wanted to attain. An animal caught in a trap seemed promising but too vague until he discovered how ermine is hunted in the Arctic. Salt is put out on the snow and when the ermine licks it, its tongue is caught fast in the ice. Kenneth Tynan eloquently captured the reaction of the spectators and critics:

> I know that from the first I was waiting breathlessly for the time when the rack would move into the final notch, and the lyric cry would be released: but I never hoped for so vast an anguish. . . . The two cries were torn from beyond tears or shame or guilt: they came from the stomach, with all the ecstatic grief and fright of a newborn baby's wail.[33]

Missing from the reviewers' comments is a sense of the *mise en scène*: where were Oedipus, the other characters, the chorus? To be that powerful, the moment had to be strong visually as well as aurally. It is worth returning to the blocking notes to see how Saint-Denis envisaged the scene. Let's begin with the circumstances that precede Oedipus's recognition. Jocasta having apprehended the truth of Oedipus's birth reentered the palace, followed by the guards, leaving the messenger (who withdrew into the furthest corner stage left) and the chorus on stage with Oedipus. As she exited, Oedipus in a change of attitude turned to the chorus, symbolically repudiating his mother as he declared himself "the child of luck." The chorus, caught up in his mood, approached him from either side in two groups singing:

Oedipus's nurse, mountain of many a hidden glen,
Be honoured among men;
A famous man, deep-thoughted, and his body strong:
Be honoured in dance and song.

They formed a circle around Oedipus while dancing and chanting the last four lines of the ode, their arms outstretched, palms up, each half moving in a different direction. As they danced the pitch of the scene increased, its intensity abetted by Yeats's compressed lyric. The effect of the scene was twofold: on the one hand, the chorus was allying itself with Oedipus, seemingly entreating him; on the other, he appeared victimized, entrapped in the circle, his august distance of the earlier scenes vanished. Oedipus broke free, rushing towards right center where the awaited herdsman was entering as the chorus moved left and up.

Arriving upstage center they divided once again in two groups, the chorus leader slightly center and down of them. When the herdsman was fully on stage, an agitated Oedipus backed up center. His two guards (who had reentered) remained behind him as a menacing presence. Throughout the interrogation of the herdsman, Oedipus advanced on him deliberately, watched carefully by the distanced chorus whose response was muted. For example, as Oedipus came closer to the truth they lowered their heads. On the herdsman's last line to Oedipus, "You are the most miserable of men," they backed up, distancing themselves even more from Oedipus who was downstage center, his body turned out, his head twisted and thrown back at his climactic moment. Thus he had a long cross as he rushed to the palace exit, pushing by the Corinthian messenger, followed at a distance by his guards. The draperies, specified for the first time as red (perhaps a lighting effect), snapped closed.

Olivier's reentrance, with its change of tone and rhythm, was as gripping in its own fashion. As the draperies slowly opened, the blinded Oedipus, his body enveloped in black robes, blood streaming down his cheeks, groped his way to a pillar. But perhaps "grope," with its nuance of clumsiness, does not fully characterize his physicality. Photographs reveal that Olivier's Oedipus was as majestic in adversity as he was in his glory. Frozen in time by the camera, his movements seem dance-like, more so after his blinding than before. As in the opening of the play, he resembles a living statue, but one conceptualized by the actor and his director. He became the idealization of an emotion or condition. This scene exemplified Saint-Denis's ideas of poetic realism.

Reputation has it that "the only part of the production to receive unanimous acclaim was the performance of Olivier himself."[34] An examination of the reviews proves that assertion imprecise. While Olivier's acting was widely applauded—"a performance of passion, anguish and pathos that places him on the highest pinnacle among modern tragic actors"—there were critical reservations.[35] It was noted that Olivier "occasionally threw away all restraint and dignity"; that there was "a certain awkwardness of posture during some of his earlier speeches"; that he was sometimes given to "ranting"; and that he had not yet "fully expanded [his] tragic powers."[36] I cite these comments not to denigrate Olivier's performance, but to set the record straight. Olivier's performance was a *tour de force*, but it was part of a production architected by Saint-Denis.

The acting was almost universally well-received. Sybil Thorndike was lauded for her heroic presentation and "courage to let out the emotional stops."[37] One dissenting voice—not heard at the time—was Kenneth Tynan's. An eighteen-year-old Tynan recorded his impressions that were published five years later. He felt that she was pompous and anachronous—in a word, *hammy*. "She treated every line as if were the crucial line of the play: it was all so ponderously weighted that when the big hurdles approached, the horse couldn't jump."[38] "Dignified," "impressive," "distinguished," "noble" were the adjectives used to describe the performances of Ralph Richardson (Teiresias), George Curzon (Creon), Harcourt Williams (the priest), Miles Malleson (the shepherd), and Nicholas Hannen (the chorus leader).

A small number of reviewers found the chorus problematic, while about a third found it effective. Others barely noted its presence; one suspects that being unaccustomed to the conventions of Greek tragedy, they lacked the critical tools. The ever-cranky Ivor Brown proclaimed that "Saint-Denis has produced the chorus with deliberate poses that have High Art written rather self-consciously all over them."[39] Judging from the photos and Saint-Denis's directorial notes, the chorus's gestures were stylized and hieratic. Saint-Denis chose to "reduce the choreographic movement to a bare minimum."[40] That is, the choral movement, devoid of athleticism, depended on gesture rather than dance, perhaps to emphasize age and dignity.

With the exception of the few negative comments on the chorus, critics enthusiastically praised the direction, even those for whom Greek tragedy was exotic and/or archaic. The *Daily Telegraph*'s comments typify the latter category:

> Greek tragedy is perhaps the most difficult of all forms of drama to render effectively on the modern stage. Its grandeur is inescapable, but its formalities make it alien in spirit to our own way of thought. I doubt whether the problem has been solved better by any director than Michel Saint-Denis at the New Theatre last night, or the play better acted than by the Old Vic Company.[41]

For *Time and Tide* the production was "vivid and thrilling theatre"; the *Birmingham Post* enthused that "Michel Saint-Denis's intensely dramatic production brought the ancient tragedy pulsatingly to life"; the *New Theatre* wrote that Saint-Denis had "achieved a sense of darkening and malignant destiny which was lost in Reinhardt's more austerely classical production."[42] This last remark is puzzling given that Reinhardt's *Oedipus* seems to have been neither austere nor classical. A few reviewers observed that six years of absence from the theatre "had not dulled Saint-Denis's genius."[43]

Writing to Copeau just after the opening, Saint-Denis admitted that taking up his profession after all that time had been difficult.[44] In directing *Oedipus*, he had confronted a situation fraught with uncertainty. The production reunited him with Olivier, who regarded their previous venture together (*Macbeth*) as a debacle; he had to readjust to working with members of the profession, many of whom did not share his standards and ideals, and most importantly, once again he had to prove himself as an artist. The premiere, a euphoric experience, validated Saint-Denis's views and his talent. He was acclaimed by the audience who invited him onstage to take a curtain call with the cast. All that was lacking for him was Copeau's presence. In his letter, Saint-Denis stressed that this production and his work with the Old Vic was a continuation of the tradition begun by Copeau. Saint-Denis's need for his uncle's approval did not diminish with time.

If Copeau continued to withhold his approval, the same cannot be said for the public. The production, which sold out for its entire run, was the talk of London. For those lucky enough to have seen it, the play remained an indelible memory.[45] Its emotional impact was such that smelling salts were kept at the theatre.[46] Directly after its closing, the Old Vic Company left on tour for New York. There, the play met with similar enthusiasm. In order to meet the demand for tickets special matinees were added. Nonetheless, according to its press agent, "at least 30,000 persons were unable to obtain reservations."[47]

Oedipus's triumph may have created a more welcoming climate for Greek tragedy on Broadway; the following year John Gielgud played Jason and directed Robinson Jeffers's adaptation of *Medea* in New York with Judith Anderson in the title role. But more interesting from our point of view was the arrival in the United States of Tyrone Guthrie's Habima production of *Oedipus Rex*. Guthrie's *Oedipus* received mixed reviews. Ironically, it was compared unfavorably to the now legendary Saint-Denis production.[48]

NOTES

1. CEMA originated as a private organization.

2. James Forsyth, *Tyrone Guthrie: A Biography* (London: Hamilton, 1976), 192.

3. Laurence Olivier, *Confessions of an Actor: An Autobiography* (Middlesex: Penguin Books, 1984), 143.

4. Ibid.

5. Anthony Holden, *Laurence Olivier: A Biography* (New York: Atheneum, 1988), 205.

6. Ivor Brown, *The Observer* (21 October 1945).

7. Karen Dorn, "Stage Production and the Greek Theatre Movement: W. B. Yeats's Play *The Resurrection* and His Version of *King Oedipus* and *Oedipus at Colonus*," *Theatre Research International* 1 (1976): 194.

8. The reasons for terminating the collaboration are obscure. They remained friendly and Margaret Harris headed the design section of the Old Vic School.

9. Michel Saint-Denis, "The Way to Conduct Rehearsals of Plays of Different Style," lecture notes for technical courses, 27 June 1947.

10. *Sunday Graphic* (21 October 1945).

11. Alan Dent, *News Chronicle* (20 October 1945).

12. Jacques Copeau, unpublished letter to Michel Saint-Denis, 15 July 1945.

13. Audrey Williamson, *Old Vic Drama* (London: Rockcliff, 1957), 190.

14. Presumably, Olivier, whose legs were thin, was wearing padded tights.

15. Sophocles, *King Oedipus*, trans. W. B. Yeats, in W. B. Yeats, *The Collected Plays of W. B. Yeats* (New York: Macmillan, 1935), 513.

16. Interview with Sybil Thorndike, *Theatre World* (November 1945).

17. Saint-Denis broadcast periodically for the BBC during the postwar years, functioning as a cultural commentator, often giving his view of the political situation.

18. Alan Moorehead, *Daily Express* (25 October 1945).

19. *Tribune* (2 November 1945).

20. In the original Greek, the play's title uses "*tyrannos*" rather than the word for "king." *Tyrannos*, which is translated as "tyrant," does not have the negative connotations of the English word and means an absolute ruler who did not acquire his power through hereditary means.

21. Desmond MacCarthy, *New Statesman and Nation* (undated).

22. Michel Saint-Denis, "English Theatre in Gallic Eyes," trans. J. F. M. Stephens, Jr., *Texas Quarterly* 4 (autumn 1961): 43.

23. *Sunday Graphic* (21 October 1945).

24. W. A. Darlington, *Daily Telegraph* (19 October 1945).

25. C. M. Bowra, *Sophoclean Tragedy* (Oxford: Clarendon Press, 1944).

26. C. M. Bowra, "*Oedipus Rex*," unidentified newspaper article.

27. This device, borrowed from the Japanese Kabuki, was judged as an efficacious means of bridging the gap between audience and actor found in Western theatre.

28. Peter Arnott, *Public and Performance in Greek Theatre* (London: Routledge, 1991), 22.

29. *King Oedipus*, 475.

30. Michel Saint-Denis, blocking notes.

31. *King Oedipus*, 477.

32. Olivier, 144.

33. Kenneth Tynan, *He that Plays the King* (London: Longmans, Green, 1950), 46.

34. Fiona Macintosh, "Tragedy in Performance: Nineteenth- and Twentieth-Century Productions," in ed. P. E. Easterling, *The Cambridge Companion to Greek Tragedy* (Cambridge: Cambridge University Press, 1997), 309.

35. A. W. *New Theatre* (October 1945).

36. Philip Page, *Truth* (26 October 1945); *Sunday Graphic* (25 October 1945); *Tribune* (9 November 1945); *Time and Tide* (27 October 1945).

37. Williamson, *Old Vic Drama*, 190.

38. Tynan, 47.

39. Brown, *The Observer*.

40. Ibid.

41. Darlington, *Daily Telegraph*.

42. *Time and Tide* (27 October 1945); *Birmingham Post* (21 October 1945); A. W., *New Theatre* (undated).

43. Beverly Baxter, *Evening Standard* (21 October 1945).

44. Michel Saint-Denis, letter to Jacques Copeau, 22 October 1945.

45. Martin Esslin, telephone interview, 24 February 1998.

46. Michel Saint-Denis, BBC interview, January 1960.

47. Quoted in Charles Railsback, "Michel Saint-Denis and the Organic Theatre," Ph.D. dissertation, Indiana University (1996), 111.

48. Dwora Gilula, "The First Greek Drama on the Hebrew Stage: Tyrone Guthrie's *Oedipus Rex* at the Habima," in *Theatre Research International*, vol. 13, no. 2 (summer 1988): 142.

◆ chapter nine ◆

Triumph and Disaster: The Old Vic Theatre Centre

T HE CHRONICLE OF THE OLD VIC THEATRE CENTRE is composed of inter-twining narratives: the rise and fall of Saint-Denis's reformist program, and the machinations of the Old Vic's Board of Governors to transform the company into the National Theatre. It involves differing visions, finances, missed opportunities, rivalries. The complexities make it difficult to tease out the separate strands; even Saint-Denis—the major player—never fully understood the chain of circumstances.[1]

Even as he began directing *Oedipus*, Olivier, Richardson, and Burrell had given their support for the creation of a drama center conceived and headed by Saint-Denis. During the preliminary stages Saint-Denis must have deemed the center the most risk-free enterprise he had ever undertaken. Here was an opportunity to develop a school and company on the back of an established institution, whose reputation had been enhanced by the triumvirate's first two brilliant seasons. Given the postwar optimism and available government funding, the Old Vic's expansion seemed inevitable. What Saint-Denis did not suspect was how deeply imbedded in cultural politics that expansion was to prove.

In June of 1945 Olivier submitted Saint-Denis's proposal for the Old Vic Theatre Centre to the Board of Governors with the proviso that they respond within a month, a stipulation they did not honor. If the project were rejected Saint-Denis would have to find another means of earning his livelihood. (His financial commitments included the support of his two remaining children.) While waiting, he directed *Oedipus*, then returned to France accompanied by Suria Magito, whom he had grown close to personally and professionally. In January, on the anniversary of his son Jérôme's death Saint-Denis suffered a severe stroke, the first of a series that would eventually kill him in 1971.[2] His speech was impaired and his right side paralyzed, but after six months' rest he apparently fully recovered. During Saint-Denis's recuperation George Devine and his wife Sophia Harris joined him in France to assist in planning the Centre.[3] At approximately the same time, the Board gave the Centre the go-ahead, appointing Saint-Denis as general director with responsibility for its overall policies.

Notwithstanding their approval, the governors, engrossed in stratagems to make the Vic the national theatre, did not grasp the plan's ramifications. Theoretically, while under the wing of the parent organization, the Old Vic Theatre Centre would operate as an independent entity. The Centre had a measure of fiscal autonomy—it received direct government funding—but was responsible to the Board, an arrangement that would destroy it. Neither Saint-Denis nor his associates appreciated until too late the danger the national theatre posed to their Centre.

Because the Old Vic Theatre Centre was a more complex operation than the London Theatre Studio (LTS), Saint-Denis engaged Glen Byam Shaw, whom he had directed in several productions, as the school's director. While Byam Shaw and Devine played pivotal roles, Saint-Denis was the Centre's undisputed authority. The Centre was conceived as a three-tiered structure that Saint-Denis fondly called "the wedding cake": the bottom layer was the drama school run by Byam Shaw; at mid-level, a theatre aimed at a youthful audience (the Young Vic) headed by Devine in association with Suria Magito; and the crown, the top tier, was Saint-Denis's experimental theatre.[4]

Saint-Denis conceptualized the Young Vic with Suria Magito, who had trained in Russia where there is a children's theatre tradition and spent the war directing young people's theatre. The Young Vic, directed at youth, suited the Centre's ladder system by providing professional experience for the school's most talented graduates as they climbed towards its pinnacle, the experimental theatre. For Saint-Denis, the experimental theatre was the organization's most significant component, his laboratory whose research would be tested before the public. Its purpose was to develop a group of professionals capable of reinvigorating the theatre through the creation of experimental plays, innovative production techniques, and new stage architecture.

The Centre benefited from newly established government subventions for students, especially veterans who received special consideration. A few American students attended the school, some on the G.I. Bill, others on scholarships from private American foundations. The most important funding agency was the Arts Council (formerly CEMA), which subsidized the Centre directly in the amount of £9,500 per annum for two years. This limitation hindered long-term planning, effectively preventing the school from instituting a three-year program. With approximately 60 percent of its students receiving financial aid, the Old Vic School could be more selective than LTS. Scholarships also allowed underprivileged students to attend, fulfilling one of Saint-Denis's ambitions. The school prided itself on its atypical student body; good-looking would-be actors were, for the most part, conspicuously absent, so much so that the quintessential student experienced reverse prejudice. A member of Group 1 recalls: "People who apparently had everything going for them were dismissed as not very interesting."[5]

As a result of financial aid, Saint-Denis's enhanced reputation, and favorable publicity, four hundred applicants vied for forty places in 1946. Another thirty were selected for the one-year technical-production course. Saint-Denis would have preferred to limit acceptances to twenty acting and fifteen technical students, but budgetary considerations made this impossible.[6] The school's inauguration, delayed because of Byam Shaw's directing commitments, was held in January of 1947 in the bomb-damaged, almost roofless Old Vic. Seated on the stage—the auditorium was unusable—students, faculty, and dignitaries shivered in their winter coats throughout the ceremonies. Among the dignitaries was Laurence Olivier, who greeted the students with an inspirational speech aimed primarily at the young actors.

In spite of the celebratory atmosphere surrounding the opening, Group 1 encountered difficult circumstances. The first term was held in the unheated Froebel Educational Institute at Barons Court lent by the Sadler's Wells Ballet School. Following Saint-Denis's request, the Board of Governors transferred the school to the Old Vic theatre. Planning to make the renovated building the Centre's headquarters, Saint-Denis engaged the French architect Pierre Sonrel to collaborate on the design. However, initial funding provided barely enough money for such minimal repairs as covering the gaping hole in the roof with a tarpaulin. Consequently, only the school was housed there; the Young Vic (once formed) toured, and the experimental theatre was deferred. A graver difficulty for the students was their truncated course work. Since Group 1 started in January, they had to complete their two years' work in five trimesters rather than six. "We were continually aware," says Edgar Wreford, "that we were fighting against the clock. We were working twenty-six hours in twenty-four and feared we would not be able to do it."[7]

Fear of failure was endemic during their first year, beginning with the students' initiatory exercise, the "test play," one of Saint-Denis's curricular additions. It consisted of presenting a Shakespearean play for the faculty before their training had really begun. For several weeks they rehearsed *Antony and Cleopatra* under the eye of Byam Shaw, who had just directed the same play with Edith Evans at the Piccadilly Theatre. They were given little tutelage, since the faculty wished to evaluate "the student's shortcomings."[8] The pupils' weaknesses and talents were immediately obvious giving, the staff the opportunity to develop individualized plans of action. To the end of his teaching days Saint-Denis remained fond of the procedure as a means of assessing new students, but even he admitted that "it was like throwing someone into deep water to make him discover what he can do to help keep himself afloat."[9]

Since the school still had no performance space, on the day of their show the intimidated students were brought to the Piccadilly Theatre where they performed on the set of Byam Shaw's production. Fifty years later, Lesley Retey remembered her feelings clearly: "They shoved us onstage—it was just terrifying. I had this huge voice which had won all the elocution festivals in England. But on the Piccadilly stage no one could hear me."[10] A critique followed in which Saint-Denis explained that they were all engaged in a perpetual search to find "the truth about the theatre, acting, and the meaning of a play."[11] He cautioned against working for "results," reiterating that the process was all important. In a key metaphor used at the school, the students had "entered the tunnel." Saint-Denis characterized the training as a journey into the unknown from which, it was hoped, they would emerge into the light. After the *Antony and Cleopatra* experience, students *knew* they were in the dark, unsure of their direction. Under the pressure of those early weeks, students worried that they were being weeded out, especially as the school's brochure stated that the first term was probationary. Three students did not return at the term's end, validating suspicions that the "test play" was indeed a test.

Criticism was a fundamental part of their education; evaluations attended by the whole class and faculty were held at regular intervals. Students found it a brutal ordeal. They awaited their turn, often for hours, as critiques could last an entire day. The order of presentation reflected the organizational hierarchy. Saint-Denis was the last to speak and his word carried enormous authority. His perceptiveness could be very helpful, but sometimes emotionally devastating.

It was part of the process of stripping everybody down psychologically and then rebuilding them. This was the principal reason for preferring young students. Those who profited from the experience emerged very different, "greatly enlarged."[12] In keeping with a somewhat therapeutic function, the staff assumed that they could intervene in the students' personal lives if it meant improving their work. Norman Ayrton recalls Saint-Denis breaking up relationships he considered unproductive.[13] One of the charges brought against the school was that it meddled in psychoanalysis. Paradoxically, years later Saint-Denis leveled the same complaint against the use of the Method in the United States.

The school strove for an organic training where all aspects of the instruction fed into one another, with the ultimate goal of creating the complete artist. Some felt Saint-Denis was ruthless in the service of that goal. His standards were so high that not infrequently students felt paralyzed by them. Although Michel taught less than at LTS, his was the dominating presence. George Devine, Glen Byam Shaw, and Saint-Denis were referred to as "the three boys" to distinguish them from the triumvirate managing the Old Vic. But, as Wreford asserts, "that was a kind of familiarity which meant the two boys and Michel. No one really thought Michel was one of the boys."[14] Norman Ayrton recalls the awe Saint-Denis inspired. Upon entering the school students would ask, "Is God in today?"[15] Nonetheless, Ayrton, who became director of LAMDA (London Academy of Music and Dramatic Art), deplores the lack of that old-fashioned discipline in today's theatre. As evidence of Saint-Denis's peculiar combination of exacting standards and hypnotic charm, former students are fond of citing his remark to Gielgud at the closing performance of *Noah*: "At last you are beginning to find the way to play the first act." Gielgud accepted the statement without rancor for "by that time I had such a respect and admiration for the ideal for which he never ceases to strive in his work that I was encouraged rather than depressed by his remark."[16]

The work was demanding, the discipline strict, but most of the students would agree with Chattie Salaman's assessment of the Saint-Denis training: "I knew it was going to be the most exciting time of my whole life and it bloody well was."[17] Students and faculty alike considered themselves a part of a brave new experiment taking place in the legendary playhouse. In the words of Lee Montague of Group 1: "From the very beginning we lived and breathed the real live theatre. We rehearsed on the stage of the theatre, had history of drama lectures in the dress-circle bar, learnt about makeup in the dressing-rooms, discussed stage management in the corridors."[18] In the six years of its existence, the Old Vic school became the foremost theatre school in the Western world. And throughout that period, it continued to grow and change.

One of Saint-Denis's innovations was the directing program, the first in England, where directing was still a rather haphazard craft. It is noteworthy that Saint-Denis's model is followed—whether consciously or not—in most professional directing programs today. At the end of the stage-management course approximately five students were invited to continue. The additional year or two concentrated on creativity in contrast to the prior focus on technique. Even more than the other disciplines, the program emphasized synthesis and the relationship of the arts. Directing students acquired a thorough grounding in the visual arts to build a knowledge of color, composition, and style, which would help them develop a personal directorial approach. They worked closely with the design students with whom they were paired. Together, they took theoretical classes in acting, production, architecture, and design, plus Saint-Denis's seminars. For most practical classes they were separated. Directors had intensive training in acting, improvisation, movement, and voice to learn about the actor's work from the inside out. During the first term, directing students observed acting classes and rehearsals; during the second, they functioned as assistant directors of the school shows. Design students, by contrast, were responsible for designing entire shows while being supervised by advisers. In their weekly seminar the young directors studied three plays of contrasting styles, eventually joining with the design students to prepare production books. They did not work with live bodies on their own until after the school shows, when they directed one-act plays or scenes from full-length ones.

The Centre was closely watched by the theatre world and the government agencies funding it. Due to everyone's hyper-awareness of being part of an experiment that had a lot riding on its outcome, the students felt an exceptional need to succeed. The specter of the national theatre hovered close by. It was in this emotional climate that the first end-of-term show was produced. As at LTS, it was a varied program displaying as many aspects of the training as possible. Generally, the three directors divided the productions among themselves; plays they were unable to undertake because of time constraints were parceled out to the staff. Devine directed comedies; Byam Shaw, Shakespearean productions; and Saint-Denis, modern dramas. After receiving adverse notices for his 1930s Renaissance productions, Saint-Denis's only English foray into Shakespeare occurred following Byam Shaw's departure when Saint-Denis mounted *King John*.

Wanting to develop a collaborative process between emerging writers and his actors-in-training, Saint-Denis brought in James Forsyth, anticipating that he would replicate Obey's role in the Quinze.[19] Forsyth came to Saint-Denis's attention when the dramatist sent him his play, *The Bronze Horse*. Although written in prose, Forsyth's dramas contained the quality Saint-Denis called "realistic poetry": a lyricism that "reached at times the rhythmical beat of verse," while "penetrating and enhancing reality."[20] After productive sessions with the improvisation classes devising scenarios from their explorations, Forsyth was requested to write a script for the school show. *Penthesilea* had all of the ingredients for a Suria Magito work: it was drawn from myth, was heavily movement-based and dependent on choral work. She sketched out the original treatment in movement before giving it to Forsyth. They collaborated with the composer and designer.

Two distinct programs made up the inaugural show: the first, acts from *The Winter's Tale*, *Macbeth*, and *The Merchant of Venice*, staged by Byam Shaw; a condensed version of *Our Town* directed by Saint-Denis; and *A Musical Item*, songs arranged and conducted by Jani Strasser. The second included a cutting of *The Plain Dealer* directed by Pierre Lefèvre, Chekhov's *The Wedding* mounted by George Devine, and Magito's *Penthesilea*.

As still inexperienced directors, Lefèvre and Suria Magito were under close scrutiny by the "three boys." Lefèvre encountered difficulty with the Restoration comedy, which the cast deemed beyond their capacity. Several days before opening "the three boys came in and had an absolute fit. Michel told us it was dreadful."[21] A pattern was established whereby at a certain point, one or more of the trio would come to rehearsal, criticize the proceedings, and then take over—a demoralizing experience for director and cast. From the students' perspective, Saint-Denis, the final arbiter, seemed unconcerned about sparing people's feelings.

The spotlight was undoubtedly focused on the Centre's opening night of the school show, May 30, 1948. Repairs made it possible to obtain permission to present it at the Old Vic Theatre. Three hundred temporary seats were installed for the first performance there in eight years. It was a stressful occasion for the performers because the audience included critics, directors, producers, and leading actors such as Peggy Ashcroft, Edith Evans, and Ralph Richardson.

Notices were mostly favorable; the directors were complimented on "the excellence of staging, production, decor, and general high standard of performance."[22] As expected, Lefèvre's Restoration production was problematic; the *Times* reviewer found the performance "ragged in timing," but praised it for being "well set and well dressed." The same critic relished "the good fun" in the Chekhov farce.[23] Saint-Denis's *Our Town* was "deeply moving."[24] Group 1 participants had divergent perceptions, depending on which play they had performed in. The most negative were the actors who took part in *Penthesilea*, which they judged trite and pretentious.[25]

It is unclear whether the faculty agreed with the students' evaluation of *Penthesilea*. While the experiment was never repeated, George Devine, in a radio interview, described the production as a model of teamwork.[26] To the students' surprise, *Penthesilea* aroused the greatest public interest. The play was lauded, however, for its choreography and ensemble, not its script. Typical of the comments was Arnold Haskell's, the director of the Sadler's Wells Ballet School: "What impressed me most was the way the pupils moved on the stage. . . . I will remember the corps of Amazons for a long time."[27]

Some of the critics used their reviews to evaluate the work and the spirit of the school as a whole:

> For sheer promise, this is the most exciting group of students I have yet seen. They are a varied group of individuals, yet all seemed to have learned one important thing in common—the right approach to acting. There was no evidence of technique for technique's sake, or subordination of one aspect of the production for another. . . . The result was a fusion of sincerity and technique, which led to some wonderful moments.[28]

Even as the directors looked back on a fruitful year, the Centre had begun sliding toward its collapse. Its demise had nothing to do with the quality of its work, which remained high throughout its difficulties. The Centre's existence had been predicated on the profit-making ability of the company and the support of the management, especially Laurence Olivier. However, after two dazzling seasons, Richardson and Olivier, the Vic's money-makers, began acting in film and abroad. The artistic rewards of the Vic were satisfying but exacted financial sacrifice on Richardson and Olivier. In consequence, the directors, who had an informal twelve-year mandate, devised a schedule whereby the two stars would give half their time to the Vic. In their absence, John Burrell would take sole charge in London. Olivier and Richardson remained committed to the Vic and, like the governors, anticipated its metamorphosis. At a Board meeting in 1947, in a move to make the Old Vic the strongest contender for the national theatre,

Olivier and Richardson had been charged with forming a permanent company of qualified actors. Later, as Olivier enthused about the future, the more skeptical Richardson demurred. He pointed out that their vision of the national theatre and that of the governors diverged, and that the theatrical profession was not represented on the Board: "They're not going to stand for a couple of actors bossing the place around any more. . . . We shall be out, old cocky."[29]

Their dismissal took place sooner than Richardson anticipated. The following season the two stars went abroad, Richardson to Hollywood, Olivier, by request of the British Council, to tour Australia with the Old Vic. Without them, the 1947–48 season was lackluster and the theatre lost money. A lot of criticism was aimed at the unfortunate John Burrell, caught in a situation not of his own making. The Board, pushed by its new chairman, Lord Esher (a harsh critic of Saint-Denis), determined not to renew Olivier, Richardson, and Burrell's contract. Esher ousted all three while the most powerful of them were overseas. He may have been prompted by Tyrone Guthrie, whose biographer suggests that Guthrie, still smarting over the Saint-Denis/Olivier *Oedipus*, was agitating in the wings for their removal.[30]

Another managerial configuration was formed: Llewellyn Rees was appointed administrator of the entire Old Vic Theatre organization, and Hugh Hunt was made the artistic director of the company. The two men were part of an old-boy's network from which Saint-Denis was excluded by virtue of his nationality and background. Rees, an arts administrator, had close ties to Lord Esher. He had worked for the Arts Council, where Esher was on the Executive Board, and had served on the Old Vic Board of Governors. In what appears to be a self-serving recommendation, Rees proposed establishing the powerful and long-term position of administrator, emphasizing that a crucial aspect of the job would be "to restore the dwindling prestige of the company."[31] Certainly, there was speculation that he had manipulated the situation to gain the appointment.[32] Saint-Denis and his associates were to find that Rees's interest was the bottom line. Hunt, who had been the first artistic director of the Bristol Old Vic, was essentially promoted. Although Hunt was no hack, he was unquestionably more malleable from the governors' point of view than either Richardson or Olivier. He also was driven by ambition and coveted the directorship of the National.[33] The stage was set for a confrontation between "the three boys" and the new administration.

There are two versions of what happened next, Charles Landstone's and Byam Shaw's. According to Landstone, who was a confidant of Rees and Hunt, the initial threat to the Centre's existence came from Hunt who believed that the Vic would strengthen its candidacy if it gave up its performance space at the New and returned to the Waterloo Road theatre. He argued that the company could only develop its identity in its own home. Fully aware the playhouse had been promised to the Centre, Hunt turned the problem over to Rees, remarking "that's Llewellyn's worry. He will have to solve that one."[34] The governors concurred with the cost-saving measure; a grant from the Arts Council to restore the playhouse facilitated their decision. In Byam Shaw's version, it was he who suggested that the Company be brought back to the Old Vic Theatre, since there were insufficient funds for the theatre's remodeling.[35] He acted under the assumption that money would be easier to raise if the Centre and the company shared the theatre. According to Byam Shaw, Hunt, Rees, and the governors were all in agreement with the plan.

It was decided to amalgamate the Old Vic Centre and the company. The administration was top-heavy with Saint-Denis, Devine, Byam Shaw, and Hugh Hunt responsible in principle for the Centre and the theatre, all of them reporting to Rees. This arrangement raised anxiety among "the three boys," although all the repercussions were not immediately evident. As a memorandum from George Devine attests, they feared that "the Theatre Company coming to the Old Vic will make them redundant before they even had a chance to show their full worth."[36] As if to confirm their fears, a report in the *Times* unwittingly predicted the Centre's collapse:

> The present directors, Mr. Hugh Hunt, director of the Old Vic Theatre Company, Mr. George Devine, who is in charge of the Young Vic Theatre Company, Mr. Glen Byam Shaw, who runs the school, and M. Michel Saint-Denis, will work as a joint directorate, each director remaining, as at present, responsible to the governors for his own department.[37]

It is striking that even at this juncture, Saint-Denis's experimental theatre is not mentioned. He is for all practical purposes superfluous, the only director without a department. Without the experimental theatre, the thrust of the Centre was lost.

Still, Saint-Denis, Devine, and Byam Shaw determined to try to make the arrangement work. One consequence was that they began directing for the company. Likewise, Saint-Denis saw a chance to realize a third-year training scheme through an apprentice system that would promote the most promising graduates. Those selected would spend an additional year attached to the company playing small parts or appearing in the ensemble. John Blatchley and Pierre Lefèvre were assigned to supervise their training. However, when the third-year students made their debut in Saint-Denis's production of *Electra*, Actors' Equity objected. The students were neither Equity members nor receiving the minimum salary. Notable was Llewellyn Rees's attempt to nullify the project. To resolve the dispute, he advised eliminating students in speaking roles in future productions. A compromise was reached that limited the students' participation to one year as well as the number of appearances. In lieu of salary, they would receive grants from the Ministry of Education.[38]

The most profound disruption to the Centre's plans was the school's move to Dulwich, theoretically temporary, so that the remodeling could take place. When the Centre amalgamated with the Old Vic Company, the school lost its financial independence and incurred higher costs, partly because of its dislocation. Its deficit was used against it at a later date.[39]

During this period Saint-Denis and Sonrel forged ahead with the remodeling, another of the ironies in Michel's life. The renovation of the Old Vic Theatre had been an integral part of his concept for the Centre. Saint-Denis believed that the British theatre was in a state of transition. Part of the Centre's mission was to hasten the birth of new forms. Fundamental to this birth was a new and adaptable theatre architecture. Now he found himself renovating the theatre for another company whose needs differed. Moreover, the design was compromised because of funding cuts. Saint-Denis was trying to bridge the gap between audience and performers. But working within his budget and in a historical space restricted the changes he could make. He kept the proscenium arch but extended the forestage, which militated against naturalism and allowed the action to be brought closer to the spectators. This forestage was flexible—a hydraulic elevator allowed it to be lowered so that for realistic or naturalistic plays a box set could be used. The result was controversial in some quarters; doubtless, any modification would have been greeted with suspicion. Peter Newington, Sonrel's assistant, felt that "there was an awful lot of unnecessary fuss over the change. Michel was trying, quite rightly, to conjoin the Victorian Old Vic with a more flexible modern concept of the use of the stage."[40] Tyrone Guthrie, one of its critics, wrote in his 1959 autobiography:

> The result looks handsome and dignified but bears no stylistic relation to the architecture of the auditorium; and more serious, it makes a number of seats unsaleable because from them actors on the forestage cannot be seen. It also fails to solve the main problem because behind this dignified forestage there remains a proscenium arch; and inside that arch—here's the rub—is a perfectly conventional stage, framed by the arch which the whole audiences faces, inside which they have been conditioned to expect "a picture." So long as that picture remains, some kind of a picture has to be put inside it.[41]

Guthrie's comments were not groundless. The original design called for a major reconfiguration of the auditorium that had to be curtailed because of the budgetary restraints. The outcome was poor sight lines in certain sections of the house. Nevertheless, upon viewing the refurbished Old Vic, theatre critics were "favorable, even enthusiastic."[42] Particularly gratifying to Saint-Denis and Sonrel was the *Architects' Journal*'s appraisal, which cited the design as "the most significant innovation in the history of the British theatre for the last fifty years."[43] The article counters Guthrie's argument, stating that the stage "freed producer and author from the limitations of the picture frame."[44] An unexpected champion was Lord Esher, who esteemed the reconstruction "a happy blending of the old and new."[45]

Saint-Denis had chosen *Electra* (March 1951), starring Peggy Ashcroft, as his first vehicle to display the remodeled stage. He was delighted to return to Sophocles with an actress of Ashcroft's distinction and talent. Although Ashcroft had never essayed the Greeks, she had been impressed by Saint-Denis's production of *Electra* at LTS, "thrilled by a remarkable girl playing Electra," and was eager to try her hand at the part.[46] And the new Old Vic, his own instrument, provided directorial opportunities unavailable five years earlier when Saint-Denis mounted *Oedipus* on a proscenium stage. Because of the Vic's expanded apron, he could explore staging traditions of ancient Greece: the chorus of Argive women played on the forestage, which functioned similarly to the orchestra of Greek theatre, the circular space on which the chorus sang and danced. The character–chorus relationship was further reconfigured by the addition of a raised stage behind the chorus' playing area on which the actors performed. Here also, Saint-Denis looked to the ancient Greek theatre, where scholars believe such a platform was used. The narrow, raised stage, four feet high, served to formalize the production, but perhaps at the expense of distancing the audience emotionally, contrary to his intention. The fifth-century Athenian chorus played a vital theatrical role through its dancing, singing, and chanting. Placing the chorus in the foreground in a modern production increases its prominence in a theatrical culture where audiences find characters more interesting. It, therefore, became incumbent upon Saint-Denis to find twentieth-century counterparts in terms of movement, staging, and sound that would create comparable theatricality and meaning for his audience.

As with *Oedipus*, Saint-Denis experimented with techniques that would respect the tragic tradition while simultaneously creating a production that would "speak" to contemporary audiences. Accordingly, he again chose a designer, Barbara Hepworth, from the world of abstract art. While the noted sculptor lacked any theatre experience, within her art she found a meeting ground between modernism and classicism, surely a determinant in Saint-Denis's decision. Although Hepworth's credentials were indisputably abstract, critics frequently compared her sculptures to classical works because of their serene majesty. Stark and innovative for its time, Hepworth's set was completely white except for a black central door on the raised stage. No attempt was made to create a realistic facade; massive architectural blocks and tall pillars suggested the palace. The only other set piece was an angular, twisted wire sculpture at stage right symbolizing Apollo. This being Hepworth's first stage production, Margaret Harris translated the designs into a theatrically realizable form. Harris's canvas rendition, with its lack of weight and texture, shocked the sculptor, who had envisioned a stone set.

Difficulties surfaced early in the rehearsal period. Their source was Ashcroft's inability to reach the emotional heights Saint-Denis (and possibly the role) demanded. It is a notoriously tricky part, a tragedy in which the protagonist embodies the spirit of vengeance. Apart from the prologue, Electra is onstage throughout, but even in this first scene her presence is felt as the audience and other characters hear her lamentation. The role begins at an emotional peak and remains there. Electra exists at the extreme edge: she is in a constant state of rage, grief, and frustration, unyielding in her determination to exact retribution for her father's murder. Yet circumstances force her to be passive, to await her brother Orestes's return so that he will destroy their mother Clytemnestra and stepfather Aegisthus. Adding to the difficulties, the character's obsessiveness and capacity for cruelty render her unsympathetic despite her victimization by her mother and stepfather.

Rehearsals became a struggle, with Saint-Denis pushing his actress to the point of nervous collapse. Ashcroft, who had "always been fully accepting of Michel as a director," strove to fulfill his vision.[47] Presumably, Saint-Denis was convinced that Ashcroft had the resources to withstand his driving her. After all, this was the fifth production in which they had worked together. However, halfway through the rehearsal period while struggling with the recognition scene, she lost control, screaming hysterically, and was taken to a clinic where she remained for a week.[48]

Saint-Denis, understandably upset, met with his troubled actors the follow-ing day to analyze the situation. He might have been forewarned, since a paral-lel incident had occurred during the LTS production. Always sure of what he wanted, Saint-Denis had forced his young student beyond her capabilities. Chattie Salaman, then a student at LTS, remembers: "She was a frail girl. Michel admired her very much as an actress, but he had this idea of enormous strength and volume and was trying to reach this image. And she couldn't do that; she was too inexperienced. But he kept compelling her. Finally, she collapsed."[49] Ashcroft, of course, was no novice but an accomplished actress of proven versa-tility. Still, Saint-Denis was noted for breaking down actors' defenses in order to probe a character's psyche. That he realized he pushed too hard is apparent in his comment that Ashcroft was dealing with "atavistic memories."[50] Painful feelings that she did not want to explore may account for part of the problem, but she might also have been incapable of expressing rage of the kind and size Saint-Denis envisaged. And much as she trusted Saint-Denis's artistic vision, she had a different conception of Electra. All these factors could have prevented her from fully realizing the role.

Electra did not replicate *Oedipus*'s success. While its critical reception was generally favorable, *Electra* failed to generate the same excitement. The question arises: Why did concepts that operated so successfully in *Oedipus* not produce a similar effect in *Electra*? I would postulate that despite *Oedipus*'s triumph, Greek tragedy had yet to be accepted by the British. The political climate had changed since *Oedipus*, the sufferings of the war were receding into the background, and *Electra* was to many a study in irrelevant misery. Not atypical was Kenneth Hur-ren's reaction: "I fear it does not altogether escape that hint of the ridiculous which impinges any chronicle of unrelieved horror and abnormality in these days when the mind tends to reject as implausible events which are beyond contemporary experience."[51] Second, the fusion of classicism and modernism in *Electra* was more startling, particularly in the use of the forestage as a Greek orchestra in conjunction with Hepworth's set. In an era in which British stage design remained representational, her abstractions, most notably Apollo, incurred critical mockery. Because of the forestage, Saint-Denis created more elaborate choreography for the chorus than in *Oedipus*. It participated in the action, responding to and portraying the emotions enacted by the principals above it. During the choral odes, Saint-Denis invoked a classical mood through his formal imagery as in this example: "Miss Ashcroft achieves a moving picture of grief personified as she stands in static relief against the sun-swept wall of the palace."[52] Dissonant music by Henry Boys, orchestrated for percussion and woodwinds, accompanied the odes and some of the characters' speeches. However, those critics for whom the chorus was "an eternal problem" found Saint-Denis's aesthetic choices embarrassing and ludicrous.[53]

Reaction was divided concerning Ashcroft's Electra; her detractors felt she was miscast, since "her great talent [lay] in the lyrical and sweetly sad."[54] Those who held this opinion considered her slight stature, physical delicacy, and mellifluous voice impediments that made it impossible for her to master the character of Electra. "Electralette" was one critic's harsh judgment.[55] But even those who admired her performance appeared surprised that she "turned it into one of her finest achievements," given "her radiant charm" and "fascinating gentleness."[56] The human quality for which Olivier was applauded, in Ashcroft's case was regarded as a substitute for heroic attributes: "If Peggy Ashcroft is a very human Electra, Sophocles depicted not just an ethical problem but a human being confronted with such. It can be said that she convinces in what must be, for her, a grueling hour-and-a-half's performance."[57]

With reviews as our only evidence, it is difficult to assess Ashcroft's performance. It should be pointed out that, in general, women express rage differently from men; that female roles calling for extended rage are rare; that consequently, there were few models; and that male critics were bringing masculine standards to bear. At least two items seem to corroborate this latter view: the critique "perhaps it still needs a man to give full weight to the women of Greek tragedy," as well as Ashcroft's interview with *Stage* in which she defended her portrayal.[58] Her Electra was not an archetypal figure of power, but "the embodiment of a strong spirit in a body broken by physical and spiritual suffering," a concept she believed to be supported by the text and Saint-Denis's production.[59] If indeed Saint-Denis had reached that conclusion, then his original vision evolved or was compromised over the rehearsal period to meet Ashcroft's.

As far as Saint-Denis's work was concerned—chorus apart—critical reaction was on the whole laudatory. Notices were similar to those he had received for

Oedipus: praise for his composition, build, pacing, and austere style. "The atmosphere of doom and vengeance were magnificently conveyed by Michel Saint-Denis's production."[60] "The production by Michel Saint-Denis develops an exciting intensity."[61] "Saint-Denis, the producer, has obviously aimed at classical simplicity of style, and has achieved it. This tragedy mounts uninterruptedly, propelled by acting which, without exception, is keen and taut with finely restrained emotion."[62] T. C. Worsley was impressed by the integration of the dignified style into every aspect of production: large and simple gestures, speech that lay "well beyond naturalism, but was never pseudo-poetical."[63] The principal exception was Kenneth Tynan, who found the production "slow and curiously unrhythmical."[64]

That *Electra* did not achieve the success of *Oedipus* cut deep for Saint-Denis. Had it done so, he might have been in a stronger position to defend the Old Vic Theatre Centre. Instead, "there was no longer a unity of purpose inside the organization."[65] Following the amalgamation, tensions fed by competing ambitions grew into antagonisms. Llewellyn Rees, focused on promoting his own career, had neither the desire nor the ability to provide the leadership to make the directorship function. Exploiting his position, he undermined the Centre in numerous ways. He became the liaison for the Old Vic at Board meetings. Cut off from contact with the governors, the Centre trio had to depend on Rees to negotiate for them with the Board. Correspondingly, Saint-Denis, Devine, Byam Shaw, and Hunt excluded Rees from their own meetings covering artistic policy.

Perhaps in retaliation, perhaps to demonstrate his theatrical expertise, Rees began observing classes at the school. The directors, faculty, and students regarded him as a spy. Confirming their suspicions, Rees reported to the governors that "students in the improvisation class did nothing but spend the morning on the floor pretending to be animals."[66] Such comments fueled the governors'—in particular Lord Esher's—distrust of the school's methods, raising questions about the training's value in developing classical actors. Saint-Denis, Devine, and Byam Shaw expended considerable effort in vainly countering these allegations.

The intrigue became more complicated when Hugh Hunt made a bid for power, informing his co-directors that he would have authority over them. Lord Esher thwarted Hunt's attempt when, a week later, he denied having made the offer. Cooperation between the "three boys" and Hunt was now impossible. In April, just three months before the king of England was to lay the foundation stone of the national theatre, the situation reached a climax. Rees persuaded the governors to terminate the directorship, further separating the Centre from the company. Hunt's contract was due to expire the following year; Rees and Esher suggested Byam Shaw fill his position for a season.[67] Further reductions seemed probable, Saint-Denis being most at risk for elimination. Stoking their fears was Rees's remark that "in the event of real financial stringency, it might be hard to justify Saint-Denis's position as 'Overlord.'"[68]

Convinced that the Centre was in jeopardy, the trio sent an ultimatum to Lord Esher on April 23: either the governors find a solution to the problems posed by Rees's interference into artistic decisions or they would resign. Contrary to their hopes, Esher accepted their resignations. Loyally, the faculty members tendered their resignations in a joint letter.

Saint-Denis, Byam Shaw, and Devine thought that if they could rouse public opinion they might prevail. Therefore they wanted to release their version of the staff's resignation before the other side could get to the press. Jeremy Geidt, an acting teacher, delivered the letter of resignation to the Old Vic and broke the news to the press. Geidt remembers skulking into the theatre, depositing the document on the administrator's desk and racing out the stage door. The next stop was Fleet Street, then back to the school in Dulwich where he was greeted by an ebullient Michel, delighted to have won that round.[69]

And indeed he had, but only for the moment. Public opinion was now firmly on the side of the Centre; letters and statements published by the press favored its retention. Llewellyn Rees, incapable of coping with the situation, offered a feeble explanation: "There is no row at all. It is just that the directors have a policy and the governors another. What their different policies are, in clear terms, it is impossible for me to say. The differences are over artistic matters."[70] To the governors' chagrin, press coverage continued for weeks. Letters of support continued to pour into the newspapers, accusing the governors and the Old Vic's administration of having acted irresponsibly. Following a mass meeting the students wrote to Llewellyn Rees, demanding the reasons for the resignations. Having waited in vain for a response, they sent a letter of protest to the *Times*. Actors' Equity urged the Minister of Education to appoint an inquiry committee to investigate the Old Vic. The British Drama League entreated the governors and the Arts Council "to resolve the differences so as to maintain the progressive policy created by the three directors."[71]

The governors did not bend. Unfortunately, Saint-Denis and his associates did not help their case by maintaining silence. Saint-Denis's lack of response was not atypical of him. When, during the war, his patriotism was impugned by Radio France, he refused to counterattack because "he hated lies and vulgarity," preferring to let his integrity speak for him.[72] Still refusing to divulge details, Saint-Denis, Byam Shaw, and Devine only answered their attackers once the governors contended that they had quit rather than continue working with Rees. In a press statement, the three protested: "We could not properly accept a negative attitude and absence of disposition to plan and work resolutely for the artistic entity which we had undertaken to create with the approval of governors, including the continuance of the Old Vic School and the Young Vic."[73] The governors had attempted to reduce the issues to a clash of personalities, whereas the problem was the change of policy that occurred after the theatre reopened.

The Old Vic was in turmoil, its reputation damaged, its status as candidate for the national theatre weakened. Needed now was a strong figure who could set it on course again. Hugh Hunt sent Stephen Arlen, the company manager, to persuade Tyrone Guthrie to prevent the theatre from possible collapse. Guthrie agreed, with the proviso that he be granted "power to make wide decisions in respect of future policies."[74] Hugh Hunt remained as administrative director. Saint-Denis, Devine, and Byam Shaw were pleased with the appointment, although they had not been consulted. They believed that the Centre was now saved; the public supported them and their old advocate Guthrie was at the helm. After his appointment, Guthrie took the "three boys" out to dinner and announced he was closing the school. Appalled, Michel asked why and was astounded by the reply, "I don't believe in schools." Michel reminded Guthrie of the financial and moral help he had given to start LTS. Guthrie retorted that he had changed.

Shocked by Guthrie's decision to close the Centre, "one of the most tragic things that has ever happened in our theatre," Peggy Ashcroft met with him.[75] An acrimonious discussion followed in which Guthrie said, "I don't know what you are fussing about. Michel has had more influence than anyone else. So it does not really matter about the school."[76] Unquestionably, Saint-Denis had influence; power is what he lacked. Guthrie offered another explanation to Marius Goring: "Pity. Two sports masters in love with the head. Very unhealthy. Got to be stopped."[77] Whatever the implications of Guthrie's statement, there is no question that with the closure of the school, British theatre incurred a blow. Although the school's influence continues to this day, how might the theatre have been transformed if the Centre had been allowed to flourish? Many would support Peter Duguid's contention that "another three years and we could have revolutionized the theatre."[78]

An outpouring of affection and sympathy for Saint-Denis followed his dismissal. Protests from the public continued even after the press coverage subsided; artists, theatre practitioners, and admirers wrote to him directly. A slew of letters from his staff expressed appreciation for his work and their concern for his future. For Jani Strasser, the years spent teaching at the Old Vic Centre were the most satisfying of his life.[79] Marion Watson was moved to send a sum of money to Michel and Suria for their personal use.[80] In an effort to show how much he meant to them, Saint-Denis's friends and colleagues joined together to buy him a car, his first.[81]

The official reason given for the closure was the debts incurred by the theatre's reconstruction and the need for devoting to the theatre's operation the school's annual subsidy of £4,500. Undeniably, the lack of funds played a significant role. But personal antagonism towards Saint-Denis was also a factor. As we have seen, he inspired strong feelings; in addition to loyal friends and admirers, he had implacable enemies. In an era when chauvinism was more openly acceptable, his nationality was held against him. Saint-Denis's very presence at the Centre aroused suspicion. His colleagues all attest to the prevailing prejudice found among those in power, particularly Lord Esher, who apparently did not trouble to hide his disdain for Saint-Denis. Esher is said to have "dismissed him as a foreigner . . . whose proper place was somewhere else."[82]

For Esher, that place was as far away from the nascent national theatre as possible. Fixated on the national theatre, Esher viewed the Centre as the means through which Saint-Denis could seize control of it. Neither he nor the rest of the Board ever comprehended Saint-Denis's plans to promote theatrical reform through experimentation. Nor did they have the imagination to envisage a role for the Centre within the national theatre. Repeatedly, Saint-Denis's colleagues assert that "he was never interested in leading the national theatre company," a company that ultimately did not materialize until 1963.[83] For years Saint-Denis considered Lord Esher the most fully culpable, but modified his opinion, having decided that "the real villains were Hugh Hunt and Llewellyn Rees."[84] In all probability the complete story will never be told. Most of the principal figures are dead; those who remain played a secondary role and were not privy to all that was happening at the time.

Saint-Denis, Devine, and Byam Shaw agreed to continue until their last group finished—a matter of three terms. George Hall, among Saint-Denis's other students, dates "a real thaw in Michel's personality" from this period.[85] Saint-Denis was astonished and touched by his students' loyalty. The students' support succeeded in getting the matter placed before Parliament. In his book on George Devine, Irving Wardle quotes Frank Dunlop, the student leader, as saying that if the directors had put more energy into the fight, the school would have continued.[86] Contrary to Wardle's contention that Saint-Denis "had taken such a battering that he didn't want to fight any more," archival evidence demonstrates that as late as June 1952 he was negotiating with Lord Esher, investigating schemes that might save the school.[87] One was the incorporation of the school into the Shakespeare Memorial Theatre at Stratford. But the obstacles thrown up—particularly the lack of money—made it inevitable that the school would fold.

The trio was drifting apart. Byam Shaw accepted Anthony Quayle's offer to co-direct the Shakespeare Memorial Theatre at Stratford. Saint-Denis replaced Byam Shaw at the school, where he took over much of the teaching. He had offers to direct in the West End, but a career as a free-lance commercial director had little appeal. Rightly or wrongly, Saint-Denis felt betrayed by a country he loved. Before leaving England, he showed the wartime honors bestowed on him to a friend. "They gave me these," he said, weeping, "and then they took away my theatre."[88] He had decided to return to France and, during the last months of the Centre, reestablished connection with Jeanne Laurent, who was in charge of the theatre division in the French Arts Ministry. Michel left England in July of 1952 to take over the directorship of the Centre de l'Est in Alsace as part of the decentralization of French theatre. The tremendous force for change that Saint-

Denis had been for the British theatrical culture would become more evident with the passage of time and the coming to maturity of his pupils and disciples.

A parting note from Guthrie, refusing an invitation to the farewell party in Saint-Denis's honor hosted by the French ambassador, underlined the ambiguity of Guthrie's character. A ready participant in the destruction of Michel's British career, Guthrie expressed his "affectionate good wishes and the sincere hope that we shall not be losing touch with you for more than a very short while. I would simply hate to feel that our recent differences of opinion, and the fact that I felt obliged to take decisions which I knew were not in your personal interest, would stand in the way of a friendship which I, for one, value very much indeed."[89] Years passed and Guthrie made no attempt to contact Saint-Denis, although their careers sometimes ran in parallel directions.[90] Both were instrumental in the establishment of the professional theatre in Canada, and both made important contributions to the American theatre. In founding his theatre in Minneapolis in 1963, Guthrie gave impetus to the burgeoning regional-theatre movement, while Saint-Denis's American school, the Juilliard Drama Division, developed actors capable of playing the diverse repertory of those theatres.

In 1955, George Devine, for whom Michel had been a mentor, friend, and collaborator, took over the Royal Court Theatre where he launched the English Stage Company. Here, he created a playwright's theatre and, in so doing, fulfilled Saint-Denis's dream of revitalizing the theatre through the discovery of new dramatists. The kind of play he found, however, was anathema to Saint-Denis. Within the first few years of its existence the English Stage Company discovered and promoted the socially conscious but often structurally conventional works of John Osborne, John Arden, Arnold Wesker, and Edward Bond. Devine's theatre succeeded in attracting a broader-based audience precisely because of the impact created by playwrights speaking in a new political voice.

Publicly, Michel Saint-Denis praised Devine's company, which had "conquered the press and completely overthrown the old theatre."[91] But privately, he was baffled by Devine's incursion into what he called "the mud of naturalism." He was perhaps more baffled and certainly hurt by Devine's rejection of him. For despite Saint-Denis's unhappiness at Strasbourg, Devine did not request him to participate in what was pointedly called the English Stage Company. Jocelyn Herbert remembers: "George thought about asking him, but he was like a child growing up. He loved Michel, he always did. It was not a question of rejection. It was a question of having to do your own thing. Any child has to leave home."[92] The relationship between the two men had been similar to that of Copeau and Saint-Denis. As Saint-Denis had been driven to find his own identity, so Devine struck out on his own.

NOTES

1. "The Old Vic: A Discussion between Michel Saint-Denis and T. C. Worsley," *New Statesman and Nation* (2 June 1951): 617.

2. Suria Magito Saint-Denis, letter to A. C. Scott, 23 September 1976.

3. Michel Saint-Denis, unpublished letter to Jacques Copeau, 17 April 1946.

4. A similar group, the Young Vic Players, was added to tour areas not traditionally served by theatre companies.

5. Lesley Retey, personal interview, 31 May 1989.

6. Michel Saint-Denis, "Future Planning," 6 November 1947.

7. Edgar Wreford, personal interview, 6 June 1989.

8. Ibid.

9. Michel Saint-Denis, "The Juilliard Bible." This was the informal title given to the documents that form the basis of the Juilliard Drama Division's curriculum.

10. Retey, interview.

11. Wreford, interview.

12. Norman Ayrton, personal interview, 8 June 1989.

13. Ibid.

14. Ibid.

15. Ibid.

16. John Gielgud, *Early Stages* (London: Falcon Press, 1948), 24.

17. Chattie Salaman, personal interview, 8 June 1989.

18. Margaret McCall, *My Drama School* (London: Robson Books, 1978), 150.

19. James Forsyth, personal interview, 30 May 1989.

20. Michel Saint-Denis, "Naturalism in the Theatre," *The Listener* (4 December 1952): 928.

21. Retey, interview.

22. *Illustrated* (26 June 1948): 15.

23. Ibid.

24. Audrey Williamson, *Theatre of Two Decades* (New York: Macmillan, 1951), 176.

25. A. C. Scott, unpublished transcript of an interview with Peter Duguid, 25 November 1976, Bibliothèque de l'Arsenal; Retey, interview.

26. Terry Gomperty, "Interview with George Devine," 10 June 1948.

27. Quoted in Richard V. Romagnoli, "The Young Vics: The Development of a Popular Theatrical Tradition," Ph.D. dissertation, Florida State University (1980), 46.

28. Ted Willis, *Daily Worker* (London) (1 June 1948).

29. John Miller, *Ralph Richardson: The Authorized Biography* (London: Sedgwick & Jackson, 1995), 124–25.

30. Anthony Holden, *Laurence Olivier* (New York: Atheneum, 1998), 239.

31. Charles Landstone, *Off-stage: A Personal Record of the First Twelve Years of State-Sponsored Drama in Great Britain* (London: Elek, 1953), 160.

32. Ibid., 147.

33. Ibid., 163.

34. Ibid.

35. Irving Wardle, *The Theatres of George Devine* (London: Eyre Methuen, 1978), 131. The money originally allotted by the Arts Council was withdrawn.

36. George Devine, "The Old Vic Amalgamation: Notes for Private Circulation amongst Directors" (27 November 1949).

37. "The Old Vic Theatre: Reopening Next Year," *Times* (3 December 1949): 7.

38. Old Vic Report of Meeting with Glen Byam Shaw, Llewellyn Rees, and Gordon Sandison regarding Third-Year Students, 18 January 1950.

39. Old Vic Theatre Centre Budget, Transition period, 1951.

40. Peter Newington, personal interview, 8 June 1989.

41. Tyrone Guthrie, *A Life in the Theatre* (New York: McGraw-Hill, 1959), 207. Saint-Denis responded to Guthrie's criticism in his article, "Chekhov and the Modern Stage" (*Drama Survey* [spring–summer 1963]: 77–81) in which he criticized Guthrie's development of the thrust stage. Acknowledging the effectiveness of the open stage, Saint-Denis did not find it universally appropriate, unlike the more flexible Old Vic stage.

42. Pierre Sonrel, "Michel Saint-Denis and Pierre Sonrel," unpublished essay, quoted in Charles Railsback, "Michel Saint-Denis and the Organic Theatre," Ph.D. dissertation, Indiana University (1996), 73.

43. David F. Cheshire, *The Old Vic Refurbished* (London: The Old Vic Ltd., 1983), 54.

44. "The Old Vic Goes Home," *Architects' Journal* (23 November 1950): 412.

45. Lord Esher, letter to Michel Saint-Denis, 27 November 1950.

46. Peggy Ashcroft, personal interview, 5 June 1989.

47. Ibid.

48. Pierre Lefèvre, personal interview, 12 January 1989. Lefèvre played Pylades in the production.

49. Salaman, interview.

50. Michael Billington, *Peggy Ashcroft* (London: John Murray, 1988), 133.

51. Kenneth A. Hurren, *What's On in London* (23 March 1951).

52. T. C. K., *Birmingham Post* (10 April 1951).

53. Billington, *Peggy Ashcroft*, 133.

54. *Art News and Review* (24 March 1951).

55. D. V. H., *Recorder* (24 March 1951).

56. Geoffrey Tarran, *Morning Advertiser* (3 April 1951).

57. James Fielding, *The Spectator* (23 March 1951).

58. John Barber, *Daily Express* (24 March 1951).

59. *Stage* (19 April 1951).

60. *Kensington News* (23 March 1951).

61. *Sketch* (28 March 1951).

62. C. L. W., *Birmingham Mail* (10 April 1951).

63. T. C. Worsley, *New Statesman and Nation* (24 March 1951).

64. Kenneth Tynan, *Curtains: Selections from the Drama Criticism and Related Writings* (New York: Atheneum, 1961), 7.

65. Worsley, *New Statesman and Nation*, 617.

66. Lefèvre, interview.

67. Landstone, *Off-stage*, 170.

68. Ibid.

69. Jeremy Geidt, personal interview, 6 December 1988.

70. Ibid.

71. *Daily Telegraph* (22 May 1951).

72. Jean Oberlé, *Jean Oberlé vous parle: Souvenirs de cinq années à Londres* (Paris: La Jeune Parque, 1945), 60.

73. *Manchester Guardian* (19 May 1951).

74. James Forsyth, *Tyrone Guthrie* (London: Hamish Hamiton, 1976), 216.

75. Ashcroft, interview.

76. Ibid.

77. Quoted in Wardle, *The Theatres of George Devine*, 138.

78. Peter Duguid, quoted in Scott's unpublished transcript.

79. Jani Strasser, unpublished letter to Michel Saint-Denis, 17 August 1952.

80. Marion Watson, unpublished letter to Michel Saint-Denis, 25 May 1952.

81. Georges Lerminier, unpublished and untitled article.

82. John Elsom and Nicholas Tomalin, *The History of the National Theatre* (London: Jonathan Cape, 1978), 100.

83. Herbert, interview.

84. Suria Magito Saint-Denis, unpublished letter to A. C. Scott, 1 November 1976.

85. George Hall, personal interview, 7 June 1989.

86. Quoted in Wardle, *The Theatres of George Devine*, 140.

87. Michel Saint-Denis, unpublished letter to Lord Esher, 23 June 1952.

88. Hall, interview.

89. Tyron Guthrie, unpublished letter to Michel Saint-Denis, 26 July 1952.

90. S. M. Saint-Denis in a letter to Scott (1 November 1976) alludes to a reconciliation between the two men during an International Theatre Institute (ITI) meeting on "Théâtres Populaires" in Athens in 1957 that took place at a dinner party Guthrie gave for Saint-Denis. She claims that a number of people attending the ITI meeting were invited. Yet, Michel Saint-Denis's 1961 article, "The English Theatre Seen Through Gallic Eyes" (translated by J. F. M. Stephens, Jr., *Texas Quarterly* 4 [autumn 1961]), asserts that he never again saw Guthrie after leaving England in 1952.

91. Saint-Denis, "The English Theatre Seen Through Gallic Eyes," 38.

92. Herbert, interview.

◆ chapter ten ◆

Strasbourg and the Centre de l'Est

I F CULTURAL AND NATIONALISTIC POLITICS drove Saint-Denis out of England, France's political and cultural agenda created a role for him in its postwar theatre. Humiliated by its defeat and occupation, France was determined to eradicate the political practices that led to disaster. The postwar leftist government embarked on changes to develop a more egalitarian, unified, and decentralized France. Its mission included rebuilding the economy through regional development and improving the standard of living of the poor.

The theatre was perceived as a useful tool for educating the less-privileged classes. Urged on by forward-looking theatre practitioners, the government offered support for decentralization and subsidization. Ironically, in espousing the principles of decentralization, the postwar leadership continued on a path laid down by its despised predecessor, the collaborationist Vichy government. In order to promulgate its ideology, Vichy had provided limited funding for touring companies promoting traditional national culture. Although the British would have disliked the comparison, the parallels between the CEMA (Council for the Encouragement of Music and the Arts) wartime tours and the French are striking. Both endeavors foreshadowed postwar governmental backing of theatre.

Spearheading the decentralization movement was Jeanne Laurent. A thirteen-year veteran at the Ministry of Culture, she assumed the functions of director of the Division de Spectacles et Arts in 1946. This post positioned her to continue implementing theatrical reforms she had set in motion under the Vichy government. During the war, while France had been divided in two politically, administratively it remained almost unchanged—namely, centralized in Paris. This political disruption provided the civil service with an autonomy never before enjoyed.[1] Laurent, albeit antifascist and actively pro-Resistance, did not find herself morally compromised, convinced that she was working for the betterment of French culture. Influenced by Dullin's and Copeau's ideas, she conceived a postwar plan for the development of permanent subsidized theatres in the provinces, funded by the central government and local municipalities. Among her backers was Saint-Denis's BBC colleague Pierre Bourdan, who was the Minister of Education, a position then analogous to Minister of Culture.

The first of the regional theatres or drama centers, the Centre de l'Est (CDE), founded in 1946, sprang from a grass-roots effort. (Four other centers were launched between 1946 and 1952, the years of Laurent's tenure.) Alsace-Lorraine, claimed by Germany and France alternatingly for almost a century, had been "repossessed" by the Nazis during the war—the French language and cultural expression prohibited. The *Syndicat Intercommunal* of Alsace-Lorraine, an inter-city federation, regarded a regional theatre as an appropriate vehicle to help restore cultural ties with France. The federation would contribute a percentage of the expenses, provided that the national government furnished the rest. Laurent enthusiastically endorsed its proposal. Her superiors' authorization to proceed implied the national government's willingness to promote local theatre if political justification could be found.

Rather than delay the Centre's opening, Laurent appointed Roland Pétri as interim director for six months while searching for a more suitable candidate. The choice of director was mainly hers. Decentralization may have been the stated goal but Paris made most of the decisions, though granting the regions veto power. Pétri's premiere production, *Le Survivant* (The survivor), written by a playwright of local origin, was to validate decentralization and silence its Parisian critics. Hastily mounted by a harassed Pétri using Paris actors, the performance was uninspired and fell flat.

The next director, André Clavé (1947–52), had considerable regional experience, having led a wartime touring company. At the end of five years Clavé had raised production standards, organized the CDE into two troupes (each with its own circuit), built up the touring base, increased the number of performances each year, presented 49 plays, and initiated drama classes. Even with these accomplishments, Clavé failed to win the affection of the populace and the powerful Inter-city Federation.[2] The deciding factor leading to Clavé's resignation was a campaign conducted against him by the Strasbourg press after two productions failed.[3]

By 1952, decentralized theatre in France had progressed sufficiently that there were numerous qualified candidates for the position. Why then did Laurent offer the directorship to Michel Saint-Denis who had not solicited it? Saint-Denis was a theatrical unknown in France, having left the French theatre scene almost two decades earlier. The *Syndicat Intercommunal* wanted Jean Dasté, director of the Comédie Saint-Etienne, the second drama center founded, but he turned it down.[4] A series of coincidences brought Saint-Denis to Laurent's attention. Saint-Denis's architect-collaborator Pierre Sonrel, a consultant for the construction of the Centre's proposed theatre and school in Strasbourg, suggested that Clavé see the redesigned Old Vic. When he returned, Clavé reported that the Old Vic School was terminating and Saint-Denis contemplating a return to France. Letters were exchanged between Saint-Denis and Laurent and an interview arranged.

At every level Saint-Denis's credentials were unparalleled. His background included theatre design, creating two successful drama schools, a distinguished directing record, the founding of theatre companies, and an involvement with theatrical reform and decentralization dating back to the Copiaus and the Compagnie des Quinze. Politically, he was associated with the Resistance and the Liberation. But Saint-Denis was hesitant to immerse himself in a thorny situation. His ambivalence manifested itself in his unsuccessful scheme to forge an alliance between the Old Vic School and the Stratford Memorial Theatre, even as he arranged the interview with Laurent. Among the problems facing the new director were "confrontational" local politics, a population that only half of which was fluent in French (the remainder spoke a dialect and understood German better), selecting an appropriate repertory, forming an acting company, and reorganizing the Centre's administration.[5] The theatre would not be built for several years, necessitating a commute between Colmar and Strasbourg. Colmar was the base for the CDE by default because it possessed a functional theatre, rare in provincial France. However, the CDE shared the building with other cultural institutions, creating a scheduling nightmare. Because the theatre lacked workshop space, the CDE's sets were built in places as far away as Paris. On a personal level, Saint-Denis was reluctant to take a position where he had not been specifically requested and was sympathetic to Suria Magito's anti-German feelings.[6] His son's death in Alsace may have also had an influence.

Saint-Denis's preference was the as yet unrealized Centre du Nord in Lille. Officials in Lille had petitioned for him, eliminating the effort he would have to invest in gaining their trust. His knowledge of the region—he was a native of Beauvais and had been stationed near Lille during his military service—carried weight. Laurent intended that each center develop a specifically regional focus, establishing its own aesthetic and thereby enriching the broader culture. A director with a strong connection to the area he served would promote this vision.

However, the Lille center depended upon an allocation from the central government. Laurent was confident it would be forthcoming, but Saint-Denis did share not her optimism.[7] Events proved him correct. Inflation prompted Paris to adopt a fiscal policy that reduced art funding; equally important, Laurent had powerful enemies among politicians and self-interested theatre practitioners in Paris. Covetous of the grants disappearing into the provinces, her detractors labeled Laurent the "tzarina of the theatre [who] poisons us all," claiming that ending such subsidies would benefit both the national budget and the theatre.[8] In October of the same year Laurent was transferred to an unrelated civil-service position. With the removal of its strongest advocate, the growth of decentralization was delayed for almost a decade, during which time subsidies did not keep pace with inflation.[9]

By the time she left, Saint-Denis had accepted the directorship of the Centre de l'Est, where he encountered greater problems than anticipated. On a positive note, he would realize there his ideal of a company and school working in tandem. In practice, the conflicting requirements of developing a school and a company simultaneously meant that neither would have his full attention. Upon assuming the directorship, he began auditioning actors. Suria Magito remained in London to close out their affairs. She was to join him in Alsace, but in what capacity was unclear. Their letters from this period reveal as much about their relationship, personal and professional, as their stress and insecurity: hers are emotional, critical, and angry; his, conciliatory but firm. Following the Old Vic School's collapse, Magito fell ill with nervous exhaustion and its attendant symptoms, heart palpitations, migraines, and crying fits. Her demands were incompatible, causing continual discord in their relationship. She wanted recognition as a colleague on an equal footing, while also espousing the traditional female role of nurturer and mainstay. The latter, she believed, entitled her to a privileged place that she jealously guarded. Fearing that Saint-Denis was excluding her from the Strasbourg project by holding auditions without her, she lashed out, criticizing him for lacking judgment in people, undermining his ability to recruit a company. As proof, she cited George Devine as being a self-interested and "disloyal" friend who had done little to save the school.[10] Saint-Denis refuted her argument, at the same time promising her a role at the Strasbourg school.[11] How she would participate remained vague.

In addition to engaging actors, Saint-Denis used his time in France by observing firsthand the drama centers to assess their strengths and weaknesses. Besides the Centre de l'Est, he visited Dasté's Comédie de Saint-Etienne and Hubert Gignoux's Centre Dramatique de l'Ouest. He attended productions, examined the administrative organization, and studied budgets, all of which helped him to develop a working plan. As the CDE's general director he had to oversee both company and school. Management details such as budgeting were not Saint-Denis's forte. In England, George Devine had handled those affairs, leaving Saint-Denis free for creative planning. As Pierre Lefèvre explained, "Michel had the ideas and George put them into shape."[12] Saint-Denis realized that replacing Devine would be impossible, but he needed an assistant to help implement his objectives. He hired Daniel Leveugle, a director recommended by Dasté. Long-range goals involved audience building; developing a comprehensive training program whose alumni would contribute to the evolution of decentralization by raising standards at the regional theatres employing them; building a permanent home for the school and company; and creating a touring company of school graduates.

Saint-Denis found that the centers' productions suffered from insufficient rehearsal and weak companies. But finding top-quality actors proved difficult. Salaries were low and most professional actors resisted leaving Paris. It took considerable persuasion to convince even the rawest among them of the potential "real advantages: year-round work under able directors and receptive audiences."[13] Saint-Denis understood the actors' feelings; in Alsace, he too would feel isolated from what was happening in the theatre world.[14] And undoubtedly distressing to him was his theatrical obscurity in France. In England, where he had collaborated with the most talented artists of his generation, actors were thrilled to have the opportunity of working with him. Here, finding even competent people was problematic.

In 1952, Paris did not hold out any hopes for him. Saint-Denis always functioned in the theatre as part of an organization. But an organization has to be built with collaborators and requires financial support. Locating the funding to build an independent company would have been well-nigh impossible because he had lost nearly all his important contacts in France (mostly through death). And the government, interested in promoting its aims primarily through decentralization, had funded only one comparable Paris company, the Théâtre National Populaire (TNP) in 1951 and engaged Jean Vilar to head it.

To the casual observer (which Saint-Denis certainly was not), the Paris theatre world was a continuation of trends dating back to the second decade of the twentieth century. The tentative steps towards decentralization notwithstanding, Paris remained the country's theatrical center. The Comédie-Française was struggling to regain its prestige, having lost its strongest actors. Boulevard theatre continued to produce the same kind of commercial fare it had been doing for more than fifty years. The era's foremost directors were Jean-Louis Barrault and Jean Vilar, disciples of Charles Dullin. Saint-Denis felt a strong affinity with their artistic practice, which resembled his own. Among the leading playwrights were Jean Anouilh and Jean-Paul Sartre, who rose to prominence during World War II by writing works that were a veiled defiance (often using mythology and legend as subject matter) of the fascist government. Albert Camus, whose first play *Caligula* was produced at the end of the German Occupation, held a worldview similar to Sartre's. Major prewar playwrights such as Cocteau, Giraudoux, and Claudel continued to find audiences.

However, by 1950, the most inventive drama was being produced far from the mainstream in Parisian *théâtres de poche* (Off-off-Broadway-like venues). These plays that we know as "theatre of the absurd" lent themselves to minimalist productions. Small, low-budget theatres could risk producing experimental works without courting financial disaster. With their minimal plots, psychologically undeveloped characters, dream- or nightmare-like worlds, and devalued language, the absurdist plays were yet another permutation of symbolist drama. Underlying absurdist plays is our struggle to deal with the essential meaninglessness of the universe, an idea formulated by Camus in his philosophical writings. The most prominent of the "French" absurdists—Arthur Adamov, Eugène Ionesco, Samuel Beckett, Jean Genet—were all outsiders: Adamov was Russian; Beckett, Irish; Ionesco, of Rumanian origin; and Genet, a criminal. Perhaps this element contributed to their hyperawareness of the arbitrariness of existence.

Saint-Denis's repertory at the CDE, comprised primarily of classics interspersed with a few modern but not experimental plays, was consonant with that of the other centres, not simply because of a shared aesthetic but also through necessity. Each director, a spiritual son of Copeau, rejected commercial theatre and desired to reach a wide range of spectators, especially the culturally marginalized. Reputable plays that had passed the test of "universality" could be guaranteed at the very least not to drive away potential patrons. New works were difficult to introduce because the unsophisticated audiences were "more sensitive than the Parisian public to religious, moral, or political prejudices."[15] Consequently, absurdist plays took a long time to win acceptance. Saint-Denis, like Jeanne Laurent, was convinced that the centres' future depended on the creation of indigenous work. To hasten that day, the directors' charge was to upgrade production quality and educate the public through readings, lectures, and other forms of outreach.

In March of 1953, two months after becoming the CDE's director, Saint-Denis debuted with *A Midsummer Night's Dream*. Years of studying Shakespeare had made Saint-Denis a more confident Shakespearean director, as demonstrated in his final student production at the Old Vic, a fascinating *King John*. Saint-Denis opted for a Shakespearean comedy rather than tragedy because the comedies' unity of style rendered them more congenial to French taste. His metaphor for the production was an orchestra in which each sphere represented an instrumental section: the nobility, the brass; the fairies, harps and flutes; the lovers, strings; the mechanicals,[16] trombones and percussion. Original music was provided by his English colleague Henry Boys; Suria Magito choreographed the movement and dance.

Abd'el Kader Farrah began his collaboration with Saint-Denis with this production. Since the productions toured, they required a flexible, easily transportable set, much like the Compagnie des Quinze's. For *A Midsummer Night's Dream*, Farrah fashioned a movable platform representing the forest. To the rear was a colonnaded Elizabethan-like structure with two entrances on both levels and several playing areas, including a railed balcony. Sliding panels opened to reveal Titania's grove, Theseus's palace, and the mechanicals' workshop.

Contrary to the lavish, ponderous Shakespearean productions customary in France, Saint-Denis's *Midsummer* was scenically simple, imaginative, rapid, and language-dependent.[17] It was enthusiastically received by spectators and reviewers, including the many Parisian critics in attendance. Reviews described it variously as "extraordinarily magical," "gracefully staged," and "enchanting" with a *mise en scène* that captured the play's poetry, irony, and mischief.[18] Generally, critics found the acting laudable—Saint-Denis's direction concealed flaws—although Paris reviewer Bernard Dort perceptively noted the actors' lack of experience.[19] While in this case reactions were unanimous, evaluating the critical commentary of the CDE calls for discernment and a certain skepticism: Paris critics brought familiarity of current trends, wide play-going experience, and cosmopolitan biases; provincial critics knew their audiences but had their own prejudices and little practical knowledge.

The brief season's second and final offering consisted of two plays, Musset's short romantic comedy, *On ne badine pas avec l'amour*, directed by Saint-Denis, and Molière's *La Jalousie du barbouillé*, directed by Jean Dalmain, a company actor. Both plays met considerably less interest than the Shakespeare. Why Saint-Denis appointed Dalmain director is puzzling; he never repeated the experiment and Dalmain left the company. Why not Daniel Leveugle or Suria Magito? Leveugle was already in Strasbourg and Magito would have leapt at the opportunity.

Furious and hurt by her ambiguous role at the CDE—"to my great surprise I discovered that the 'faithful companion' of fifteen years of your work is the only person who has no position"—Magito hectored Saint-Denis with requests for greater responsibility.[20] Saint-Denis appointed her school director after she threatened to resign if she were made director of movement. Magito's appointment established a policy, whereby the CDE's general director was responsible for choosing the school's director, which eventually had negative consequences. Leveugle became the school's assistant director and the following season Magito and Leveugle directed one play apiece for the company.

In January of 1953, the Ecole Supérieure d'Art Dramatique opened its acting division in Colmar; the technical division awaited completion of the Strasbourg institute. Tuition was free and students were eligible for government grants because of the school's hard-won designation as an *école supérieure*. Because of the limited facilities, the first term presented a bare outline of the training. Improvisation, general culture, theatre, and art history were taught by Saint-Denis, movement by Magito, and acting by Leveugle and Magito. As a disciple of Charles Dullin, Leveugle's training had commonalities with that of Saint-Denis, but "he did not know Michel's techniques and lacked the background of the teachers who had worked with him in England."[21] Saint-Denis had originally intended to exploit the presence of the professional actors by having them teach as well as act. In practice it did not work out, given the actors' unfamiliarity with Saint-Denis's methods, their constant touring, and their base at Colmar during the school's first years. For these reasons, the CDE took on an international stamp. In October of 1954, when the school moved to Strasbourg, the faculty expanded to include Old Vic veterans Jani Strasser (vocal technique and singing) and Barbara Goodwin (dance and movement). Pierre Lefèvre and John Blatchley joined the faculty and company the following year. The school's mission—to train local actors—broadened to include all French nationals and "foreigners capable of working in French."[22] Initial auditions confirmed that it was as difficult to recruit talented students as it was actors, for similar reasons. So little interest was manifested that it took twenty auditions to find twelve acceptable students.[23] Few candidates investigated Saint-Denis's background;

they knew nothing of the London Theatre Studio and the Old Vic Theatre Centre. Thus reality set the school on a different course from that originally envisaged by Saint-Denis. Not only was regional emphasis put on hold, but the CDE's foreign enclave alienated many of the locals.

The new school followed the prototype of the Old Vic with a few important changes. The acting program was extended to three years; Saint-Denis had always considered two years inadequate for the teaching of voice and speech. He deemed the extra year even more crucial for French students because of the peculiar demands of the French classics. To his surprise, more movement classes were needed. Even though the French students were generally more graceful, their movement tended to be more stereotypical than that of the Old Vic students. And in a departure from the norm, auditions were and are held two out of three years, limiting the number of groups present at any one time to two.

Through the concerted effort of Saint-Denis and the staff, Les Cadets (later renamed Les Tréteaux), a touring company resembling the Young Vic, was created in 1956 for the top graduating students. The young actors brought live drama to far-flung villages, most of whose inhabitants had never before seen a play staged. Because the facilities in these areas were so rudimentary, the CDE's regular touring companies were unable to perform there. The Cadets, whose sets and costumes were made by the school's technical students, carried their own equipment.

The Ecole Supérieure d'Art Dramatique was unique in France in offering a comprehensive technical division. Until then, only the Centre d'Apprentissage in Paris gave aspiring technicians a formal method of learning their craft. No other school had a directing program. In Strasbourg, technical training comprised one, two, or three years depending on the student's course of studies. As at the Old Vic, the best students were asked to remain a third year for further studies in design and directing. Understandably, there was no playwriting course; the complexities of establishing one would have overtaxed the meager resources. But in view of Saint-Denis's total-training concept and desire to foster regional dramatists, its omission in later years is less comprehensible. Once the school moved to Strasbourg, Saint-Denis's day-to-day participation lessened; he was enmeshed in company responsibilities and supervision of the theatre's construction. He did not teach on a regular basis, but oversaw student work. As in England, students found his perspicacious criticism an invaluable part of their training.[24] During the first year at Strasbourg the school was largely in Suria Magito's hands.

In their first full season, he mounted Jean Giraudoux's *Tessa* and Fernand Crommelynck's *Une femme qui a le coeur trop petit*, lesser-known works of these celebrated French-language dramatists. During the interwar years these two writers had been acknowledged masters of a new literary drama movement. Saint-Denis was attracted by their rich language and imagery. Moreover, he may have anticipated that *Tessa* would have the same popular appeal it enjoyed in

Louis Jouvet's original incarnation. The reviews indicate that it did; critics describe full houses and the perfection of Saint-Denis's staging. Noteworthy are the favorable comments of the *Dernières Nouvelles d'Alsace*, the influential Strasbourg newspaper that had crusaded against Clavé. Its critic applauded Saint-Denis's direction as a complete break with the methods of André Clavé.[25] Crommelynck's more difficult play encountered a less enthusiastic response. Certain reviewers thought the script baffling; audiences are variously cited as appreciative, enchanted, restless.

The next two productions extended the CDE's circuit beyond its customary perimeters. Daniel Leveugle's *The Misanthrope* traveled to Switzerland and Belgium where it won approval. In Brussels, Saint-Denis was commended for his struggle in bringing about "a renaissance of quality theatre in the French provinces."[26] This tour, through introducing the company's work to somewhat more sophisticated audiences, provided a test that revealed its healthy growth.

Its next excursion was less successful. The Comédie de l'Est was selected to participate in the first Paris International Theatre Festival in June of 1954.[27] More a command performance than a request, the invitation was issued by the Ministry of Arts and Letters. Regardless of his misgivings, Saint-Denis dared not refuse what amounted to his funding agency. He decided on *The Seagull*, a reasonable choice considering his Chekhovian expertise. But surprisingly, Suria Magito directed it. Why present Magito with a psychologically realistic play when her strengths lay in movement skills? Perhaps overburdened by a pressing schedule, insufficient staff, and the complexities of the move to the Strasbourg facilities, Saint-Denis simply did not have the time to undertake the third play. It is unlikely Magito mounted the play without Saint-Denis's supervision, since he had always kept a close eye on her work.[28] How much of the final production was her work remains a question.

The Seagull premiered in Alsace, the first time the CDE had produced a full-length play by Chekhov. Some local reviewers found it too foreign: "The mentality of these unfortunate people is too far from our daily lives for us to be interested in their unhappiness."[29] Negative or mixed reactions in Alsace, though painful, were to be expected. Saint-Denis understood that his educationally diverse audiences would develop a collective appreciation only through repeated exposure to what they perceived as challenging material. At the Paris International Festival, where the CDE would be matched against renowned companies, it would be held to a different standard. However, Saint-Denis recognized that his actors' deficiency in discipline, experience, and talent constituted an almost insurmountable problem.

Decentralization still had its Paris detractors who were unwilling to accept it as a work-in-progress. André Clavé's comments regarding his company's 1952 visit to the capital merits citing, since it sheds light on the inhospitable atmosphere the CDE confronted:

> Our trips to Paris became more and more difficult. When the Centre was
> founded the theatrical profession in Paris did not take our attempt very seri-
> ously. On the other hand, difficulties that did not escape them made our
> experience one to sympathize with. Ever since we passed that trial stage and
> our base became secure, we have been considered rivals to be envied. Espec-
> ially because we are subsidized.[30]

The Seagull was not the only Chekhov work Paris saw in 1954. Numerous
productions were mounted in honor of the fiftieth anniversary of his death, permitting a base of comparison lacking in Alsace-Lorraine. Notices of the CDE
production were almost evenly divided; of seventeen reviews, nine were positive.
But they were so contradictory, one wonders whether they were more representative of their authors' positions on decentralization than the actual performance.
It was both praised and damned for its Russian atmosphere. One critic thought
Suria Magito's translation "precise, flowing, and even elegant"; for another, it was
"heavy, often awkward."[31] The staging was commended for its "attention to clarity" and criticized for its disorganization.[32] The divergent views extended to the
acting: Maria Ribowska "threw herself into Nina's tragic flight, with all her soul"
in one review, while another wrote that "she had not yet taken wing."[33]

So concluded a season that Saint-Denis termed "successful in its first half, a
fight in the second."[34] Despite the CDE's continuing progress, each season was
a struggle. While in theory the CDE was noncommercial, the marketplace was
still to be reckoned with, although government subsidy shielded it from the fiscal crisis that destroyed the Old Vic Theatre Centre. Awarded special status
because of its nationalistic objective, the CDE received the largest portion of the
sum allocated to the drama centers. Yet, in comparison with the prestigious
Comédie-Française, it had little political clout. In 1952, the total amount split
among the five centers was 75 million francs, whereas the Comédie-Française
received 291 million, almost ten times more than the CDE.[35] Furthermore, the
CDE's subsidy could not exceed 50 percent of the budget; box-office sales had
to make up the rest. Spectators had to be sought, seduced, retained.

If Saint-Denis had a model for making theatre attractive to a mass audience
it was Jean Vilar, director of the TNP. Vilar had overcome similar but not identical hurdles. Vilar's company was based in Paris and composed of gifted actors.
Saint-Denis admired Vilar's ability in "reaching a public which had forgotten
what a theatre was" with a repertoire of classics and modern dramas that became
box-office hits.[36] But he understood that achieving the same results in Alsace-
Lorraine would take time. One way to develop an audience-base was to keep
ticket prices low, approximately one-third the price of a ticket in Paris. Obviously, this strategy created its own problem, since revenues were inadequate.
Another was to adjust the dramatic offerings to appeal to a broader audience
while maintaining artistic integrity, often a double-bind. These competing
demands bring into question Saint-Denis's function at the CDE. What was his

role as a theatrical leader? Was it to explore form and establish high standards, to act as a curator of a cultural museum, to pander to popular taste? Or a combination of the three?

These were questions Saint-Denis confronted as he worked out an aggressive strategy for the 1954–55 season. He planned to bring the company into regions where entertainment was a novelty. During this period, inhabitants of isolated areas rarely had access to television, movies, or even automobiles. However, glancing at the titles, one wonders what relevance the plays had for this audience: Anouilh's *La Sauvage* (The restless heart), Marivaux's *La Première surprise de l'amour* (Love's first surprise) and *L'épreuve* (The test), *Romeo and Juliet*, and Calderón's *The Alcalde de Zalamea* seem aimed at the professional classes. Saint-Denis appears to have looked for plays that paralleled thematically and stylistically his CDE's successes. Cocteau's and Anouilh's plays were considered close in spirit to Giraudoux's—witty, poetic, whimsical, thought-provoking (but not too intellectually taxing)—qualities that also applied to Marivaux's eighteenth-century comedies. *Romeo and Juliet* was aimed at young spectators who made up a large percentage of Saint-Denis's public. Calderón's plays, like Shakespeare's, with their combination of aristocratic and comic, low-class characters had appealed to all strata of their societies.

Saint-Denis strove to improve production quality, but most of the actors consistently fell short of his standards. Cast lists indicate a more than 50 percent turnover each season. The low retention rate was caused by Saint-Denis's dissatisfaction with the actors' abilities and the actors' dissatisfaction with the modest remuneration, the absence of other professional opportunities such as radio or film parts, and grueling touring conditions. Continual change hindered the growth of an ensemble grounded in a shared technique.

To reach a wider public, during 1954–55 the number of plays was increased and the company of twenty split into two. The rehearsal schedule was lengthened to six weeks, "the minimum time necessary if a production is to have some polish and not run risks on tour."[37] Touring required detailed planning, scheduling, and coordination. Few towns or cities had working theatres; where they existed, they were frequently booked because they had multiple uses. More often, the venues used were cinemas, municipal auditoriums, or function halls without technical equipment or proper stages. Routinely, two sets were constructed, one for professional-sized stages, and a diminutive one for small platforms. This forced adjustments to the blocking and playing. Transportation was made difficult by long distances and poor roads. The actors traveled by bus, the stagehands in a van; the sets and costumes were sent by truck.

In August of 1954 the two companies began rehearsing; one worked on *La Sauvage*, the other on the Marivaux double-bill. In mid-October both went on the road for ten weeks, playing fifty performances of each production and covering fifty cities and towns in an area roughly defined as east of the line from

Lille to Reims to Dijon to Lyon. In mid-December the companies returned to Colmar, rehearsed for the second part of the season, combining for *Romeo and Juliet* and *The Alcalde de Zalamea* and left for another ten weeks' tour.

At the end of the formal season they reprised Saint-Denis's *Romeo and Juliet* and Leveugle's *The Alcalde de Zalamea* for a mini-outdoor tour and the Strasbourg Festival, performances that served as tryouts for their second appearance at the Paris International Festival, where they played at the Théâtre National Populaire.[38] They were greeted more warmly than the previous year. *Romeo and Juliet* was a hit and Saint-Denis welcomed as a Shakespearean expert: "No one in France has such a deep understanding of Shakespeare, or such a thoughtful and harmonious technique, no one is as close to the source as he."[39] Leveugle's "dynamic staging" was praised as were "the actors' lively performances."[40]

Unquestionably, Saint-Denis had accomplished much. However, his attempts to impose artistic rigor upon the company met with hostility. Maurice Ducasse, a long-time CDE actor, sabotaged the ensemble Saint-Denis was trying to build. Ducasse's chief interest was the promotion of the actors' union and his own career within it.[41] Betrayal, overwork, anxiety, perfectionist tendencies, and insufficient and sometimes unreliable staff took their toll on Saint-Denis, who began drinking heavily. He was frustrated, "imprisoned by multiple tasks," precipitating a second stroke, so severe it temporarily paralyzed his right side and impaired his speech.[42]

Saint-Denis's illness set the organization adrift. Managing the school had been more than Suria Magito could handle; now she had the added responsibility of nursing Saint-Denis. The company was left in the hands of the still inexperienced Leveugle. The arrival of John Blatchley and Pierre Lefèvre alleviated a grim situation. While both were capable teachers and directors, Lefèvre had the added advantage of being a competent actor and administrator. As Blatchley and Lefèvre took on more of the school's responsibilities, Leveugle's teaching load was lessened and his directing duties expanded. Although Magito remained the school's titular head, Lefèvre and Blatchley "made all the real decisions." They "had to fight Suria who was a bit like an amateur doing it."[43]

Still, the organization looked to Saint-Denis for the leadership that he was physically and psychologically unable to provide. Those loyal to Saint-Denis endeavored to fulfill his vision, but without his supervision development came to a halt. He was bitter, ashamed, depressed, and lost interest in work. Under the care of his doctor, he rallied and within two months could walk, speak, and pick up the threads of the CDE. But his participation was limited by the consequences of the stroke. He never again enjoyed the energy that propelled his earlier projects, though to an outsider the effects might be indiscernible.

Several months after his stroke he heroically directed *Voleur d'enfants* (Child stealer) by Jules Supervielle for the company. A "bitter sweet" twentieth-century surrealistic drama, it featured Pierre Lefèvre making his CDE acting début. The play was well-received and Lefèvre's acting praised, but rehearsals were difficult. The anti–Saint-Denis faction among the actors, taking advantage of his weakness, continued to resist him, threatening to strike.[44]

Unable to continue, Saint-Denis tendered his resignation with the condition that he remain until the Centre's home was fully operational. During his last year, he undertook an original play titled *Le Pays noir* written by his assistant Jean-Claude Marrey, but was forced to turn it over to Lefèvre when he found himself too debilitated. Though no longer capable of directing a multifaceted institution like the CDE, he did not consider retirement. Nor could he afford to financially. He was mulling over options when Robert Chapman arrived in Strasbourg. Commissioned by the Rockefeller Foundation to research actor training for the future Juilliard Drama Division, Chapman had visited drama schools in England where he was advised to contact Saint-Denis. Saint-Denis's training was the embodiment of everything Chapman felt a theatre school should offer.[45] After reading Chapman's endorsement, Rockefeller himself and members of his planning committee paid a follow-up visit that resulted in a consultancy for Saint-Denis. In 1957, Hubert Gignoux, former director of the Centre de l'Ouest in Brittany, replaced Saint-Denis. Saint-Denis worked with Gignoux for four months to facilitate the transition. His rancor towards the Centre and his poor health notwithstanding, Saint-Denis's departure, as Gignoux recalled, "wasn't very easy for him; he was sad to leave."[46]

The facility housing the theatre building and school was completed at last. Built on the bombed-out site of the Strasbourg Conservatory of Music, it was modern and functional, superior to any of Saint-Denis's earlier facilities. The 750-seat theatre, the first built in France after the war, was an acoustical marvel; the stage with its jutting apron drew on Sonrel's Old Vic design. Other features included spacious dressing rooms, rehearsal spaces, classrooms, workshops for school and company, a library, and cafeteria. One rehearsal room contained a scaled-down replica of the mainstage.

Saint-Denis had not raised the Centre to the level he hoped to achieve, but the elements were all in place. There is a certain irony in his leaving behind a healthy, functioning institution when he was no longer either. It is a mark of the esteem that he had gained that Saint-Denis's departure prompted an article by his severest critic Jean Guinand of the *Dernières Nouvelles d'Alsace*. In it, he cites Saint-Denis's accomplishments, the most important of which was "setting the Centre de l'Est on its true course," an achievement "unremarked by Paris."[47] Fiercely attached to him, Suria Magito also resigned, effectively giving up her career. She became Saint-Denis's representative and protector, never again to direct or hold a teaching post. Another Saint-Denis legacy was Pierre Lefèvre. When Gignoux, who had no pedagogical experience, was hesitant about continuing the school, Saint-Denis recommended Lefèvre run it during the changeover. The two-year transitional period stretched into fifteen as Saint-Denis's disciple fashioned the school into the pattern of the earlier English models. Under Lefèvre and Gignoux, Saint-Denis's vision of school and permanent company working synergistically was implemented, although the research component was de-emphasized. With the company based in Strasbourg, numerous instructors were drawn from the troupe. Students benefited from close exposure to the professionals; company members were pushed to excel under the exacting gaze of the students. The ladder system planned for the Old Vic School was realized in Strasbourg. Five years after Lefèvre assumed command of the school, 60 percent of the company consisted of former students. Other graduates worked in the regional theatres proliferating throughout the country and also taught in the growing number of French drama programs. The school's reputation grew, the faculty expanded, and the number of applicants rose to more than a thousand. Today's incoming classes are still small, but for pragmatic reasons. In a shrinking theatre, fewer graduates stand a better chance of working.

Despite many changes, Saint-Denis would recognize the curriculum. His system of placing the incoming acting students into groups still exists, each one functioning as an independent production company. The three sections work together on projects. (The directing program ceased to exist years ago.) Although the curriculum is no longer coordinated, elements remain. The following are only a few examples: mask is taught; each student studies a musical instrument; nondramatic text is a teaching tool. It is not so much that the school respects or even recognizes the Saint-Denis tradition, but rather that his philosophy and methods have permeated the teaching of theatre in France, a measure of the school's success.

NOTES

1. Marion Denizot-Foulquier, *Jeanne Laurent, le théâtre et les arts* (Association pour l'Animation du Château de Kerjean, 1997), 31–32. This freedom applied only to ministries in which the Germans did not have a vested interest.

2. Michel Saint-Denis, letter to Suria Magito, 26 March 1952.

3. Jean-Claude Marrey, "Strasbourg: d'André Clavé à Michel Saint-Denis," in Robert Abirached, ed., *La Décentralisation théâtrale*, vol. 1: *Le Premier Age 1945–1958* (Paris: Actes Sud-Papiers, 1992), 71.

4. Saint-Denis, letter to Suria Magito.

5. Ibid.

6. Ibid.

7. Ibid.

8. Hubert Gignoux, *Histoire d'une famille théâtrale* (Lausanne: Editions de l'Aire, 1984), 313–14.

9. Pierre Bourdan had died several years earlier, replaced by a minister uninterested in the theatre.

10. Suria Magito, letter to Michel Saint-Denis, 27 September 1952.

11. Michel Saint-Denis, letter to Suria Magito, 30 September 1952.

12. Pierre Lefèvre, personal interview, 20 June 1989.

13. Michel Saint-Denis, *Training for the Theatre: Premises and Promises*, ed. Suria Saint-Denis (New York: Theatre Arts Books, 1982), 57.

14. Lefèvre, interview.

15. Michel Saint-Denis, "The French Dramatic Centres," in Frederick Lumley, ed., *Theatre in Review* (Edinburgh: Richard Paterson, 1956), 40.

16. The "mechanicals" or "rude mechanicals" refers to the lower-class characters (the craftsmen) in *A Midsummer Night's Dream*, who play important roles in the play-within-a-play.

17. Bernard Dort, *Théâtre Populaire*, no. 1 (May–June 1953): 80.

18. Reviews quoted in Lumley, *Theatre in Review*.

19. Dort, *Théâtre Populaire*, 80.

20. Suria Magito, letter to Michel Saint-Denis (undated).

21. John Blatchley, personal interview, 2 June 1989.

22. Michel Saint-Denis, program notes, Centre de l'Est (1954).

23. Lefèvre, interview.

24. Claude Petitpierre, personal interview, 20 June 1989.

25. Jean Guinand, *Les Dernières Nouvelles d'Alsace* (undated review).

26. E. Becker, *La Nation Belge* (undated review).

27. The festival, which became the Theatre of Nations in 1957, was organized by Aman Maistre, a former member of the Compagnie des Quinze and Saint-Denis's brother-in-law.

28. Christine de la Potterie, personal interview, 15 March 1996.

29. *L'Alsace* (Mulhouse edition) (undated review).

30. Denis Gontard, *La Décentralisation théâtrale en France 1895–1952* (Paris: Société d'Édition d'Enseignement Supérieure, 1973), 179.

31. Marcelle Capron, *Combat* (undated review); *L'Express* (undated review).

32. *Paris-Presse* (undated review).

33. Georges Lerminier, *Le Parisien Libéré* (undated review); *Franc Tireur* (undated review).

34. Michel Saint-Denis, program notes, *La Sauvage*, 1954.

35. In 1952, 450 francs were worth approximately $1.

36. Michel Saint-Denis, "The French Dramatic Centres," 41.

37. Ibid.

38. Supplementary actors were jobbed in for the large-cast plays.

39. Kenneth S. White, *Les Centres dramatiques nationaux de province 1945–1965* (Berne: Peter Lang, 1979), 104.

40. Undated CDE program.

41. Lefèvre, interview.

42. Michel Saint-Denis, *Faisons le Point*, 10 January 1955.

43. Lefèvre, interview.

44. Blatchley, interview.

45. Robert Chapman, personal interview, 11 October 1988.

46. Hubert Gignoux, personal interview, 27 June 1989.

47. Jean Guinand, reprinted in *La Vie du CDE*, vol. 12 (15 March 1958).

chapter eleven

Extending the Influence: The Juilliard Drama Division

I N THE 1950S THE ROCKEFELLER FOUNDATION began developing the multi-purpose Lincoln Center performing arts complex in Manhattan, which was to include a new repertory company headed by the prominent director Elia Kazan in association with the producer Robert Whitehead. Subsequently, the project was expanded to include the training of performing artists. The Juilliard School, renowned for music and dance, was offered facilities in the Center, provided that it create a drama division. Opposed was Kazan, who fought to have the acting program led by Lee Strasberg, the father of the American Method, attached to his Lincoln Repertory Center Company (separate from Juilliard).

Given the Method's hegemony in the American theatre, the obvious question is how Michel Saint-Denis, alien to this tradition, was selected to develop Juilliard's program. Apparently, the Foundation had reservations about linking the drama program with the Method, since Robert Chapman, a Harvard professor and dramatist, was engaged to conduct an international investigation of drama schools. It was almost inevitable that Saint-Denis became involved once the search moved beyond the Method and the United States.

Chapman's investigation began in New York where he attended classes at the Neighborhood Playhouse, the Actors' Studio, and Stella Adler's school, all Method-oriented. In Chapman's view: "They were teaching psychology, which I didn't like. I have always felt that an actor is a sort of mountebank who has to be able to do everything—to sing, play an instrument, juggle. And they were teaching none of that."[1] He continued his observations at universities throughout the United States, where again "psychology" rather than technique predominated. In England, Chapman was impressed by the preeminence given to technique at the London Academy of Music and Dramatic Art and the Central

School, whose faculty included Saint-Denis protégés. Among the practitioners he encountered were Glen Byam Shaw and George Devine, who spoke passionately of Saint-Denis's impact on British training. The result was Chapman's visit to Strasbourg.

Although the Juilliard project seemed tailored to Saint-Denis at this period, age and experience had made him more cautious. Thus he was only willing to commit to an examination of the American theatre scene and "prepare a plan for a *professional* drama school of an advanced kind."[2] He had acted in a similar capacity at other institutions, for example, at the Institut National Supérieur des Arts du Spectacle (INSAS) in Brussels. The Juilliard New School of Drama (its name at that stage) was not slated to open until 1961, permitting Saint-Denis the luxury of time in which to make a decision. Although no formal offer of a directorship had yet been made, it was not long in coming.

Saint-Denis arrived in 1958, open to learning about a theatre he knew only by reputation but wary about the grip of Method training and the role of the university as the repository of training and tradition.[3] To test the response to his ideas, Saint-Denis gave a series of lectures on style—four in New York's Plymouth Theatre, sponsored by the American Shakespeare Festival and Academy, and one at Harvard—to audiences of practitioners and intellectuals. Those ideas were further disseminated when the lectures were published, at which time the concept of style entered the American theatrical vocabulary.[4]

Saint-Denis's examination was to be a three-month tour, with only a brief period in New York to familiarize himself with Broadway and off-Broadway and to meet major theatre figures. Deeming it critical that a drama school reflect its country's traditions, beliefs, and aims, he wanted to observe American culture close-up, to scrutinize theatre training, and to acquaint himself with the emerging regional-theatre movement. So important was this understanding that he undertook two similar tours the following year, one with Suria Magito, who now at last was Madame Saint-Denis (see figure 11.1).

He found that "there was no professional standard of theatre," the chief reasons being that the theatre received less support than the other arts and also the quality of training.[5] Even where opportunities existed for actors to study technique, training was usually fragmented. Acting, movement, and speech were taught as if each was a discrete and unrelated discipline. University programs varied: some were theoretical, some more vocational, some recreational. But even in the most vocationally oriented programs, training was part of a broad liberal-arts education. A school, such as the ones founded by Saint-Denis with their single-minded intensive training, could not function in a university setting. Because of the dictates of the academic curriculum, Saint-Denis did not find "enough time given to the indispensable work on essential techniques necessary for a student concentrating on acting."[6]

At those institutions that claimed to offer professional training, Saint-Denis

FIGURE 11.1 *Michel and Suria Saint-Denis at home in Seine-Port.*

deplored the almost universal reliance on the American Method. More attention was paid to orthodoxy than to exploration, each teacher offering his or her own interpretation of what Stanislavsky meant. All too often classes revolved around discussion of acting theory. This overintellectualization of the acting process disturbed Saint-Denis, as did the training's psychoanalytic emphasis. In his view, affective memory—championed by Lee Strasberg—was often pushed well beyond the domain of art, forcing the student to probe publicly into painful, sometimes shameful emotional experiences. Acting crossed the line into therapy, at times crippling actors. Saint-Denis was not opposed to Stanislavsky's teachings; indeed, British critics had long considered him the Russian's chief exponent in England. Stanislavsky's System was the point of departure for the Method and much of Saint-Denis's work, but their applications differed. The Method's apparent lack of concern for text and characterization were antithetical to Saint-Denis, for whom the author's text was sacred and transformation the actor's ideal.

While much in the American theatre of the 1950s was alien to Saint-Denis's experience, there were commonalities with the postwar French theatre of the

1940s. As in France, there was a movement to decentralize that hearkened back to the early days of the century. Likewise, decentralization's ultimate realization sprang from amateur and semiprofessional sources. But government support for decentralization was lacking in the United States, a situation not to be remedied until the establishment of the National Endowment for the Arts in 1965. Paradoxically, decentralization was easier to achieve in France because the country was so much more centralized and politics and art far more intertwined.

Despite chronic funding problems, American regional theatre was on the rise, which increased Saint-Denis's faith in the Juilliard project.[7] He did not want the school's graduates to discover "that the theatre they have been trained for doesn't exist," a criticism hurled at him by his British detractors.[8] By his second trip, subsidization no longer appeared to be an idle wish. In a historic decision, the Ford Foundation had awarded grants to three regional companies. However, with few exceptions, Saint-Denis was dismayed by the regional productions he attended. Their directors eschewed commercial fare in favor of dramas that Saint-Denis termed "big style" and for which the actors lacked the skills. Neither their training nor the typecasting of commercial theatre, film, and television prepared American actors to play the diverse roles required by permanent companies. Clearly, actor training had to evolve to meet the changing needs of the American theatre.

Saint-Denis watched with interest the development of the repertory company at Lincoln Center, whose intent was to become a national theatre based on the European model. (Feelings of cultural inadequacy prompted American idealists of the 1950s to look to Europe for guidance.) Saint-Denis wanted to establish a reciprocally advantageous relationship between the Lincoln Center Repertory Company and Juilliard. Robert Whitehead, who embraced similar values—a permanent company, an eclectic repertory of classical and experimental modern drama, a belief in a rigorous training program—was in agreement. They collaborated on a design to link the institutions so that Juilliard would "supply the Repertory Theatre . . . with talented and well-trained personnel," while maintaining its autonomy.[9] The plan was doomed because of Elia Kazan's prejudice against Juilliard. As for Saint-Denis, his Old Vic experience had taught him that a school had to remain financially and artistically independent in order to survive.[10] Kazan prevailed and in March 1961, Whitehead requested that the Drama School be placed under the control of the Repertory Company. The request was denied. Had the school been placed under the aegis of the theatre, Kazan might have been able to overrule Saint-Denis's curriculum design.

The Lincoln Center Repertory Company's sole season (1964) under Kazan and Whitehead justified Saint-Denis's reservations. Critics attacked an ill-considered program of plays that neither promoted a vision of the company's purpose nor aimed at a specific audience. Kazan and his actors were out of their depth when they moved beyond contemporary psychologically realistic dramas.

Years later, Kazan's autobiography, perhaps unwittingly, made a case for Saint-Denis's views: "We never really succeeded in wedding the necessary vocal force, clarity of speech, dexterity with words, and love of the language to the emotional techniques of the Stanislavski–Strasberg [*sic*] method. . . . We all needed to be trained, I as much as anyone, in the techniques of what's called style."[11]

Juilliard had requested that Saint-Denis prepare "an advanced school of theatre."[12] In his address to the American National Theatre and Academy (ANTA), he purported to be bemused by the term "advanced." Saint-Denis often masked his intentions behind an assumed role—here, the naïve foreigner in the hope of dispelling any impression that he was a threat to American theatre professionals. The address was a forum for him to lay out the arguments for the school he envisaged. He began by defining an advanced school as one "where work would be of authentic quality, which should have a creative attitude and be of significance for the theatre." This purposely loose definition permitted him to broaden the parameters of the acting training. His solution, which was only partially executed, consisted of a two-track acting program. The more important track would offer three years' training to a group of twenty students of college age. With cultural adjustments, this course would replicate the best of the Old Vic and Strasbourg paradigm. The second course, to begin in Year Three, would accept a dozen older students with previous training and/or professional background. In the fourth year, the two groups—having shrunk to twenty-three actors through the process of elimination—would unite to form a touring company. The company that was to play at universities would serve a dual function, providing career opportunities for the performers while establishing "a professional standard of acting . . . missing in the very places where it would be most essential." His plans included parallel programs in directing, design, and playwriting.

Even as he reported to ANTA, Saint-Denis continued to investigate options other than the Juilliard directorship. Publicly, he down-played the opportunity, stating that "the director of the organization should be American." Saint-Denis's assertion was disingenuous for someone whose *modus operandi* had always been to hire the most qualified person, irrespective of nationality. And his assertion notwithstanding, Saint-Denis supported the candidacy of the Rumanian-born, French-reared, British-educated John Houseman.

Privately, Saint-Denis confided to Suria his doubts about the viability of the Juilliard project. Worrying him were Juilliard's failure to proceed on schedule, insecure funding, and salary disagreements. These were familiar problems he no longer had the energy to contend with, particularly since he "would not be in a position to pursue the artistic policy which was agreed on without the most hectic fight."[13] Among his other prospects was the possibility of "realizing something in France."[14] Saint-Denis still yearned to have an impact on French theatre, and with the government under André Malraux's artistic leadership investing heavily in theatre, it appeared that he might be awarded one of the new well-endowed cultural centers. Instead, Saint-Denis was appointed Conseiller Artistique to the Comédie-Française and Inspecteur Général des Arts et Spectacles—prestigious sinecures rather than positions where he could effect change. England also beckoned with an invitation from a former Old Vic colleague to direct Stravinsky's oratorio *Oedipus Rex*.

Nonetheless, Saint-Denis did not want to sever ties with Juilliard, a decision motivated partly by economics. After an unremunerative life in the theatre Saint-Denis had little money put aside for his retirement.[15] Now in his sixties, with his health compromised, he could not afford to let go of his consultancy fee. And as a consultant he could implement his vision without becoming involved in the politics and day-to-day operation of the school. If heads were to roll, his would not be among them. Weighing more heavily than other considerations, however, was Saint-Denis's conviction that he had an essential role to play in the reformation of the theatre, be it as director, educator, adviser, or design consultant. In this latter role Saint-Denis advised the internationally renowned but theatrically inexperienced modernist architect Pietro Belluschi on every aspect of the Drama Division's facilities: classrooms, rehearsal space, dressing rooms, and the school's two theatres, particularly the Drama Workshop. Seating between two and three hundred, the Drama Workshop is a variant of Saint-Denis's earlier theatres, with a flexible acting area and an optional thrust stage.

As the Drama Division took shape on paper, Saint-Denis divided himself among his many projects, commuting between Europe, Canada, and the United States, as he pondered the Juilliard decision. In 1961 he veered towards acceptance, negotiating his salary and duties as director of the Drama Division.[16] A year later he withdrew and signed a three-year contract with the Royal Shakespeare Company (RSC). His reasons were myriad: Juilliard's frustrating delays, the resignation of William Schuman as president of the school, an ongoing concern about "a possible artistic disagreement with the Direction of the Repertory Theatre," and disapproval of granting academic degrees in the field of drama.[17]

So intense was Saint-Denis's resistance to making the Drama Division a degree-granting institution that a glance at his rationale is in order. Obviously, the unfavorable impression made by American university departments was one factor, another was cultural bias. In England and France, university theatre departments were unknown; a student desiring a theatrical career attended a drama school or conservatory. Moreover, in France, where university programs are akin to graduate schools, a degree does not carry the same meaning as in the United States. A diploma from an advanced specialized school can be more prestigious. Saint-Denis worried that the addition of degree requirements would eviscerate the program. He feared that a too intellectual training approach might limit the actor's imagination. Yet, as Robert Chapman noted, students graduating from a Saint-Denis school were well-grounded in the liberal arts, having studied literature, fine arts, and cultural and theatre history.[18] The defining difference was the relationship of the cultural studies to the practical work. Saint-Denis lost the argument; Juilliard's Dance Division already offered a Bachelor of Fine Arts (BFA); the Music Division, a Bachelor of Music.

Peter Mennin, Juilliard's next president, wooed Saint-Denis over the next three years. In order "to make the offer as tempting as possible," he assured Saint-Denis that "your ideas would be given complete support from the outset" and proposed that Michel become artistic director, thus removing any administrative burden.[19] Other inducements included holding the position until Saint-Denis's contract with the RSC expired. Mennin abandoned his pursuit only when Saint-Denis signed on for another three years with the RSC. Even without his other reasons, the ongoing construction and administrative setbacks would have made it impossible for Saint-Denis to await the Drama Division's opening.

As artistic consultant, Saint-Denis was key in choosing the Theatre Division's director. After considering candidates of varying backgrounds, Saint-Denis settled on John Houseman, who had wide experience in alternative theatre as an administrator, producer, and director. Houseman's theatrical career began in association with Orson Welles in the Federal Theatre Project and then at the Mercury Theatre where they presented works by Büchner, Dekker, Shaw, and Shakespeare. As artistic director of the Shakespeare Festival in Stratford, Connecticut, and the Theatre Group in California, Houseman had been deeply involved in the developing regional-theatre movement. His lack of pedagogical experience notwithstanding, Houseman, with his "usual mixture of arrogance and modesty," leapt at the chance to direct what was potentially the country's most effective theatre program.[20] Perhaps this same arrogance led him to assert that he was the only one offered the post, despite documentation to the contrary.[21]

As Houseman's deficiency in training made Saint-Denis's expertise indispensable, the two met in Stratford-upon-Avon and in France to discuss their collaboration. Although Saint-Denis's European responsibilities had decreased, he would not be free until the spring of 1968. Since the Drama Division's opening was now projected for the fall of 1968, Suria Saint-Denis spent several weeks in New York in 1967 to participate in faculty hiring, a process that took Houseman almost a year. Once the teachers were provisionally selected, Michel and Suria Saint-Denis (accompanied by their Strasbourg assistant Barbara Goodwin) joined Houseman for a two-week audition of the faculty. The "retreat," held at a boarding school in Connecticut, allowed Saint-Denis to gauge the faculty's competence.

Regrettably, Saint-Denis was still suffering from the unpredictable effects of another serious stroke suffered two years earlier; at times, he was lucid, at others confused, his speech garbled. Understandably nervous because of his speech impairment, he faltered during his first talk, unable to follow his notes. But with

Suria's help he recovered himself and "his old authority and charm returned."[22] Together, they outlined the curriculum, much of which was new to the assembled teachers. A high point was Saint-Denis's mask demonstration. Those present long remembered his instant transformation into the semi-tragic, semi-comic personage of Oscar Knie. Under Saint-Denis's guidance, four students brought in from the National Theatre School of Canada (another of Saint-Denis's schools) demonstrated the neutral mask.

His first interviewee was Michael Kahn, Houseman's choice to head the acting department. Kahn was perplexed at finding himself a candidate for what was arguably the most influential faculty position at Juilliard. He was aware of Saint-Denis's prominence, "but knew nothing about his system. And so I thought it was rather strange being asked to run the acting department of the school that Michel was starting."[23] Kahn's training, which included studying with Method teachers Michael Howard and Lee Strasberg, might have predisposed Saint-Denis to reject him. But after talking with Kahn at length, Saint-Denis realized that their viewpoints regarding the needs of the American theatre converged. Kahn, who was about to become artistic director at Stratford in Connecticut, had encountered difficulty casting actors who could speak and play classical material. For his part, Kahn was pleased to note: "The idea that self-expression was unavailable to the artist unless he had the tools to express himself was very attractive to me since I was doing classical theatre at the time."[24]

From the outset, however, Kahn had questions about the acting program. Valuable as the sequence of courses with its emphasis on technique was, he felt that the acting student ran the risk of being shortchanged. He voiced this fear at the retreat when he asked the Saint-Denises, "When do we *teach* acting?" and received a response "that didn't quite satisfy him."[25] His question might have been amended to *how* rather than *when*. The curriculum, which Saint-Denis brought to the United States (dubbed the "bible" by Juilliard), did not include scene classes, considered to be indispensable in American training. Suria Saint-Denis and Kahn would clash repeatedly on this issue in the future.

In this, his fifth school, Saint-Denis had adjusted aspects from his earlier institutes to fit the society and theatre the students would enter. Certain adaptations were concessions. The Drama Division has always been a four-year, degree-granting program. Had he remained, Saint-Denis's misgivings regarding the BFA might have been laid to rest, for Juilliard has always prided itself on being a professional school in the best sense. Taking the degree is elective and the number of students earning a BFA varies; nondegree students receive a diploma. As many as 50 percent of an entering class may opt out of the degree program because they already hold a Bachelor's.[26] In contrast to Saint-Denis, the faculty prefers college graduates because "it is difficult to find seventeen-year-olds who are ready for the kind of training we offer."[27] At the time of the Division's opening, Saint-Denis's comprehensive course of study had been reduced to an acting program. Other amendments followed his death. In spite of the changes made to the original plan, Juilliard has remained faithful to the essence of Saint-Denis's vision of actor training, his curriculum still providing the guidelines.

The Juilliard Drama Division opened in September of 1968, ten years after Saint-Denis first associated himself with the project. The intervening decade had wrought considerable change in all domains, the theatre included. A new American drama was erupting in the works of Edward Albee, Sam Shepard, Amiri Baraka, Maria Irene Fornes, to name only a few. Stylistically and philosophically, these playwrights were, to a greater or lesser degree, indebted to the French absurdists and England's Harold Pinter. Often their works were devoid of traditional narrative structure and psychologically developed characters, calling for divergent acting approaches.

Almost concurrently, several companies moved well beyond naturalistic techniques, investigating alternative visions of acting. Though their experimentation frequently paralleled that of Saint-Denis's early career, these companies were reacting to the period's societal transformations. Some, such as the San Francisco Mime Troupe and the Bread and Puppet Theatre, both still in existence today, drew on popular traditions to (re)create theatricalist and populist theatre. The San Francisco Mime Theatre, established in 1959, creates political satires in a musical-comedy format. Topically contemporary, its style has its origins in commedia dell'arte, clowning, and vaudeville. The Bread and Puppet Theatre, founded in 1961, explores the world of myth, utilizing gigantic puppets in combination with live actors, often masked. Possibly the most influential companies in terms of the development of acting were the Living Theatre and the Open Theatre. However, their training was designed to teach skills in service of their companies' artistic objectives, not to prepare young actors for a general theatrical career. The era's experimentalism prepared fertile ground for Juilliard's drama program.

The controversial Living Theatre was committed to social, political, and artistic change. Founded by Julian Beck and Judith Malina, the company first attracted attention with its production of Jack Gelber's *The Connection* in 1959. The performance combined detailed naturalism and an exploration of Artaud's theatre of cruelty. Artaud's theories, which the Living Theatre was the first American company to apply, remained fundamental to its work (although the directors also explored other avenues). They aimed to create ritual rather than traditional theatrical production. They eradicated the barriers between actor and public, making the spectators part of the performance. They frequently replaced dialogue with sound and gesture. Over time, their practice and their politics became more radical. Collective creation almost completely replaced conventional scripts. After leaving the United States in 1964, the troupe—whose lifestyle and practice resembled an anarchic Compagnie des Quinze—toured almost continually for the next twenty years, living communally, almost always on the edges of existence. Their influence in Europe, especially France, was strong.

Joseph Chaikin left the Living Theatre in 1963, dissatisfied with the company's intense focus on using theatre for political ends. Chaikin wanted to discover techniques for handling nonnaturalistic theatre in a more deliberate way than the Living Theatre. He founded a theatrical laboratory—the Open Theatre—with a group of like-minded artists more interested in research than performing. Together, they explored physicality and voice—with an emphasis on physical transformation—through sound-and-movement exercises, theatrical games, and improvisation. Nontheatrical sources such as Yoga and contemporary psychology, in particular Eric Berne's role-playing theories, also informed their work. After his visit in 1967, the company experimented with the Polish director Jerzy Grotowski's techniques. Their diverse exercises led to the creation of plays developed collaboratively among the actors, directors, and playwrights who comprised the Open Theatre. The plays delved into large themes—war, death, evil, freedom—portrayed metaphorically and abstractly. Despite Chaikin's rejection of the Living Theatre's political activism, he believed that the theatre artist should respond to the society in which he or she lived.

The decade also wrought considerable change in Saint-Denis; his health and cognitive abilities had deteriorated. Juilliard's ten-year delay in opening effectively limited Saint-Denis's hands-on contribution to intermittent classes, advice, and one project, a reading of *Oedipus Rex*. Participating students count themselves fortunate to have had this exposure to him and his methods. In June of 1969, Suria was alarmed to discover that Michel had suffered irreversible brain damage resulting from his strokes. She took him back to England with the understanding that she would continue to act as consultant to Juilliard. In London, he continued to decline as he watched his world slipping away. Many of his closest friends and colleagues were already dead (George Devine in 1965). His daughter Christine, who nursed him in London, remembers him crying as he watched the funeral of his old adversary, General de Gaulle, on television.[28]

For Suria Saint-Denis, consulting meant making sure that Juilliard did not deviate from the path Saint-Denis had laid out. But as long as Michel was alive, she was torn between her desire to minister to his health and her duty to his work. She managed to get to New York twice a year for three-week periods until Saint-Denis's death in 1971, a heroic effort under the circumstances. Within such a circumscribed situation it was difficult for her to have a major pedagogical influence.

Saint-Denis's death complicated existing problems. His curriculum had been designed in accordance with a plan that he had developed and perfected throughout his professional life. His loss, first to illness and then to death, created a pedagogical gap. Copies of the Saint-Denis bible had been distributed to the faculty, who needed clarification of its details. They were frustrated in their attempts to speak to Saint-Denis directly because Suria generally acted as her husband's surrogate even while he was still at Juilliard. After he died, Michael Kahn stepped in to fill the void. And in so doing, put forth several different concepts.

Kahn challenged the Saint-Denis bible during Suria's first consulting visit in November of 1969. Until then, he had adhered to the first-year program of silent improvisational exercises. Kahn viewed them as "sort of variations on sensory and task exercises," but with a somewhat different intent.[29] While recognizing the value of the silent improvisations in providing a stimulus to the imagination, Kahn felt the program did not fully respond to the first-year students' needs. Saint-Denis believed emphatically that "the student learns to act by improvising," making the transition from improvisation to interpretation through rehearsal.[30] Kahn contended that students had previously acquired bad acting habits that rehearsal technique alone did not correct. Instituting scene classes, he insisted, would enable the instructor to isolate problems. Suria was fiercely opposed and Houseman supported her. A compromise was reached whereby in addition to the major productions, one-act plays of diverse styles would be rehearsed intensively. Ultimately, Kahn and other acting instructors succeeded in adding scene classes.

Michel Saint-Denis, who always questioned assumptions, "had a tremendous suspicion of method, any method which stopped questions, any method which discouraged change."[31] Had he been able to continue at Juilliard the training program would have evolved, albeit in a different manner. But after his death Suria became even more protective; any deviation from her husband's plan was heresy. Moreover, she regarded herself as Saint-Denis's collaborator who had served an important function in all of the Saint-Denis schools as a teacher, director, and administrator. She was a woman of many talents; however, her commitment to furthering her husband's work overshadowed her admittedly less significant gifts. Michel's death diminished her confidence and left her superfluous in the eyes of many.

Despite her practical knowledge she scarcely taught at Juilliard. According to Kahn she frequently expressed the desire, but when given the opportunity "she was panic-stricken and would start trembling"[32] in front of a class. Her discomfort did not prevent her from criticizing "unorthodox" procedures, resulting in strained relations between her and various instructors. She was not above intriguing and being divisive. Still, she had her supporters, among them Margo Harley, Houseman's administrator and currently producing director of the Acting Company. For Harley, she was "the conscience of the school."[33] Houseman also backed Suria in most controversies; it was largely due to his efforts that the school kept her under contract as consultant director.

Some years before her death Suria Saint-Denis made New York her home, and Juilliard became even more her special charge. She arrived at the school each morning meticulously dressed, observed classes and rehearsals, attended faculty meetings, and wrote reports. Increasingly, she was excluded from the decision-making process. The staff was outwardly respectful of her; she was treated as something of an icon but not heeded. Her reports protested that "the training is just not Saint-Denis's, and I wanted it recorded at least."[34]

Houseman's resignation in 1976 accelerated changes already in progress. After several years, many of the faculty concurred that the school was turning out actors who were perhaps too technical for the American theatre. To remedy this situation, Michael Howard, and then John Stix, members of the Actors Studio, were recruited. Both men introduced Method exercises including sense memory, infuriating Suria Saint-Denis.

In all probability Saint-Denis would have initially resisted any inclusion of the American interpretation of the Stanislavsky System. He considered his own use of Stanislavsky's theories at the London Theatre Studio (LTS) and at the Old Vic more effective. However, Kahn felt strongly that the school needed to be responsive to the practical needs of the American actor. While it was important for actors to be able to perform in plays of all styles, it must be remembered that the majority of roles actors play in the United States are in realistic drama. Equally important is the acting teachers' belief that Method work as taught at Juilliard is congruent with Saint-Denis's techniques, particularly as Strasberg's practices were modified by the school's instructors. Saint-Denis's *bête noire*, emotional memory, is not taught at Juilliard.[35]

Other changes included redefinition of the "test play" as the less threatening "discovery play." The test play's aim was "to shock the student into a realization of how essential the training of the voice and body is to his development as an actor."[36] The discovery play, still largely an undirected production of a Shakespearean work, no longer overwhelms students with their own inadequacy. During the four-week rehearsal the director, who functions as a combination stage manager/ideal audience, encourages students to realize their creativity as fully as possible. The discovery play serves two purposes: it is the first step in forming the group into a cohesive whole, and it allows the faculty to assess the students' strengths and weaknesses without overt criticism. Armed with this information, the instructors can more easily deal with individual problems in the classroom.

Each change of administration increased Suria's anxiety that the school would stray farther from its model. Houseman was replaced by Alan Schneider, whose brief directorship was rife with administrative conflict. In 1979, Michael Langham, a former protégé of Tyrone Guthrie, was brought in to head the division. Saint-Denis had met him in England when Guthrie brought Langham to the Old Vic to direct *Othello*. Langham's first day at the Old Vic coincided with the departure of Saint-Denis, Byam Shaw, and Devine. Since Guthrie bore responsibility for closing the Old Vic Theatre Centre, the initial encounters between Langham and Suria were filled with mistrust. Langham's contention, reminiscent of Guthrie's, that he did not believe in actor training did not help the situation. For Suria, it seemed that the old battle lines were being redrawn—this time, with Langham and herself as surrogates for Guthrie and Michel. On his arrival, Langham found a "spiky and embattled" Suria, who later proved helpful as a guide to the training, although she remained intrusive.[37] But she approved the changes Langham introduced. He humanized what was sometimes a harsh discipline and brought the school closer to its original intention. Langham, being British, was committed to approaching character through text, like Saint-Denis. The kinder, gentler ambience instituted under Langham has continued to evolve. Not everyone agrees that the change has been for the better. The director Gerald Gutierrez, a member of Group 1 who has taught at Juilliard, missed the old discipline, finding that "the atmosphere has become less serious."[38]

Further changes followed Suria Saint-Denis's death at age eighty-five on December 29, 1987. Most significant was Michael Kahn's 1993 appointment as director of the Drama Division that ushered in a new era, bringing with it innovative programs. Interestingly, Kahn's career parallels Saint-Denis's in numerous ways. He has divided his time between training and directing. Although he has successfully mounted plays of various styles, his principal interest is English Renaissance theatre. Artistic director of the Shakespeare Theatre in Washington, D.C., he juggles the Juilliard directorship and the company. Kahn finds the positions "symbiotic since a lot of Juilliard students ultimately work in Washington, and some of the actors from the company teach at Juilliard."[39] This affiliation would have been applauded by Saint-Denis who had hoped to forge a similar connection with Lincoln Center. In an era where classical theatre is increasingly rare, the company provides a positive model for the students who are regularly bussed down to see productions.

Under Kahn, the entering class has shrunk to twenty, down from thirty-five during the beginning years. At the Division's inception, the faculty expected to winnow the class size down to half by the fourth year. With over a thousand candidates applying for those twenty places, the Drama Division enjoys a selectivity that equals, if not exceeds, that of Ivy League colleges. Impressive as that fact is, Kahn protests that at least half of those auditioning lack any notion of the craft of acting. Still, entering classes are so strong that as few as three or four students are now eliminated from the program. Juilliard's only serious competitors are the graduate acting programs at New York University (NYU) and Yale University, mainly because these programs offer a Master's degree. The administration and faculty at Juilliard considered instituting a graduate acting program but vetoed it because, in contrast to the three-year Master's program at the universities, the Juilliard model consists of four years.

Auditions, which take place in New York and key cities nationwide, approximate the procedure devised by Saint-Denis for the London Theatre Studio almost seventy years ago. Following a warm-up and brief orientation, applicants present a classical and a contemporary monologue for a panel of several faculty members representing the acting, movement, and voice/speech departments. If the audition sparks their interest, the auditors work with the applicant directorially, sometimes asking for an improvisation. Applicants are asked to prepare a song *a capella*, although a trained singing voice is not requisite for admission. Callbacks can be initiated by the enthusiasm of even one panel member.[40] The panels converge to review the finalists, and those who have not been eliminated are interviewed.

Does the student demonstrate imaginative powers, energy, a trainable voice and body, mental and emotional flexibility, sensitivity to language, risk-taking ability? These are the qualities the faculty members search for during the audition. The faculty is also on the lookout for talented minority students; under Kahn's leadership, attracting a diverse student body became a priority. This is not to say that standards were lowered in order to reach out to minorities, but rather that the Division became more sensitive to the issue. Conversely, the ratio of admitted males to females is two-to-one. The rationale is the preponderance of classical plays performed at the school in which women have many fewer roles.[41] Yet, the presence of so many minority students necessitated expanding the repertory; why not find a way to do the same for the female student body? One obvious inequity is that entrance requirements are more stringent for women, who also make up a larger percentage of the applicants. When JoAnne Akalaitis taught at Juilliard, the Division "began to practice a little gender reversal."[42] Laudable as this practice was, it did not translate into greater numbers of female students.

Another consideration in accepting students is whether in the faculty's best judgment the candidate has the resources to work professionally. In other words, would this person be cast? Presumably, the occasional applicant is turned away on the basis of personal appearance. Harold Stone, the administrative director, admits that their most commercially successful graduates are not only "very talented, but beautiful in some way."[43] Of course, the competitiveness of a school depends in large measure on the success of its graduates.

During Kahn's tenure, the Drama Division has expanded its purview to include playwriting and directing programs on the graduate level (but nondegree granting), bringing it more in line with Saint-Denis's original scheme. Saint-Denis's earlier schools were predicated on changing the theatrical culture in which they were located; Juilliard, while maintaining standards, had become more pragmatic, teaching students to fit into the "real" world. That paradigm has been modified by Kahn who, like Saint-Denis, believes that a good drama school must develop more than actors in order to make a meaningful contribution to the theatre as an art. While it would be foolish to contest the centrality of the actor, the contemporary theatre has seen few actors who led the profession in new directions. That function has primarily been the province of directors and playwrights.

A previous attempt to develop playwriting had been made by Michael Langham, who created a dramatist's residency with desultory results. In 1993 it was restructured by Kahn, who thought "the money could be put to better use to have an actual playwriting program with two well-known dramatists as teacher/mentors and to invite three student playwrights to spend a year here."[44] The program, presently chaired by Marsha Norman and Christopher Durang, has grown to two years and has six playwriting fellows, three first year, three second year. As part of their development process the playwrights have biweekly readings of their plays, followed by discussion. Upon completion, their plays are given full productions. Thus actors and playwrights, brought together in a working situation, learn from each other. Graduates of the program such as Adam Rapp (*Nocturne*) and David Lindsay-Abaire (*Fuddy Meers*) have begun to make their presence felt professionally.

Kahn inaugurated the Directing Program in 1995 in collaboration with JoAnne Akalaitis and Garland Wright, funded by the Andrew W. Mellon Directing Fellowship. (The directorship of the program was put into Andrei Belgrader's hands in 2000 after Wright's untimely death.) Originally a two-year program, it has been extended to three, with no more than three directing fellows per cycle. The highly selective program seeks gifted individuals with leadership qualities and substantial directing experience. As in the Playwriting Program, mentoring is the principal pedagogical tool. In addition, the directing fellows follow a rigorous course of study that includes acting, movement, and design. The latter is taken at NYU's Tisch School for the Arts, since Juilliard has no scenography department. On the practical side, during the first year they stage scenes with third-year acting students; during the second they act as assistant directors to the professionals mounting school shows; and during the third they stage full-length plays on their own. Initially, the acting faculty resisted the program, fearing that the young actors' progress might be impeded through working closely with the directing fellows. This attitude disappeared by the end of the first cycle. Allowing the directing students to team up with professional actors was an important consideration in developing the program. Directing programs often fail because they do not address the students' need to work with experienced actors. Juilliard is fortunate in having created an alumni pool of its graduates—working actors who volunteer to collaborate with the emerging directors.

Despite these accretions, the acting program remains the heart of the Division. Each year's training has its own goal, although some classes, such as Alexander technique, are constants. The first or the "discovery" year develops the student's awareness of his or her acting instrument: "The student . . . discovers what talents—physical, vocal, and imaginative—nature has given him [and] what he has to do to develop them."[45] Basic skills are emphasized—relaxation, concentration, and control of the body and voice—to help the student become more expressive. First-year actors work with full neutral masks on silent individual improvisations in which they are pushed to transform themselves as fully as possible. Play analysis examines two scripts of varying styles and gives the student tools to understand dramatic structure and character relationships. First-year students are cast in plays that function as rehearsal projects to explore the actor's process. The finished project is shown exclusively to fellow class members and faculty, using basic rehearsal clothes, props, and furniture.

In the second or "transformation" year, students move from self-awareness to character awareness. In acting class and rehearsal projects, they delve more deeply into the world of the play. Text study focuses on Shakespeare; comic techniques are played with. In second-year mask class, characterization becomes more complex—even exaggerated—as students improvise with half-masks that allow them to speak as well as move. Rehearsal projects are brought to a somewhat fuller realization than those of the previous year.

In the third or "interpretation" year, the emphasis is on performance. Students appear in full productions of four-to-five plays, each of which is rehearsed for six weeks. So that students gain an understanding of the conditions of professional life, one production tours the New York public schools for a two-week period. The other plays, presented in the Juilliard Theatre, are open to a limited public. Classes are integrated with the performance work whereas previously, the reverse was true. Text study explores the canon from the Jacobean and Restoration periods to contemporary works. A course in makeup is added during this year when, for the first time, it becomes important in the students' performance work.

In the fourth year, students form a repertory troupe, the capstone of the training. The group has now been shaped into an ensemble that can work closely and profitably together. Group cohesiveness is fostered from the outset and is one of the factors that may figure in a student's being cut from the program at the end of the second year. Four plays of distinctly different styles are given full-scale productions and mounted twice, first for an invited audience over a few days. At the end of the school year there is a repertory season of several weeks during which the plays are presented to the general public and members of the theatrical profession. Ideally, the year is planned so that each student may have the opportunity of playing a variety of parts in a variety of styles. And while less time is spent in class and more in rehearsal, an audition class is added in preparation for the world the student will confront.

The Acting Company, founded by John Houseman and loosely affiliated with Juilliard, was created to keep the very talented actors of Group 1 together after graduation and foster their growth. In the spirit of the Quinze and the Young Vic, the Acting Company brought professional productions of classical drama to universities and areas not usually served by touring companies. Through its tours, the Acting Company demonstrated the results of Juilliard's training. Consequently, one of its unexpected benefits was the changes it wrought in the teaching of acting. Gradually, Juilliard's association with the

Acting Company grew more tenuous. As regional theatre shrank, graduates became wary of leaving New York and its professional prospects—not only those in television and film, but also in theatre. In 1998, however, the connection was revived when the graduating class joined the Acting Company as a group. Juilliard's further connection with the Acting Company and the company itself are both linked to the future of the American theatre.

The American theatre has undergone many changes since Saint-Denis was brought to the United States to create the Drama Division to serve what was then a growing movement. Juilliard's graduates are now found more often working in television and film than in theatre, although the training has not made concessions. And while a theatre school naturally laments the loss of theatrical opportunities for its graduates, its famous television and film alumni help to keep Juilliard in the public eye. It is generally felt by the Juilliard staff that, although there have been changes, often due to the personalities of the individual instructors, the school has remained faithful to the systematic, layered training that was Michel Saint-Denis's greatest legacy. Pierre Lefèvre, who taught Mask at Juilliard from 1970 to 1997 and is the closest living link to the Saint-Denis training, is convinced that "Michel would be very proud of this place."[46]

NOTES

1. Robert Chapman, personal interview, 11 October 1988.

2. Michel Saint-Denis, *Training for the Theatre: Premises and Promises*, ed. Suria Saint-Denis (New York: Theatre Arts Books, 1982), 64.

3. Michel Saint-Denis, "Address," 3 December 1959, *Newsletter of Greater New York Chapter of ANTA*, New York (April–May 1960), 3.

4. The book, of course, was *Theatre: The Rediscovery of Style*.

5. Saint-Denis, "Address."

6. Saint-Denis, *Training for the Theatre*, 66.

7. Ibid.

8. Ibid.

9. Plan for the Juilliard School of Drama, March 1960.

10. Letter from Mark Schubart, dean of the Juilliard School, to Michel Saint-Denis, 9 March 1961.

11. Elia Kazan, *Elia Kazan: A Life* (New York: Doubleday, 1989), 610–11.

12. Saint-Denis, "Address," 3.

13. Michel Saint-Denis, letter to A. C. Scott, 23 March 1962.

14. Michel Saint-Denis, letters to Suria Saint-Denis, 2 and 14 November 1959.

15. Ibid., 14 November 1959.

16. Michel Saint-Denis, letter to William Schuman, 14 September 1961.

17. Michel Saint-Denis, letter to Peter Mennin, 30 July 1962.

18. Robert Chapman, "Centre Dramatique de l'Est," Report for the Rockefeller Committee (1955), 19.

19. Peter Mennin, letter to Michel Saint-Denis, 14 February 1963.

20. John Houseman, *Final Dress* (New York: Simon & Schuster, 1983), 301.

21. Ibid., 299.

22. Ibid., 349.

23. Michael Kahn, personal interview, 13 April 1998.

24. Ibid.

25. Houseman, *Final Dress*, 349.

26. The auditions are so competitive that many students prepare by training at other schools and enter as college graduates.

27. Harold Stone, personal interview, 13 April 1998.

28. Christine de la Potterie, personal interview, 10 March 1996.

29. Michael Kahn, personal interview, 13 December 1988.

30. Saint-Denis, *Training for the Theatre*, 150.

31. Peter Hall, "Juilliard Tribute to Michel Saint-Denis," *Juilliard News Bulletin*, vol. 10, no. 2 (1971–72): 3–4.

32. Kahn, interview, 13 December 1988.

33. Margo Harley, personal interview, 27 March 1989.

34. Quoted by Henry Tarvainen, director and instructor NTS, telephone interview, 10 February 1989.

35. John Stix, personal interview, 14 April 1998.

36. Michel Saint-Denis, "The First Play Rehearsal," "The Juilliard Bible," 2.

37. Michael Langham, personal interview, 13 January 1989.

38. Gerald Gutierrez, personal interview, 10 April 1989.

39. Kahn, interview, 13 April 1998.

40. Callbacks are not held on the road where the same three auditors see all the candidates.

41. Stone, interview.

42. Ibid.

43. Ibid.

44. Kahn, interview, 13 April 1998.

45. Saint-Denis, *Training for the Theatre*, 86.

46. Pierre Lefèvre, personal interview, 13 April 1998.

Epilogue

ALTHOUGH SAINT-DENIS never again held a full-time, long-term position after resigning the directorship at Strasbourg in 1956, his career expanded in scope, becoming even more international. During the last fifteen years of his life, though his health was battered, he continued to undertake new projects. Still recovering from his 1955 stroke, he journeyed to Moscow to attend a conference and observe Soviet theatre firsthand. This trip was a precursor to his association with the International Theatre Institute. He continued to establish training programs and to direct. Although in directing Chekhov's *The Cherry Orchard* Saint-Denis returned to familiar territory, he pursued his explorations of different forms.

THE NATIONAL THEATRE SCHOOL OF CANADA

The emergence of a vital professional Canadian theatre is due in large part to the National Theatre School (NTS) of Canada founded in 1960 under the guidance of Michel Saint-Denis. His initial contact with Canadian theatre occurred in 1937 when he accepted an invitation to adjudicate the amateur Dominion Drama Festival (DDF) (1932–78). By his third adjudication (1952) he was struck by "a theatrical renaissance which allows us to envisage . . . the establishment of professional organizations."[1] But how to proceed? The DDF had been unable and/or unwilling to make the transition to professional theatre. Several amateur drama groups appealed to Saint-Denis to set up a much-needed school. Without a reputable training institute, actors and directors had little opportunity to develop their craft in Canada. A school could do much to end the depletion of national talent; the usual Canadian scenario entailed artists going abroad to study and remaining there to seek work. Though interested, even enthusiastic, Saint-Denis declined because of his commitments at the Centre de l'Est. The idea lay dormant for almost six years. Its supporters could not envision the creation of such an institution without Saint-Denis's leadership.

The year 1957 was propitious for the future of a theatre school in Canada. Saint-Denis had left the Centre de l'Est and associated himself with Juilliard. The possibility of his availability, coupled with the prospect of a Canada Council grant, revived the dream of a Canadian theatre school. Saint-Denis was invited to adjudicate the DDF spring finals in Halifax and to discuss the school. He refused, partly because of ill health, partly because of his Juilliard responsibilities. Still, he was anxious "to be of service to Canadian drama" and so gave the festival's keynote address.[2] In it, he reiterated the need for a national bilingual theatre school. Subsequently, in Ottawa he met with Vincent Massey, governor-general of Canada, to discuss the school's feasibility. Massey, a former amateur actor and honorary president of the DDF, was supportive, as were other influential people.[3] Consequently, a temporary committee composed mainly of DDF members was set up to carry the school forward. The committee's make-up disconcerted the small professional community who feared the school falling into amateur hands.[4]

It need not have worried. Saint-Denis was now thoroughly committed to bringing forth what was to become the National Theatre School. Therefore, despite health concerns, he agreed to adjudicate the 1959 DDF finals because "it would give a very useful push to the school plan."[5] As the movement gained momentum, Saint-Denis became more actively involved, devising training guidelines, responding to questionnaires, submitting sample budgets, planning the organization's "blueprint," and making himself available for meetings in Europe and North America. At the same time, he made clear that his participation would be limited to "advice and guidance."[6] The demands on his time were heavy and he feared overtaxing himself. Juilliard was his chief priority, but he was also picking up his directing career, revising his lectures in book form, compiling Copeau's papers for publication, and beginning another book about his schools, supported by a Rockefeller grant. In addition, he had scheduled a lecture tour in the United States for the fall of 1959.[7]

Although the Juilliard project restricted Saint-Denis's time in Canada, the Rockefeller Foundation effectively subsidized the Canadian school. Financing the early work on the school was a constant struggle; even flying Saint-Denis to Canada from France was problematic. However, since in his advisory role at Juilliard he traveled frequently to the United States, courtesy of the Rockefeller Foundation, the temporary committee was able to pick up the check for the Canadian leg of the trip.

Financial problems hindered progress until 1959 when the Canadian Theatre Centre, an association of theatre organizations, was formed in order "to assist in the promotion and development of professional and educational theatre in Canada."[8] The Centre appointed yet another committee to draw up a plan for a national theatre school and to help expedite its creation. This group was comprised of the leaders of Canada's fledgling professional theatre, Francophone and

Anglophone, assisted by a few DDF stalwarts. Saint-Denis worked closely with them throughout the writing of the "Blueprint," retaining final approval.

The National Theatre School's curriculum would follow the lines of the Old Vic School and the Ecole Supérieure d'Art Dramatique in Strasbourg. Saint-Denis was to tailor the training methods to suit Canada's particular conditions. Dealing with those conditions would prove much harder than he anticipated. The school's mandate was to develop "an approach to the theatre . . . both unique and Canadian," and to promote a theatre that would serve the needs of Canada's two separate cultures, the Anglophone and Francophone.[9] There was a strong sense of embarking on a unique experiment. At its inception, there were few venues and approximately a hundred professional actors in the country, most of whom did not earn a living at their craft. The school was in the ironic position of training artists for an almost nonexistent theatre.[10] Probably at no other time in theatre history has a responsibility of that magnitude been placed upon a drama school. Saint-Denis opined that "such a bold undertaking could not have happened in any other country but Canada."[11]

In assessing the school at the beginning of the twenty-first century, two questions arise. How closely has it adhered to the Michel Saint-Denis model? And how is it viewed by its teachers, students, competitors, and the profession? It is noteworthy that the school has remained closer to the Saint-Denis ideal than the Ecole Supérieure d'Art Dramatique in Strasbourg. That this is true, notwithstanding the fact that Saint-Denis's role in the school was an advisory one, is testimony to the faculty's and administration's confidence in his vision. After the establishment of NTS, Saint-Denis's presence was limited to a yearly visit, during which he and Suria would spend several days attending classes, appraising student work, and meeting with the faculty. With his infallible instinct, Saint-Denis frequently solved long-standing problems. A former instructor at the school remembers the occasions vividly: "Often I had been working with someone for months and Michel would put words to something I had been groping towards all that time, but never fully put my finger on. He said what he thought, often in a very charming way, but certainly very directly."[12] After Michel's death, Suria continued the visits until illness made them impossible.

In most ways, the school is an exemplar of Saint-Denis's principles: it offers a holistic and broad-based training in acting, scenography, technical production, playwriting, and directing. The relationship among the various disciplines is emphasized; through frequent contact, students discover the interdependence between technicians and artists.

IGOR STRAVINSKY'S *OEDIPUS REX*

Saint-Denis's 1960 production of Stravinsky's opera-oratorio typifies his interest in exploring new domains. He returned to London to direct England's first staging of *Oedipus Rex* for Sadler's Wells at the invitation of Stephen Arlen, the administrative director. Saint-Denis had long been fascinated by the possibilities of a fusion of music and drama.[13] His preparation, which started almost a year before the premiere, involved learning the music through recordings—he had no musical training—and discussion with the composer. (Saint-Denis's usual textual study was not applicable, as Sophocles' play had been adapted by Jean Cocteau, then translated into Latin.) The composer's chief comment was that the *mise en scène* should be "monumental and static."[14] Stravinsky envisioned a motionless, seated chorus, their faces obscured, reading from scrolls, and the characters, except for Oedipus, hidden from view when not singing.

Saint-Denis modified Stravinsky's ideas, drawing upon the classical French tragedy of Racine that demands a similar "discipline, rigor, and simplicity."[15] Traditionally, little movement is employed in staging Racine; the plays are so taut and distilled that any gesture has tremendous theatrical impact. Saint-Denis staged *Oedipus Rex* with comparable formality. His organizing image of "destiny fixed in stone," was carried through in the design as well as the blocking.[16]

This production differed markedly from the 1945 Olivier *Oedipus*. Perhaps because of the ritual quality he sought, perhaps partly to compensate for the singers' acting limitations, Saint-Denis returned to masks. He wanted them to evoke awe, dream and myth. Abd'el Kader Farrah designed impressive half-, three-quarter, and full but open-mouthed masks, complete with headdress. The degree of realism the masks portrayed varied from character to character; the chorus appeared grotesque, the shepherd and messenger the most human. In one reviewer's words, the masks expressed the personages "fundamental characteristics like a hieroglyph."[17]

Color was used more extravagantly than in the earlier *Oedipus*. The reds, greens, purples, and yellows of the costumes and masks were scattered through the basic blue and white of the set. Oedipus and Creon were dressed in leather that caused them to move stiffly, accentuating their nonhuman quality. Tiresias and the chorus wore gauze costumes grafted with rough material to give the impression of pockmarked stone. Farrah's anti-illusionistic set was composed of a staircase to the left of stage center, an elevated platform to the left of the stairs, and at stage right, scaffolding of abstract design held twenty-two chorus members arranged in tiers. The chorus and principals each had their own acting space that emphasized their isolation. An actor, dressed in a dinner jacket and standing apart from the singers, narrated in English. He was at once a distancing device and a link with an audience similarly dressed. Saint-Denis's intent was that the events be viewed through the narrator's eyes, thus intensifying the opera's dream-play characteristics.

His meticulous staging worked well for opera, every movement planned to suit the tempo. Although lacking action, *Oedipus* was carefully choreographed. The chorus, acting as one, moved only from the waist up, sometimes swaying, sometimes only inclining their heads to the right or left. The effect evidently "was riveting," although Saint-Denis was dissatisfied with it.[18] At the opening Oedipus stood at the top of the stairs; as the tension increased, he descended, symbolically portraying his downfall.

Music critics had questioned the value of staging a work they felt was essentially undramatic. The production changed their minds. Despite its hieratic nature, the acting—rare in opera—was emotionally truthful. The masked and shrouded chorus that listened and reacted is a telling example. If Saint-Denis's earlier Oedipus was a very human figure, the latter presented a picture of "harrowing grandeur."[19] *Time and Tide* summed up the impression it made: "The result is a production which preserves the formal facade of a classical oratorio of tragic dignity yet stretches and even tears it down in several places to allow the tense drama to pass through unhindered."[20]

Interestingly, the opprobrium "arty" that had dogged Saint-Denis's British career was all but absent from the critical commentary. Conceivably, critics were less inclined to reject the work because opera is so obviously outside the realistic realm. Equally likely is that his earlier work had paved the way for acceptance by the traditional critical establishment. *Oedipus Rex* played to packed houses, toured internationally, and remained in Sadler's Wells' repertory for fifteen years.

INTERNATIONAL THEATRE INSTITUTE

In 1961, Saint-Denis's life as an intercultural emissary entered another phase when he became a member of the International Theatre Institute (ITI). Founded in 1948 and sponsored by UNESCO, the organization's mandate is to promote international cooperation and exchange of theatrical knowledge and practice in order to foster creativity and growth. Through Saint-Denis's participation as a delegate, articles for the house organ *World Theatre*, conference lectures, and, most importantly five actor-training symposia (1963–67), his influence became even more widespread. John Houseman, attending the 1967 meeting, was struck by the respect and admiration exhibited towards Saint-Denis whose knowledge, experience, and perceptiveness made him the star of the event.[21]

The symposia attended by the leading drama teachers and practitioners of more than twenty countries were practical as well as theoretical. Saint-Denis set the agenda—style. Concepts were imparted through student demonstrations, followed by questions and discussion. Issues beyond training were examined, as in the final symposium that considered how cultural background affects performance. Schools of five different countries presented two scenes: the first from the national repertory of that school, the second, a foreign play. The consensus was that students from the Strasbourg School, then under Pierre Lefèvre's direction, were the most effective, giving further evidence of the soundness of Saint-Denis training methods.[22] Although there were no definitive conclusions, the interchange of ideas was particularly valuable on a political as well as theatrical level. During an epoch in which the Soviet-bloc countries and those of the West lived in mutual artistic ignorance, the meetings offered rare opportunities for dialogue, since they were attended and twice hosted by delegates from Eastern Europe.

THE STUDIO AT THE ROYAL SHAKESPEARE COMPANY

At approximately the same period, Saint-Denis was encountering a less reverent reaction from the Royal Shakespeare Company's actors. In 1962, Peter Hall, then artistic director, impressed by *The Cherry Orchard*, had invited Saint-Denis to join with him and Peter Brook in running the company. Ironically, reforms that Saint-Denis pioneered became a reality after he left England in 1952. At the Royal Shakespeare Company (RSC), Hall created a permanent company of actors, acquired a second theatre in London to present modern plays, established a stable of dramatists, and renovated the Stratford stage. The new stage with its large apron had much in common with Saint-Denis's redesign of the Old Vic.

Saint-Denis's charge at the RSC was to organize and supervise a studio for training junior members of the company in verse-speaking, movement, improvisation, and mask work. It was also a resource for the main company, many of whom took classes. The studio's larger aim was to find contemporary techniques of acting Shakespeare and other English Renaissance playwrights that, in turn, would lead to discovering alternative methods of staging current drama. Saint-Denis, Brook, and Hall hoped to engender a unity of approach so that "directors and actors would know what was meant when they used such terms as 'alienation,' 'motivation,' 'tactile memory,' a 'Brechtian,' or an 'Ionesc' (after Ionesco) way of acting."[23] Confusion about these terms and current trends was resolved through working on scenes, and then, full productions. They were mounted in a variety of manners: on thrust stages, in the round, and out-of-doors. The studio's research was to nourish the main company and, by extension, the British theatre.

The thrust of the work, therefore, was the search for style, a notion some of the younger actors found passé. In the early sixties the American Method, first brought to Great Britain in 1957, was in vogue. Frequently badly taught and misapplied, its abuses were even more flagrant than in the United States. Saint-Denis had to struggle with his students to gain acceptance for his views. But he prevailed and a distinct Royal Shakespeare Company style emerged, attributable in part to the training of Saint-Denis's studio. During his tenure at the RSC Saint-Denis directed the main company in Brecht's *Puntila and His Servant Matti* in 1965, his last production.

COPEAU AND SAINT-DENIS

The originality of Saint-Denis's contribution to theatre has been questioned: How much of what he achieved was attributable to Copeau, how much his own creativity? Saint-Denis perceived his life's work as a cultural journey "through conventions and styles" ranging from "the Greece of Sophocles to the Japan of the Noh plays; from the Italy of the *Commedia dell'Arte* to the England of Elizabethan days."[24] Guiding him at the beginning of that metaphorical journey was Jacques Copeau. They parted when Saint-Denis moved to continue the quest alone and create an artistic identity distinct from that of Copeau. At the same time, he committed himself to succeeding where his uncle had failed. Copeau provided Michel with an ideal of theatre, taught him to direct, and shared the results of his experimentation. Saint-Denis acknowledged his debt in articles, radio broadcasts, and books written after Copeau's death (1949)—perhaps reflecting his ambivalence—extolling his uncle's contribution to twentieth-century theatre.

But Saint-Denis viewed himself as a pioneer whose goal was to find a place in which to put down artistic roots and build a community of theatrical experimenters working under his direction. Yet like his uncle, Saint-Denis never reached his goal. Copeau's idealism, austerity, and fanaticism would not allow him to accept commercial success. In the case of Saint-Denis, his enterprises frequently crumbled beneath him. The reasons are manifold: lack of money, events beyond his control, and ill-health, but also Saint-Denis's self-defeating inner conflicts. For Copeau passed on his drive for perfection, thus handicapping his nephew. Michel's intimates—his son, his cousin Marie-Hélène Dasté, his wife Suria—speak of an intermittent lack of confidence, a trait hidden from outsiders behind a mask of commanding assurance. In moments of hesitancy he looked to Copeau's teachings for guidance, particularly in his directing. A case in point is Saint-Denis's 1938 *Twelfth Night*; pressured to succeed with Shakespeare, he recreated Copeau's *mise en scène*—a borrowing that failed him. Conversely, Saint-Denis's directorial triumphs, Chekhov's *Three Sisters* and Sophocles' *Oedipus*, Stravinsky's opera-oratorio *Oedipus Rex*, and Obey's *Le viol de Lucrèce* and *La bataille de la Marne* are not only works never undertaken by Copeau, but areas into which he did not venture.

In almost fifty years of struggle Saint-Denis was unable to inhabit a theatrical home; he completed one for the Old Vic Theatre and another for the Strasbourg National Theatre, but others enjoyed their use. His career was characterized by frequent beginnings, triumphs, and disasters or, as he expressed it, "curiously composed of periods of five or six years; every five to six years I start again from zero."[25] He brought to each beginning courage, imagination, and determination. Saint-Denis is often credited with bringing a French theatrical tradition into England. What he brought was a vision; Saint-Denis fathered a modern English tradition. Experience led him to revise Copeau's ideas, adapting them for different theatrical cultures.

Like Copeau, Saint-Denis attracted disciples, but unlike his uncle, Saint-Denis was willing to delegate responsibility. Devoid of Copeau's need for total power, he trained and encouraged his followers to assume leadership roles. Through his disciples his ideas and principles have been emulated and widely disseminated. At the same time, none of his disciples has taken the breadth of Saint-Denis; rather, they have selected aspects of his teaching on which to build their careers.

LEGACY

Saint-Denis's theory and practice were closely woven into the fabric of George Devine's English Stage Company at the Royal Court Theatre, whose experimentation made it a pioneer in postwar British theatre. The Royal Court Company brought about theatrical changes long advocated by Saint-Denis who was, however, disturbed by the company's choice of new material. Saint-Denis still championed the poetic drama that had enjoyed a rebirth in the 1930s and '40s. To mount naturalistic plays such as *Look Back in Anger* was, paradoxically, in his view, retrograde.

Nevertheless, Devine, faithful to Saint-Denis's teaching, incorporated training and workshops into the company. Saint-Denis's early experiments with André Obey had convinced Devine of the value of group improvisation for discovering new forms. William Gaskill and Keith Johnstone's Writers' Group at the Royal Court was an outgrowth of Saint-Denis's concept of developing plays and playwrights through improvisational study. Through the Writers' Group, dramatists at the Royal Court were able to tap into their creativity in new ways. Among those who participated were Ann Jellicoe, John Arden, Arnold Wesker, Edward Bond, and Wole Soyinka. With the exception of Joan Plowright, few Old Vic School or London Theatre Studio actors appeared at the Royal Court; however, their designers (alumni and teachers)—Margaret and Sophie Harris, Jocelyn Herbert, Clare Jeffrey, Alan Tagg, Stephen Doncaster—made significant contributions.

Perhaps truest to the Saint-Denis legacy of the institutions developed by his former students is the Royal Exchange Theatre in Manchester. This was not the first attempt by Old Vic students to form a company; a core group of idealists, including actors Dylis Hamlett, Rosalind Knight, Avril Elgar, and James Maxwell as well as directing and design alumni Casper Wrede and Richard Negri, wanted to stay together to produce work that grew out of a unified aesthetic of theatre. Career paths crossed and recrossed as companies were created and dissolved for the usual reasons: haste, lack of funding, insufficient audience support. However, over a ten-year period the group regularly met to formulate the theatre they wanted in terms of repertory, production, architecture, ethical values, and how to realize it on a practical level. They rejected the Royal Court model of a writers' theatre, judging its new drama too sociologically oriented.[26] The Royal Exchange founded by Maxwell, Wrede, and Negri in association with Braham Murray and Michael Elliott was the result.

The theatre's objectives were to alter the traditional audience–performer relationship by eliminating the formal barriers between them, to create a regional theatre, and to produce plays whose values were "universal and enduring."[27] (In practice, it meant that the repertory leaned heavily on the classics, although new drama has been encouraged through the creation of a writers' workshop and playwriting competitions.) While not a collective, they rejected the conventional hierarchical leadership, opting instead for a collaborative artistic directorship.

Their theatre company began life in 1968 as the 69 Theatre based at Manchester University. In 1976, the company (its name changed to the Royal Exchange) opened a modernist steel-and-glass theatre-in-the-round—designed by Richard Negri in collaboration with the architects—in an eighteenth-century cotton exchange in Manchester. The company has achieved a national reputation for high-quality productions. Despite the departure of four of the founding directorate (through death or retirement), the company's work remains informed "by the convictions . . . of Michel Saint-Denis."[28]

At least two children's theatres were developed by Old Vic alumni. Catherine Dasté returned to Paris, establishing and directing the Pomme Verte (1970–81), whose imaginative productions were geared towards working-class children. Frank Dunlop founded, in connection with the National Theatre, the second Young Vic, a theatre that updated the ambitions of its predecessor while adhering to its principles. Its repertory consisted of classical, experimental, and specially written works that reflected the youthful audience's concerns.

Charles Joris, a graduate of the Strasbourg School, founded and ran the Théâtre Populaire Romand from 1961–2000. The experimental company that operated as a collective was very much in the spirit of the Compagnie des Quinze.

Of the four countries where Saint-Denis worked and built training programs, England, where he spent most of his adult professional life, is ironically the only one where his original institutions have disappeared. Yet his impact on English training is comparable to that of Stanislavsky in the United States; the defining difference is that Saint-Denis implemented his own techniques there, while in the United States, Stanislavsky's work was filtered through early devotees (such as Richard Boleslavsky and Maria Oupenskaya) and (mis)translations of his books. There is scarcely a drama school in England of importance that is not imbued with Saint-Denis's practices. Many of his disciples became teachers who went on to train other teachers. Even a cursory look at Britain's leading drama schools reveals the extent to which Saint-Denis's disciples dominated English training from the 1960s through the 1990s. They, in turn, trained other teachers. George Hall, an alumnus of the Old Vic School, was director of acting at the Central School of Speech from 1963 to 1987. Norman Ayrton, another former Old Vic student, was principal of LAMDA (London Academy of Music and Dramatic Art) for a number of years. John Blatchley was one of the founders of the Drama Centre, which regarded itself as the heir of the Old Vic School. Virginia Snyders, who was director of drama at the Guildhall School of Music and Drama (1992–97), studied at the Old Vic School.

Other alumni brought Saint-Denis's practice to the United States and Canada, and countless others disseminated his ideas in countries as diverse as Australia, Greece, and Jamaica, just to name a few. Although the Juilliard Drama Division is the principal U.S. institution carrying on the Saint-Denis legacy, other British practitioners working in the United States independently of Juilliard implemented his training methods earlier. Among the most significant: the actor Jeremy Geidt was professor of acting at Yale University (1966–79) and presently teaches comic improvisation, Shakespeare, and Chekhov at the American Repertory Theatre Institute and Harvard University; and Duncan Ross taught drama at the University of Washington (1964–79) before becoming artistic director of the Seattle Repertory Company.

The extent of Saint-Denis's legacy, direct and indirect, is perhaps immeasurable. His students and followers work throughout the world as actors, directors, designers, film-makers, and teachers. His ideas and practice have permeated every branch of the theatre. Margaret Harris, who with her associates revolutionized British design, claimed that it was "all based on the work of Michel Saint-Denis."[29] Significant contemporary directors such as Peter Hall and Peter Brook attest to his effect on their work. Specifically, Saint-Denis influenced Hall's productions of Greek tragedy—*The Oresteia* (1981) and *Tantalus* (2000)—through teaching him mask techniques.[30] Undoubtedly, the theatre has changed since Saint-Denis's death in ways that he could not have foreseen. His methods, however, remain valid and valuable because of their inherent flexibility and understanding of the actor's needs.

NOTES

1. Michel Saint-Denis, BBC Section Française.

2. Michel Saint-Denis, letter to Roy Stewart, 31 December 1957. Roy Stewart was an officer of the DDF.

3. Vincent Massey's brother Raymond, who had a distinguished stage and screen career in the United States, is another example of a Canadian unable to practice his art professionally in his own country.

4. Letter from Robin Patterson, president of the Canadian Players, to Michel Saint-Denis, 3 February 1958.

5. Michel Saint-Denis, letter to Pauline McGibbon, 5 August 1958.

6. Michel Saint-Denis, *Training for the Theatre: Premises and Promises*, ed. Suria Saint-Denis (New York: Theatre Arts Books, 1982), 60.

7. Ibid.

8. "Blueprint: Plan for the National Theatre School of Canada" (1960), 2.

9. Ibid., 7.

10. In 1960, there were two other training programs in Québec province, the Conservatoires d'art dramatique in Montréal and Québec, founded in 1954 and 1958 respectively. Their orientation was outdated. In English Canada, five university departments offered an essentially academic approach to theatre.

11. Saint-Denis, *Training for the Theatre*, 60.

12. Edward Gilbert, personal interview, 1 April 1989.

13. Michel Saint-Denis, "Music in the Theatre," unpublished letter at Bryanston Music School, summer 1949.

14. Michel Saint-Denis, letter to Abd'el Kader Farrah, 7 March 1959

15. Michel Saint-Denis, quoted in the *le Figaro* (16 January 1960).

16. Saint-Denis, letter to Farrah.

17. Geoffrey Tarran, *Morning Advertiser* (25 January 1960).

18. *The Times* (17 January 1960); Michel Saint-Denis, letter to Abd'el Kader Farrah, 15 March 1960.

19. *News Chronicle* (16 January 1960).

20. *Time and Tide* (23 January 1960).

21. John Houseman, *Final Dress* (New York: Simon & Schuster, 1983), 313.

22. Charles Railsback, "Michel Saint-Denis and the Organic Theatre," Ph.D. dissertation, Indiana University (1996), 548.

23. Saint-Denis, *Training for the Theatre*, 74.

24. Michel Saint-Denis, "Naturalism in the Theatre," *The Listener* (4 December 1952): 927.

25. Saint-Denis, *Training for the Theatre*, 55.

26. *Words and Pictures 1976–1998: The Royal Exchange Theatre Company* (Manchester: Royal Exchange Theatre Co., Ltd., 1998), 43.

27. Ibid., 44.

28. Ibid., 47.

29. Michael Mullin, *Design by Motley* (Cranbury, NJ: Associated University Presses, 1996), 207.

30. Peter Hall, *Peter Hall's Diaries* (New York: Harper & Row, 1984), 420.

APPENDIX: ACTOR TRAINING

Michel Saint-Denis is unique in the theatre, if only because of the many drama schools he created: the London Theatre Studio (LTS) (1936–39), the Old Vic School (1947–52), the Ecole Supérieure d'Art Dramatique in Strasbourg (1953–present), the Juilliard Drama Division in New York (1968–present), and the National Theatre School of Canada in Montréal (1960–present). But his association with training did not end here. He initiated the Stratford Studio of the Royal Shakespeare Company (RSC) (1962–67) and designed curricula for other institutions such as the Institut National Supérieur des Arts du Spectacle (INSAS) in Brussels (1962–present). Once he left England, although he continued to direct, the balance shifted and his professional life became principally focused on creating theatre schools on an international scale. The Old Vic School provided the prototype, which he then adapted for other training programs. Its program is the exemplar for this chapter. Although Saint-Denis trained practitioners in all aspects of the theatre, the chapter's focus is on the actor.

At LTS, Saint-Denis developed many of the teaching strategies that came to fruition at the Old Vic. It was there, for instance, that he began experimenting with Stanislavsky's system. At the Old Vic, the chief enhancement was the inclusion of Jani Strasser in voice and Litz Pisk in movement. When Saint-Denis established his Strasbourg school, Strasser became director of voice. Although Pisk did not join him in Strasbourg, her protégé Barbara Goodwin was a faculty member. In preparing the curriculum for the Juilliard Drama Division and the National Theatre School of Canada, Saint-Denis used Strasser's and Pisk's approach to their respective disciplines as his model. His sole improvement on the design of the Old Vic School was to increase the course of study from two years to three or four. Three years were necessary, he asserted, to cover the three phases of his training: discovery, interpretation, and performance.

In Strasbourg, Saint-Denis realized that the cultural differences between France and England called for curricular amendments. Further amendments were made in the U.S. and Canadian schools. As an example, Juilliard extended the interpretation phase to two years. However, the training's fundamental philosophy and structure remained unchanged. Half-a-century after the closure of the Old Vic School and more than a quarter-century after his death, his remaining schools still bear the Saint-Denis stamp. All, however, deviate in some measure from his design.

Saint-Denis's ongoing aim was "to serve the contemporary theatre" through the creation of a laboratory composed of a company and school, whose finest graduates would join the troupe.[1] Not surprisingly, he drew on the Vieux-Colombier school. But it was a starting point only, not a paradigm to be imitated slavishly. He changed the focus from research and experimentation to training professionals, and he integrated Stanislavsky's concepts into the curriculum. In adapting Stanislavsky's system, Saint-Denis did not reject his own theatricalist methods; rather, he blended the two. Like Stanislavsky, Saint-Denis endeavored to discover techniques to help the actor truthfully create a character's inner life through physical expression. Stanislavsky, like Saint-Denis, believed that improvisation is key to training the creative actor. Still, Saint-Denis found Stanislavsky's application of improvisation restricted in scope. He thought Stanislavsky's use of realistic themes limited the development of imaginative skills. He was also concerned that the system encouraged too interior an approach whereby the actor may become prisoner of his or her concentration, thus losing crucial critical detachment.

The philosophy underlying Saint-Denis's training "considered the author as the only completely creative person."[2] Consequently, research was geared toward finding the appropriate style for a given work. In order to develop actors qualified to handle the entire theatrical spectrum, Saint-Denis's training repertory included plays of fifth-century BCE Athens, the English Renaissance, Restoration comedy, and modern realism. He sought a process that would allow actors to merge a deep reality with what he termed "big style." A problem for him was how to apply Stanislavsky's techniques effectively in classical drama.

OTHER DRAMA SCHOOLS

Saint-Denis's competitors in London during the 1930s and '40s were the Royal Academy of Dramatic Art (RADA), and the Central School of Speech and Drama, each founded in 1904. Both were unaffected by the evolution that training had undergone abroad. They offered conventional classes in voice, elocution, dance, gesture, and physical deportment. Perhaps because of this emphasis, RADA had a reputation as a finishing school for young ladies; girls outnumbered male students by four-to-one. The Central School was similar. At a time when a university education was not an option for many girls, middle-class parents readily sent their daughters to establishments teaching the social graces. Admittedly, there were also serious students who intended to pursue a theatrical career. In these cases, the schools' ambition was to turn out actors who would be competent to earn their living in the West End or, failing that, in "weekly rep." After the success of LTS and the Old Vic School, these institutions borrowed from Saint-Denis's curricula, but taught the exercises in a vacuum. Not until his students and disciples began teaching and heading schools were his methods disseminated, changing the face of British training and, through that, British acting and *mise en scène*.

GUIDING PHILOSOPHY

Saint-Denis intended to develop practitioners capable of presenting "the classical plays of all times and all nations."[3] He hypothesized that a rigorous classical preparation would produce a versatile actor at home in every dramaturgical style, including what he called yesterday's naturalism and modern realism. Ideally, students would acquire an across-the-board approach that they could use throughout their careers, allowing them to confront unfamiliar types of drama with confidence. Despite Saint-Denis's emphasis on style and its cultural ramifications, he believed the basis of acting to be universal; that is, since the art of acting stems from the imaginative and physical faculties, training techniques emphasizing both were needed.

His policy dictated that the faculty be made up of first-rate teachers who maintained a link to the professional theatre. A small core of permanent teachers, assisted by less experienced instructors, was augmented by visiting artists whose professional involvement was usually more active. Among the advantages students gained was a realistic understanding of their future occupation as well as potential employment contacts. Disadvantageous was the rapid turnover of instructors that occasionally caused confusion and disrupted the training.

The teaching of style as a theatrical reality was demystified at Saint-Denis's schools by the concrete and pragmatic methods adopted. Because of the integrated curriculum, all the classes focused on the style being explored in a particular term. Students investigated the life, manners, customs, and art of the culture under consideration. Research was not done in the abstract; its object was always the accurate physical expression in acting terms of that culture. Sometimes a specific area was found to hold the key to a particular style. For example, Restoration comedy was taught through period dance, which proved an excellent medium for developing the elegance, spirit, and subtle responses that the era requires of actors. In reality, dance had played an important role in the period's social structure; fencing and other forms of personal combat had been outlawed, and the dance floor had replaced the field of honor. Young men were expected to prove their masculinity through winning attractive women in complicated courtship rituals.

Another significant Saint-Denis contribution was the creation of a comprehensive, integrated course of study that fused technique and imagination. Every area of instruction overlapped; skills were taught as a unified whole rather than in isolation. Students received instruction from a coordinated faculty working for a common purpose. Since training was geared to the individual, frequent faculty meetings were held to discuss student progress. Saint-Denis was convinced that the faculty had to share a training perspective so that, for instance, the voice teacher understood and built on the work of the acting or movement instructor. As a case in point: A movement exercise for the foot might evolve into an improvisation of walking on muddy terrain, then into a full-fledged scenario of a character lost at night in a swamp. At a more advanced stage, a complete play was normally the vehicle for coordinating instruction. Many of Saint-Denis's exercises have become common currency in training programs and acting books, but with few exceptions they are employed piecemeal.

Still another distinctive characteristic of Saint-Denis's schools was their creation of an ensemble. Each class trained together and functioned as a company during the final year. Classes did not intermingle in either training or production. To maintain a sense of uniqueness, each class received a number that corresponded to the age of the school. Thus the first class at the Old Vic was called Group 1, the second, Group 2, and so on. This practice fostered a sense of peer identification. Students were to work together for the good of the group and the production. The school's environment furthered self-discipline, dedication to one's art, and appreciation of the theatre as a vocation. In the London theatre Saint-Denis encountered such ideas were considered grandiose. Skeptics found pretentious his seriousness, discipline, and unrelenting search for the truth pretentious.

SCHEDULE

The academic year, October to June, was composed of three ten-week terms. While the general outline of the work was constant, each term offered modifications. The schedule was laid out in ten-day periods and posted. Classes ran from 9:30 in the morning to as late as 7:30 P.M. Monday through Friday, with an hour's lunch break, and on Saturday from 9:30 to 1:30. During the evenings school shows were rehearsed. Classes lasted from thirty minutes to two hours; rehearsals were of necessity longer.

On the first day of the term Saint-Denis and the faculty met with the student body to discuss the program and objectives for that trimester. Students with special problems could make them known and opt for special or additional classes. In theory, technical classes (movement, voice, speech) met in the morning and interpretive ones in the afternoon, but it was not always possible to adhere to this timetable. Ideally, students spent the mornings in gymnastics, fencing, dance, and voice. Fencing was an all-male class; women took supplementary courses such as voice limbering or costume technique during that time.[4] A class in special diction was taken by students with speech problems such as a nonstandard or foreign accent.[5] The school tried to schedule first-year improvisation and style in the afternoon. Rehearsal classes took place in the second half of the day. Groups were usually taught in two sections; for more individualized work, in three.

CURRICULUM

For Saint-Denis, characterization was the essence of acting; accordingly, the acting classes concentrated on the transformational aspect of performing. The program was divided into four basic elements—movement, vocal training, improvisation, and interpretation—which, in turn, were broken down into smaller units. Each element was taught from a technical and interpretive perspective, although certain classes were naturally more oriented toward technique and others toward imagination. The students' education was supplemented by informal weekly lectures on acting, theatre history and architecture, and culture. Cultural studies were linked to the plays in process.

Saint-Denis concluded that in order to become self-expressive, the actor needed first to master fundamental theatrical skills. Thus his students developed technical tools in anticipation of utilizing them in plays: students studied poetry before they did Shakespeare, did physical exercises before they spoke, and had speech classes before undertaking dramatic text.[6]

Movement

That the body is at least as expressive as the voice was an almost revolutionary notion in British drama schools. Not that other schools completely ignored physical training, but its use would have been stereotypical and limited. Contrary to traditional practice, at the Old Vic School, movement was taught throughout the entire course of study (as were all technique classes), most intensively during the first year when students took several hours of physical training daily. Under this rubric were gymnastics, dance, acrobatics, period movement, dramatic movement, and fencing. The inclusion of fencing is an illustration of a Saint-Denis cultural adaptation. At the Vieux-Colombier School fencing was considered unnecessary because French classical tragedy is static, unlike action-packed English Renaissance tragedy.

The same principles underlay all the movement classes. Students were continually reminded that emotion and character are expressed physically—or, in the words of Saint-Denis, movement "is the outer expression of the inner continuity of a role."[7] While each movement class endeavored to teach relaxation, awareness, strength-building, coordination, concentration, responsiveness, and economy of energy, its focal point varied. Fencing emphasized dexterity and reactivity; acrobatics concentrated on circus and vaudeville tricks; dance, rhythm. Integrated into the classes were ideas of scenic space and time.

Saint-Denis directed Motley to design a practice costume for movement classes; its rationale in part was to force students to confront and conquer self-consciousness. Identical for males and females, it resembled an unbecoming one-piece bathing suit that immediately revealed any physical flaws and/or difficulties with the exercises.

Litz Pisk taught period movement and dance, but it was her gymnastics class that laid the foundation for all the movement work. In it, she stressed flexibility and physical relaxation, problems for the novice who is often physically inhibited. To achieve a harmonious fluent body—neither too tight nor too loose—can seem an impossible objective. Tension is a problem that actors have always struggled with, which other drama schools had attempted to solve. That the Old Vic was more successful was due largely to Pisk, but also to its global approach.

So many of Pisk's exercises have been incorporated into mainstream programs that it may be hard to grasp how novel her work was. While rigorous, her training dealt with more than the mechanics of the body. It was a journey into self-discovery where students explored their corporeal limits and learned to extend their physical, emotional, and imaginative capacity. Central to her teaching were two images that helped shatter the students' preconceived notions. The first was that the body is a sculpture in process that actors, regardless of shape, can metamorphose into the configuration of any character they are called upon to play. The second, the human body as a musical instrument. As musicians control their instruments, so actors must be in command of their bodies. For like sound, movement projects. The bones that act as the "keys" have to move freely. Connecting the keys are the ligaments representing the "strings" that must have the proper tension. Continuing the metaphor, the muscles must be "tuned," that is, strengthened to produce an effect.

All the gymnastic exercises employed three basic mechanical functions: stretching, bending, and rotating. The starting point was the spine: Pitz's ruling belief being that "movement emanates from your center to your periphery and beyond and shares itself out in space."[8] As emotional expression emanates from within, physical expression finds its impulse "as centered within the body as possible, moves to the limbs, and finally projects out into the audience." Accordingly, classes began with a repetitive series of whole-body exercises performed standing, kneeling, and sitting in which the spine was coiled and uncoiled. In each position, the student slowly rolled forward, the upper-body dropping forward and inward. Reversing the movement, the upper-body unrolled vertebra by vertebra. Variations, based on principles of tension and release, were practiced. An extension was the fall and rebound, a strenuous jump undertaken from a standing position, the body still, arms by the sides. In the air, the arms, hands, and legs were shaken vigorously, accompanied by a shout. As the feet touched the ground, the body collapsed, sank to the floor, recovered; the student got up, bounced, and stood relaxed, ready to replicate it.

The next phase investigated the potential of the body in space. Exercises involved myriad ways of walking, running, turning, jumping, falling—backward, forward, sideward, on all fours, on the toes, on the hands—at varying tempos. Isolations of the head, facial features, neck, shoulders, upper-arms, lower-arms, wrists, hands, fingers, hips, thighs, lower-leg, ankle, foot, toes followed. Ultimately, the exercises were injected with sound: initially spontaneous cries, then a few words, then lines of text. In this way, the students examined the effects of sound on movement and the converse.

Having attained the ability to isolate, students began gestural language; that is, to portray sensation, mood, emotion—in that order—using a single part of the body. Initial attempts were generally stereotypical and mechanical. These physical exercises required application of the internal faculties of imagination, observation, empathy, and memory. How to depict the sensation of a cold winter day or a warm summer breeze using only one part of the body? Or how to raise the shoulders to express a particular emotion? A shrug can communicate indifference, dejection, or anger. Superficially, the exercises suggest the work of the nineteenth-century teacher Delsarte, but differ in that his work was tied to theatrical convention whereas Pisk's students individuated and personalized the exercises. The student's task was to find ways of differentiating the movement to demonstrate the degree and quality of the emotion. This work was further developed in improvisation.

Vocal Training

Saint-Denis regarded vocal training as "the most time-consuming and difficult of all theatre disciplines."[9] He believed that the development of Western urban culture had had a stultifying effect on the human voice. In cultures rooted in folkloric traditions, the voice retained a vibrancy and tonal variety he wished to reclaim.[10] Modern society created a rupture between intellect and emotion, mind and body that needs to be fused for the actor whose task is to reveal feeling through words. However, too often words are associated only with the intellectual faculties. Saint-Denis strove to find a method that would bypass this association. Singing, which implies release and heightened emotion, became the point of departure, the means through which the student would gain variety and richness of tone, color, and musicality. The Old Vic School divided vocal work into singing, voice, speech, and diction.

Voice production. Jani Strasser, a former coach for the Glyndebourne Opera, developed a technique based on singing, which for him was an extension of speech. His training also had multiple objectives: to develop the speaking voice, to teach even the tone-deaf to sing, and to inculcate an approach to style through songs of contrasting periods and types.[11] By the third term, students undertook "sung improvisations," which called on their imaginative, improvisational, speech, and musical skills. Typical was the Figaro Project in which Mozart's opera served as a vehicle. Students learned a portion of *The Marriage of Figaro*, then developed their own characters and scenarios. The final step was to combine their original improvisation with the opera's music.

Where Pisk encouraged vocalizing in gymnastic exercises to liberate the body, Strasser used physical exercises, in conjunction with vocalizing or alone, to free the breathing and vocal mechanism. He taught that the key to breath control was relaxation, a dictum students found paradoxical. Yet the ability to achieve simultaneous control and relaxation is necessary in every phase of an actor's work. To his pupils' amusement, he illustrated the concept with a metaphor: the circus trainer and the poodle. The trainer represented the brain—the poodle, the instincts. The students were to teach the poodle to jump through the hoop without being told; that is, to train their vocal and breathing apparatus to produce correct sound spontaneously. Until they reached that stage the "trick" would not be successful, the "poodle" would miss the hoop. Once in command of their voice, actors must trust their skill, let go of the leash, and follow their instincts.

The muscles governing breath can be consciously controlled only through painstaking training. Strasser designed strenuous movements, seemingly unrelated to breath control and voice production, which exercised the requisite muscles.[12] There were exercises for relaxation and strength building: shaking out, pliés, stretches. Others were for muscles related to speech: diaphragm and lungs, vocal cords and larynx, resonators and articulators.

Speech. Speech, taught by Marion (Mamie) Watson, was associated with voice production and gymnastics, the teachers sometimes combining classes. Watson concentrated on diction, modulation, rhythm, color, projection, and vocal imagination. She also utilized improvisations; some were solo, others paired, and still others required small groups. Each class began with technical work in relaxation and strengthening of the speech muscles.

In keeping with Saint-Denis's philosophy of learning as process, the students progressed at a measured pace, gaining competence in one area before beginning the next. They worked in depth on brief texts, often fragments. Watson's students did not use playscripts for an entire term; nondramatic text bridged the gap between technical exercises and drama. Texts might be a newspaper column, a recipe, or a nursery rhyme; the essential criterion was a lack of intensity. The purpose was to develop the actor's ability "to bring to life each particular text in the proper character and intention."[13] Animating inherently untheatrical material aided the student in developing imaginative ability.

Initially, the students worked on communicating, phrasing, inflection, tone, pace, and rhythm. Later, they began playing with words, exploring their meaning, taking pleasure in their sound. At this juncture, a situation and/or character was added and basic acting questions addressed: To whom was the material being read, why, under what circumstances? Other exercises included speaking the text clearly while performing a complex action or establishing a mood.

Subsequently, students grappled with literary texts, both prose and poetry, that served as an introduction to the styles studied in acting. Examples included excerpts from *The Odyssey*, Plato's *Apology*, and Milton's *Paradise Lost*.

We are fortunate in having Watson's 1948–49 lesson plans for the second term of first-year speech. Below are sample exercises—by no means a complete list. Spoken improvisations approximate the silent improvisations thematically.

Weeks 1 and 2. Vocal Color.
Improvised Scenes Demonstrating Physical Sensations

1. Two people are lying under a tree cooling off after a hot climb up a hill. At first, they talk of the climb and the heat, then about the tree, the birds, the view, etc. They become more comfortable and begin discussing their childhood, remembering something that makes them laugh. After the laughter subsides, they wonder where they will be this time next year, but less confidently. They feel chilly and leave.
2. Two people are sitting up late at night during an air raid. They are stiff, cold, and sleepless. They think they hear something; they listen, but it is nothing. They try to sleep, but are too cold. Someone brings tea. As they drink, they begin to talk of trivial plans for tomorrow. The All-Clear sounds. They gather up their things and go to bed.[14]

Week 3

Students continued working on the effects of weather on vocal tone and quality. They read Act One of Elmer Rice's *Street Scene*, which takes place during a hot summer. This exercise utilized scripted material, but for a specific purpose.

Week 4. Mood

Students worked on two nursery rhymes to express differing moods, consciously varying tone, pitch, inflection, tempo, and phrasing. [Moods were a precursor to emotion.]

Week 5. Exercises for Projection. Physical Size

[Interestingly, early projection exercises were silent, since Watson did not feel the students were ready for extended vocal volume.]

1. The student is compressed into a very small box. The lid is removed and the actor gradually expands to full height.
2. The student is alternately a giant and a pigmy. The focus is not on the student's size, but on the size of the objects around him or her.

Week 6. Projection. Shouting and Whispering

1. Call to stop someone who is running away.
2. Call from the street to people on the top story of a building. Tell them to come down because you are going on a picnic.
3. Two people on a hillside are trying to find each other in a mist.

Week 7. Projection. Authority

1. Come into a room and see your small child sleepwalking, balanced on the sill of an open window. Don't startle her, but speak so firmly and authoritatively, that she obeys.
2. Two people working together, one a child, the other an adult. The adult gives three commands: "Get out of this room," "Go away," "Go." If the commands are given with sufficient authority, the child obeys. [The students reversed roles in this exercise.]
3. A group of children in an orphanage are rebelling because of bad food. Excited, they are about to find the orphanage director when he enters the room. A small person, he cannot quell the children with his size or fearsomeness. He says, "What is all this noise about?" They answer simultaneously. "Sit down quietly, I said, 'sit down.'" If spoken with sufficient authority, the children obey. [Although Watson does not comment on how having a female student play the director affected the scene, it seems obvious the dynamics would change. Her notes add that it was a challenging exercise.]

Week 8. Projection. Intensity

[Group work. The following exercise was rehearsed out of class before its first presentation. From this point on, improvisations were developed over an entire week, in and out of class.]

Portraying the leader of an underground-resistance movement, a student gives instructions for a dangerous mission. The leader first warns the group of the risk attached, but in such a way they are inspired to undertake it. The directions are detailed. Nothing can be written down, so it is vital that they understand clearly and remember. The resistance leader wishes them luck and leaves.

Week 9. A Radio Commentary of an Important Event

Solo improvisation. The Announcer describes the general scene; little is happening and he or she has to try to make it interesting. Something starts happening and works up to an exciting climax. [Watson's notes add that this exercise was geared toward Speech Delivery.]

Week 10. A Ghost Story

Solo improvisation. The story is told, not read, with emphasis on sustaining interest. [Also assigned for work on Speech Delivery.]

Improvisation

Improvisation classes were both spoken and unspoken. Silent improvisation, "the alphabet of acting where the student learns *how* to invent," was the basis of much of the training during the discovery year.[15] First-year students had silent improvisation two hours per day; in the second year, improvisation classes met through term five, but less frequently. Silent improvisation took two forms, masked and unmasked, taught as separate disciplines. Both were crossover classes where movement and interpretation shared equal focus, their objective being to learn to express action and character without words. Words, as Saint-Denis would reiterate, are the result of an inner state, which originates in the body.[16] He hypothesized that working improvisationally on characterization and situation liberated the inexperienced actor's spontaneity and inventiveness; without improvisational training, the actor would freeze when confronting the written word. Although improvisation implies extemporaneousness, class exercises were rehearsed over a long period. Improvisation functioned as a bridge to acting full-scale plays, although written texts played no part in these classes.

Unmasked Improvisation was the province of the movement director, Suria Magito, who acquired the skills under Saint-Denis's tutelage. The class was distinguished from formal pantomime, which Magito disparaged "as a series of set gestures."[17] Improvisation concentrated on the projection of the imagination through physical actions; the more inventive, the more powerful the resulting exercise. Clad in practice attire, performing without the aid of props, costumes, or text, with nothing to hide behind, students frequently found the exercises threatening. Warm-ups and sensory work were integral to the class. After exercising their hands, students might be asked to touch an imaginary cake of ice, then a hot plate, to stroke nonexistent silks, velvets, burlap, to thread a needle, to carry imaginary objects across a room. Exercises for the feet and legs included kicking a ball, climbing up and down hills, and walking on dissimilar surfaces. Exercises for the eyes involved seeing things near and far or going from light to dark.

From single tasks, the student progressed to one-person scenarios involving more complex behavior such as eating a meal or reading a letter. Specificity, dramatic build and the use of the space had to be considered. If eating, what kind of food was being consumed; if reading a letter, what were its contents, who had written it? The student had to establish the environment while using the space in a theatrically practical way. Complications were injected into the scenario—a mood, a specific incident, an obstacle in the form of a physicalization—to see how they affected the tempo and/or the actions. At first the instructor determined the details of the scenario, but with practice students invented sections for themselves.

Character Improvisation taught by George Devine was the comic equivalent of Magito's class. The greatest difference in approach was its focus on sounds. Students perfected a wide spectrum of noises, many socially unacceptable such as belching, snoring, gargling, nose-blowing, and so on, which were incorporated into improvisations.

Typical One-Person Scenario

The student is walking in a field, carrying a picnic lunch. Finds a tree, sits, and begins eating lunch. The sun shining through the leaves disturbs the student who moves into the shade, sits down again, and discovers he or she is sitting on an anthill. Leaves.

Characterization through physicalization. As the students gained mastery, they worked in pairs, groups of three, and finally as an ensemble, concurrently developing solo exercises, notably occupations and animal mime. The latter two were considered useful tools in developing not only the actor's inventiveness and powers of observation but also characterization. They required the actor to work out concretely the physical details of character. Typically, characterization was presented gradually. Until this time, the students had been asked only to play themselves in a given situation. For the occupation exercise, they had to imagine themselves working at jobs frequently alien to these largely middle-class students. The occupations were taken from the service industry, crafts, and trades. Student-actors were not yet developing a precise character, but rather discovering how the physicalizations necessitated by a profession can reshape posture, balance, gait, and gestures. The physical adjustments demanded were an elementary step toward transformation.

Animal improvisations required an even more careful and elaborate preparation. Selecting an appropriate animal was crucial; an ill-advised choice would waste an entire term. On the one hand, students were advised to make sure it provided a stretch for their abilities, but neither too challenging physically nor too threatening emotionally; on the other, they were to eschew the obvious. More than the literal imitation of the animal's physical attributes, the exercise explored its essence and dramatic possibilities. Students had to avoid getting bogged down in naturalistic detail; therefore, it was undesirable to represent a four-legged animal on the hands and knees. Saint-Denis cited the following portrayal of a cow as an exemplar: "Standing on her two legs, with her torso slightly bent forward and with her arms hanging down, the student established the cow by making a kind of comment on the cow's body: the way she chased insects away by a movement of her head; the way she munched her food, with an inward look in her eyes."[18] The student had captured the quintessential qualities of the cow. In order to achieve this level, she had minutely observed the animal's physical and emotional nature. How does it stand, move, hold the various parts of its body, what moods does it communicate? Having studied and physically worked though all these elements, she stripped away the superfluous and depicted what "reads" dramatically. Hers was an illustration of Saint-Denis's distinction between theatrical truth and naturalism. Having selected a simple action typical of the animal, students invented a brief scenario, placing it in time and space. As the term continued, the scenarios became more intricate.

Ensemble improvisation. The natural progression of the course led to group, or, in Saint-Denis's words, choral improvisations. This ensemble work trained actors to participate as group members yet retain their creative individuality. The class, divided into two or three groups, developed situations suggested by the instructor. Although similar to those of the Copiaus and the Quinze, themes tended more toward the catastrophic and/or suspenseful. Characteristic scenarios were "The Lifeboat" in which the cast of characters found themselves ship-wrecked, and "Refugees" whose characters, fleeing an invading army, tried desperately to cross a sealed border. These dramatic, some might say melodramatic, situations offered a range of characterization and conflict opportunities. As the project took shape, the instructor staged it. The better second-year group improvisations were performed publicly in the end-of-term shows.

Music, sounds, and "grummelotage" were infused into the nonverbal exercises to establish atmosphere. Sound and movement carried the story. "A Day in the Life of a Village," a choral improvisation developed by Group 2, illustrates the form.[19] This particular project incorporated the students' animal studies. Similar in content to *La Bataille de la Marne*, it was set in France at the beginning of World War II. Ten mimed scenes detailed the life of the villagers, from the dawn of a peaceful day to the German invasion and the inhabitants' flight.

Mask. Toward the end of the first year, students began working with neutral and comic masks. Each had its own instructor: Saint-Denis's domain was neutral mask; the comic, George Devine's. Both mask types have their roots in ancient theatre: the neutral derives from Greek tragedy; the comic from commedia dell'arte. Both emphasize clarity of intention, action, and feeling. The mask prevents psychologizing—anathema to Saint-Denis—since by its very nature it is antirealistic. Mask training had three practical goals: to eradicate hackneyed mannerisms, to teach the students to release creative impulses, and to prepare them to work on classical roles.

Donning the mask for the first time, students commonly feel intimidated and/or imprisoned. They have yet to learn that the mask is an inanimate object capable of absorbing the wearer's personality. But at the same time, it dictates to the actor. As Saint-Denis writes: "How to discover the meeting point between the internal and the external is one of the essential secrets of acting."[20] The mask is invaluable in bringing the actor to this point—it becomes a liberating experience, leading to a world of myth, dream, and poetry.

Saint-Denis's students worked with eight types of full-faced masks, designed by Motley—four male, four female. Although the masks were neutral, they were not completely without character. Each one represented a stage of life: childhood, youth, maturity, and old age. The mask's age clearly affected whatever movement choices the actor made. This is not to say that the actor was trapped in clichéd or predetermined movement; rather, if the actor was open, the age acted as a guide to an appropriate physicality. The mask's lack of individuality stimulated the creation of archetypal characters and situations: The oldest, perhaps a king like Lear confronting betrayal or mortality; the youths, perhaps lovers like Romeo and Juliet or Antigone and Haemon facing parental rage. Human features were represented but not emotions. It was up to the actor to fill the mask, to bring life and feeling to it through movement.

In the first exercise, the student selected a mask, contemplated it, donned it, and slowly raised and lowered the head several times. Next, the student duplicated the same sequence, but motivating the action. The student never looked in a mirror while wearing the mask, but rather let it permeate him or her while holding it. If students saw themselves wearing the neutral mask they might become overwhelmed, whereas communing with it fed their imaginations. Beneath the mask, they were deprived of those aspects of themselves they most depended on for expressiveness—the face and the voice. Their faces were covered, their bodies exposed—a reversal of the norm.

The teacher defined the dramatic actions that in their early stages were simple and brief. As they gained proficiency, students had more input, inventing characters, embellishing, and creating scenarios. Yet even in the early exercises the given circumstances were highly charged, as the following indicates:

> After choosing the male child mask, the student was instructed to enter the playing area and sit. He then repeated the sequence, but with the added circumstances that the room he had left contained the corpse of someone who had recently died. This was the first dead body he had ever seen. What kind of emotions might the child experience? How do these emotions influence the way in which the actor comes in and sits?

The problem facing the student was how to portray emotions in "the zone of silence."[21] These mimed moments resemble life, but the actor must not enact feelings in a psychological sense. They are expressed corporeally, but with the minimum of action that can show the maximum of feeling. Two elements, truth and simplicity, are at the core of the work.

The actor learns that the mask needs action to achieve its potential, but that movement must be deliberate, never haphazard. The slightest turn of the head has significance. Naturalistic gestures don't work. Sudden or violent movements prevent the audience from comprehending the moment. Over the course of the class, students developed full-fledged *études*. Themes were drawn from the world of the subconscious. One such exercise was the portrayal of a dream in which the student turned into a fierce animal.

Two-person improvisations were intricate, as in this three-character transformation exercise for two actors:

> Wearing youth masks, a newly married couple comes to a lakeshore and throws coins into the lake for luck. They then go off, their arms about each other. They go round the screen, change masks and return to the lake as adults. The husband is bored, the wife sentimental. The third time, the wife enters alone, doddering, wearing the mask of old age. A moment later her grandson appears, looking for his grandmother. Through his actions, we understand he is afraid she might have fallen into the lake. He finds her, pulls her off as she hangs back looking at the lake.

Throughout the course, the importance of the actor's *mise en scène* or self-staging was stressed. The students practiced thinking visually, developing an awareness of how to use their movement, gesture, line effectively within the dramatic composition.

George Devine developed the comic or character mask class in consultation with Saint-Denis. Devine's class differed from Saint-Denis's because of the material, the format, and his personality. Devine was accessible, whereas students stood in awe of Michel Saint-Denis. If neutral masks pushed the student-actors in the direction of magical, legendary archetypes, comic masks guided them toward the creation of farcical contemporary stock characters. And unlike their other improvisation work, this class encouraged the fabrication of dialogue. Motley constructed about two dozen Halloween-like half-masks, which adhered tightly to the face but permitted speech. Grotesque in design, they were modern counterparts of ancient commedia types. Students were permitted to use costumes, padding, and props—all aids in devising gags and shtick.

Classes began with two or three students choosing a mask and costume pieces. Unlike neutral mask, several students worked simultaneously, even in solo exercises. Once costumed, they looked into a mirror, letting their reflection suggest a character. Saint-Denis had concluded that students were more inventive with comic masks if they saw their reflection. Since the comic masks were individualized, they suggested ideas more readily than the neutral masks. The resulting characters were at once stereotypical and idiosyncratic. Students walked around the room to discover their physical life, simultaneously vocalizing to find a character voice. At this point they did not react to one another. When the instructor saw a personage emerge, he asked the actor simple questions: Who are you? Where do you live? What is your profession, and so on? The students answered in the character they were in the process of building. Those characters frequently were life's losers—a derelict, a frustrated spinster, a boy obsessed with a movie star, a spoiled brat.

The next step was playing a situation with other actors; three was the optimal number for developing and sustaining a conflict. Because of the freer atmosphere of comic mask, students tended at this early stage to depend too heavily on dialogue for characterization. In comic mask, movements and gestures are smaller and more confined than in neutral mask, but their role in the improvisations is more important than the vocal aspect. Over the long term, situations often evolved that necessitated more actors. Still, character development was more important than situation, another way in which the course differed from neutral mask. The scenarios involved mundane predicaments, but ones that lent themselves to conflict. Generally, the characters were strangers thrown together in a public place such as a dentist's office, a train compartment, a line at the store. But more than the circumstances, it was the characters with their differing needs and personalities rubbing up against one another that led to clashes.

Early improvisations were performed only once; but as the class progressed, students built on their characters much as Saint-Denis had developed Oscar Knie.

Interpretation and Rehearsal

Following the "test play," which made the inexperienced beginners painfully conscious of how much they needed to learn, work on interpreting a role was halted; the remaining first half of the year concentrated on technical classes. Nonetheless, in preparation for their future acting classes, they took dramatic text, which met once a week. Under the guidance of their instructor, students analyzed the scripts they were to work on later in the year. This course was also "used to give students the right approach toward their rehearsal work."[22] Topics covered were the way to read a play, the director's and actor's differing tasks in staging the play, how to learn lines, and rehearsal progression—and, as always, style.

In interpretation, which met daily during the latter part of the year, three plays of varying styles were worked on but not completed. Here classes focused on entire plays or, if necessary, acts of plays. The styles depended on the students' needs but generally included a realistic drama, a high comedy, and a Shakespearean play. Students learned that the approach for each type of play varied; the subtleties of Chekhov made different demands on the actor than the witty dialogue of Restoration comedy. Looked at superficially, the course seems to mandate an external approach at the expense of inner truth. The reality was that both techniques were combined. When beginning a play's study, the students wrote character histories to ground them within its world. They were constantly cautioned to look for motivation. As Lee Montague remembered: "'Look inwards,' we were told, 'think back; *why* does he do it like that?'"[23] At the end of two-and-a-half weeks they moved on to the next one, but not before the faculty had seen and criticized their work.

To help the students deal with style, Motley designed adaptable rehearsal clothes. Girls had long black woolen skirts with drawstrings through the waistband and fasteners along the sides. This arrangement allowed the skirt to be hitched up to different lengths or to give the effect of wearing crinolines or hoop skirts. The boys' trousers had fasteners down the sides that allowed them to suggest various eras through adjusting the width.

The second year was dedicated to turning the group into a performing company. Interpretation classes that were, in effect, rehearsals became the means of teaching and learning. All other classes were subordinate to and supported interpretation. If, for instance, students were rehearsing a Renaissance drama, movement classes would use dances of the period, singing classes would teach appropriate music, and speech classes would concentrate on textual or diction problems relating to the production.

Although one goal of interpretation was to simulate professional conditions, the exercise's pedagogical purpose was taken into consideration. Hence, the rehearsal conditions were considerably better than those found in "weekly rep" companies. During the first term of the second year students were still assigned roles, not necessarily because the part suited them but for learning purposes. By term five, students competed for roles that were awarded by ability. Their performances, now attended by the public, were not meant simply to showcase the actor but to present a finished piece of work.

NOTES

1. Michel Saint-Denis, "The English Theatre in Gallic Eyes," trans. J. F. M. Stephens, Jr., *Texas Quarterly* 4 (autumn 1961): 34.

2. Michel Saint-Denis, *Theatre: The Rediscovery of Style* (New York: Theatre Arts Books, 1960), 92.

3. James Forsyth, "The Old Vic Theatre School," sound filmstrip, British Council (undated).

4. There were apparently exceptions; a 1950 photo from the *Evening Standard* features two female students fencing.

5. The school was unusual in accepting students from non-English speaking countries.

6. Michael Kahn, personal interview, 13 April 1998.

7. Michel Saint-Denis, *Training for the Theatre Premises and Promises*, ed. Suria Saint-Denis (New York: Theatre Arts Books, 1982), 102.

8. Litz Pisk, *The Actor and His Body* (New York: Theatre Arts Books, 1976), 10.

9. Michel Saint-Denis, from a speech given in Brussels in 1962.

10. Michel and Suria Saint-Denis, letter to John Houseman, spring 1968.

11. George Devine, "An Outline of the Training at the Old Vic Theatre School," undated address to the students given by Saint-Denis, Devine, and Byam Shaw.

12. Sylvia Short, Group 4, personal notes.

13. Juilliard Bible.

14. A number of the improvisations used contemporary themes. World War II was fresh in the students' minds.

15. Catherine Dasté, Group 4, personal notes.

16. Saint-Denis, *Training for the Theatre*, 116.

17. Short, personal notes.

18. Saint-Denis, *Training for the Theatre*, 160.

19. Michel Saint-Denis, personal notes for the Old Vic School acting course.

20. Saint-Denis, *Training for the Theatre*, 175.

21. Pierre Lefèvre, personal interview, 1 August 1990.

22. Saint-Denis, personal notes.

23. Margaret McCall, *My Drama School* (London: Robson Books, 1978), 143.

SELECT BIBLIOGRAPHY

Abirached, Robert. *La Décentralisation théâtrale I. Le premier âge 1945–1958*. Paris: Actes Sud-Papiers, 1992.

Agate, James. *The Amazing Theatre*. London: George G. Harrap & Co., 1939.

Aykroyd, Phyllis. *The Dramatic Art of La Compagnie des Quinze*. London: Eric Partridge, 1935.

Billington, Michael. *Peggy Ashcroft*. London: John Murray, 1988.

Borgal, Clément. *Jacques Copeau*. Paris: L'Arche, 1960.

Briggs, Asa. *The War of Words: The History of Broadcasting in the United Kingdom*, vol. 3. London: Oxford University Press, 1970.

Copeau, Jacques. *Registres I: Appels*, eds. Marie-Hélène Dasté and Suzanne Maistre Saint-Denis. Paris: Gallimard, 1974.

———. *Registres IV: Les Registres du Vieux-Colombier II*, eds. Marie-Hélène Dasté and Suzanne Maistre Saint-Denis. Paris: Gallimard, 1984.

———. *Registres V: Les Registres du Vieux-Colombier III*, eds. Suzanne Maistre Saint-Denis and Marie-Hélène Dasté. Paris: Gallimard, 1993.

Denizot-Foulquier, Marion. *Jeanne Laurent, le théâtre et les arts*. Association pour l'Animation du Château de Kerjean, 1997.

Eck, Hélène. *La guerre des ondes: Histoire des radios de langue française pendant la Deuxième Guerre mondiale*. Paris: Armand Colin, 1985.

Elsom, John, and Nicholas Tomalin. *The History of the National Theatre*. London: Jonathan Cape, 1978.

Forsyth, James. *Tyrone Guthrie: A Biography*. London: Hamilton, 1976.

Gielgud, John. *Early Stages*. London: Falcon Press, 1948.

Gielgud, John, J. Miller, and J. Powell. *An Actor and His Time*. London: Penguin, 1979.

Gignoux, Hubert. *Histoire d'une famille théâtrale*. Lausanne: Editions de l'Aire, 1984.

Gontard, Denis. *La Décentralisation théâtrale en France 1895–1952*. Paris: Société d'Édition d'Enseignement Supérieure, 1973.

———, ed. *Le journal de bord des Copiaus 1924–1929*. Paris: Éditions Seghers, 1974.

Guinness, Alec. *Blessings in Disguise*. New York: Knopf, 1985.

Holden, Anthony. *Laurence Olivier*. New York: Atheneum, 1983.

Houseman, John. *Final Dress*. New York: Simon & Schuster, 1983.

Keown, Eric. *Peggy Ashcroft*. Bristol, UK: Rockliff, 1955.

Kurtz, Maurice. *Jacques Copeau: biographie d'un théâtre*. Paris: Les Éditions Nagel, 1950.

Landstone, Charles. *Off-stage: A Personal Record of the First Twelve Years of State-Sponsored Drama in Great Britain*. London: Elek, 1953.

Lee, Betty. *Love and Whiskey: The Story of the Dominion Drama Festival and the Early Years of Theatre in Canada 1606–1972*. Toronto: Simon and Pierre, 1973.

McCall, Margaret. *My Drama School*. London: Robson Books, 1978.

Mullin, Michael. *Design by Motley*. Cranbury, NJ: Associated University Presses, 1996.

Oberlé, Jean. *Jean Oberlé vous parle: Souvenirs de cinq années à Londres*. Paris: La Jeune Parque, 1945.

Olivier, Laurence. *Confessions of an Actor: An Autobiography*. Middlesex, UK: Penguin Books, 1984.

Olmstead, Andrea. *Juilliard: A History*. Urbana: University of Illinois Press, 1999.

Pisk, Litz. *The Actor and His Body*. New York: Theatre Arts Books, 1976.

Rudlin, John. *Jacques Copeau*. Cambridge: Cambridge University Press, 1986.

Rudlin, John, and Norman Paul, eds. and trans. *Copeau: Texts on Theatre*. London: Routledge, 1990.

Saint-Denis, Michel. *Theatre: The Rediscovery of Style*. New York: Theatre Arts Books, 1960.

———. *Training for the Theatre: Premises and Promises*, ed. Suria Saint-Denis. New York: Theatre Arts Books, 1982.

Villard, Jean Gilles. *Mon demi-siècle*. Lausanne: Payot, 1954.

Wardle, Irving. *The Theatres of George Devine*. London: Eyre Methuen, 1978.

Williamson, Audrey. *Theatre of Two Decades*. London: Rockliff, 1951.

INDEX

ABOUT THE AUTHOR

JANE BALDWIN, a theater historian, is a member of the Boston Conservatory faculty, where she teaches Acting, Dramatic Literature, and Humanities. She has written on acting techniques, training, and productions, and her articles have appeared in several journals including *Theatre History Studies* and *Theatre Topics*.